THE NASDAQ HANDBOOK

THE STOCK MARKET OF TOMORROW—TODAY

A Complete Reference for Investors,
Registered Representatives,
Company Executives, Researchers,
the Financial Press and
Students of Finance

PROBUS PUBLISHING COMPANY
Chicago, Illinois

Editors:
> Douglas F. Parrillo, Senior Vice President,
> > NASD Communications Group
>
> Enno R. Hobbing, Vice President, NASD News Bureau
> Margo Vanover Porter, Director, NASD Communication Services

Contributing Editors:
> Barbara Ann Dickens, Mary Kay Grimaldi, Thomas P. Mathers, Desiree W. Perkins

Researchers:
> Douglas J. MacNair, William L. Wink, D. Timothy McCormick

Production Assistants:
> Paige A. Jernigan, Pamela J. Dillon, Lisa M. Jones, Jane A. Burch, Jocelyn M. Bruns

ISBN 0-917253-54-X

Printed in the United States of America

2   3   4   5   6   7   8   9   0

In remembrance of
John H. Hodges, Jr.,
NASD Senior Vice President,
for his contribution to our industry and
the role he played in planning and implementing
the NASDAQ System.

CONTENTS

PART V: NASDAQ AS A NATIONAL ECONOMIC INSTITUTION (Continued)

PART VI: THE FINANCIAL MEDIA LOOK AT NASDAQ

PART VII: NASDAQ SYSTEMS, SERVICES AND REGULATIONS

As well as being the author of *Megatrends*, an international best seller describing major social and economic trends, John Naisbitt is Chairman of The Naisbitt Group, a Washington, D.C. company that reports on social, political, technological and economic trends for businesses and institutions. He is also a Governor-at-Large of the National Association of Securities Dealers, Inc.

Preface

by John Naisbitt

NASDAQ: Behind this information-age acronym for National Association of Securities Dealers Automated Quotations looms the future of securities trading. NASDAQ is the market for securities of emerging companies in many of the world's most innovative industries. Considering that these forward-looking ventures will continue to revolutionize the way we live, I hardly exaggerate when I say that the NASDAQ System will help make the world of tomorrow possible. The character of this market — innovative and technologically sophisticated — reflects the kinds of companies whose shares are traded on it. No wonder, then, that both the System and its companies epitomize the trends propelling our world into the future: technology, competition, diversity, growth.

As a fully automated system, the NASDAQ market belongs to the post-industrial information society that advanced technology has created. Because it represents the computerized bid and ask quotations of dispersed market makers rather than a single trading floor, the NASDAQ System is information itself. Virtually independent of space and time, this market moves instantaneously through electronics. Technology has enabled the NASDAQ System to function as the first geographically decentralized stock market. This electronic network linking market makers in hundreds of locations takes the stock market from the centralized past of specialists concentrated in a single marketplace to the decentralized future.

The NASDAQ System puts competition to work for the investor. The local investment firm in a remote location with limited resources can compete effectively with the larger multi-national firm for orders in a stock through instant electronic display of buy and sell quotations. These dealers, putting their own capital at risk in competing for investor orders, constitute the most dynamic, efficient market system yet developed.

As we move from a national to a world economy, we approach a tomorrow of countless economic centers joined in competition across the globe. In the emerging parallel development of global securities trading, electronic systems like the NASDAQ System will link securities dealers competing from numerous locations across the globe. As Bill McGowan, Chairman of MCI Communications Corporation, observed, the NASDAQ System is "the prototype of a future global stock market in which investors can trade at any time from any location through a computerized communications system." The British realized this with the launching in 1986 of the Stock Exchange Automated Quotations—SEAQ—System with its NASDAQ-derived technology. In the Pacific Basin, the Stock Exchange of Singapore Dealing and Automated Quotations (SESDAQ) System will provide the first automated system linking competing dealers in its securities.

Many companies that develop the communications technology making possible this marvel of the information age— MCI, Intel Corporation, Apple Computer, for example— maintain their stocks on NASDAQ. Still other companies foreshadow an even more dynamic information age because their fields—robotics and biotechnology, for example—are so sophisticated that their ultimate nature is really knowledge and information. NASDAQ is the market for these companies.

NASDAQ is a richly diverse market, trading the stocks of more than 4,400 companies, including those in banking, insurance, pharmaceuticals, health services, advertising, retailing and apparel. It is also the largest U.S. stock market for foreign issues, including Canon, Jaguar, Fuji, Cadbury Schweppes, Pharmacia, Gotaas-Larsen Shipping, Volvo and Ericsson Telephone. This market is also diverse both in company size and range of investors, from institutions that account for more than 40 percent of trading in NASDAQ National Market System stocks to individual investors who dominate trading in the issues of smaller companies.

NASDAQ has mirrored the growth of its companies. The statistics are dramatic: From 1976 through 1986 share volume increased 1,607 percent, while that of the New York Stock Exchange increased 566 percent and the American Stock Exchange 359 percent. During this period, the number of companies listed on the System increased 77 percent; the number of companies on the NYSE decreased 0.2 percent; and the number of Amex companies dropped 32 percent.

Companies that prize creativity and vision do not merely make the future possible; they become the future. Their market, the market of the future—NASDAQ—is here today. This book tells its story.

PART I

America's Fastest Growing Stock Market

Chapter
one

Gordon S. Macklin, during his 17 years as President of the National Association of Securities Dealers, Inc., has guided the development of the NASDAQ National Market System and computer-linked international markets. In 1987, he announced his decision to join the NASD member firm of Hambrecht & Quist as Chairman of the Board and Co-Chief Executive Officer. Before joining the NASD in 1970, he was a partner and member of the Executive Committee of McDonald & Company, a midwestern securities firm. He has served on the boards of directors of several publicly traded companies and is a former governor of the Midwest Stock Exchange.

A Primer on NASDAQ: The Market of the Future

by Gordon S. Macklin

"The over-the-counter market is gaining new prominence. Advances in electronic trading, multiple market makers, low entry cost and comparatively little paperwork have helped make it the trading forum of choice among high growth companies."

— Yla Eason
The New York Times, May 3, 1983

"Many companies eligible for exchange listing are choosing to stay in the OTC markets."

— Pavan Sahgal
Pensions & Investment Age, June 13, 1983

"The over-the-counter market offers its clients, from companies to traders and customers, a better deal."

— Susan Lee
Barron's, September 12, 1983

"NASDAQ is now the *preferred* market for a startling number of companies that could easily move to one of the exchanges."

— John Cooney
Institutional Investor, February 1984

9

"NASDAQ has come as far as it has largely because it is in effect an electronic stock market."
— Arthur M. Louis
Fortune, October 29, 1984

"By building a new equity market on a network of computers, the NASD has created what many believe to be the stock-trading environment of the future."
— Robert Winder—Nicola Stitt
Euromoney, March 1985

"The NASD has made the OTC market more alluring to institutional investors with its National Market System."
— Jeffrey M. Laderman
Business Week, December 9, 1985

"This over-the-computer, floorless stock market has not only won grudging respect from rival exchanges, but seized a formidable share of their business as well."
— Lynn Strongin Dodds
Financial World, September 16, 1986

The NASDAQ[1] market is no longer a secret. The financial press has written reams on the extraordinary growth of NASDAQ and its simple formula for success: technology, innovation and competition. As Tom Cassidy, market commentator for *Cable News Network*, recently observed, "NASDAQ is one of the most powerful financial market stories of the 1980s."

Why has this market received so much media attention? A few facts help explain why.

In less than two decades, NASDAQ has become the second largest market in the U.S. and the third largest equity

---

[1]NASDAQ is an acronym for National Association of Securities Dealers Automated Quotations.

market in the world. In 1986, more than 28 billion shares of more than 4,400 companies were traded in this market. In excess of 500 securities firms across the country, ranging from Merrill Lynch and Salomon Brothers to small broker-dealers in regional locations, make markets in NASDAQ stocks on what amounts to a "trading floor" that runs from Maine to California, from Canada to Mexico. This is a market that serves an expanding customer base of nearly 10 million individual investors and thousands of institutional investors.

A closer look at this market may help explain why it is so popular and why it represents the prototype of the stock market of the future.

The System: How It Works

The NASDAQ System is the communications facility for the NASDAQ market. The heart of the System is the Central Computer Complex in Trumbull, Connecticut. The computer complex is linked by 80,000 miles of leased telephone lines to the nearly 3,000 cathode-ray terminals in offices of securities firms and financial institutions. In late 1986, the NASD opened a total back-up, or duplex, computer facility in Rockville, Maryland, near Washington, D.C.

Through their terminals, market makers enter the highest prices at which they are willing to buy a security or the lowest prices at which they are willing to sell a security. These market makers and financial institutions can view on their terminals the quotations of all market makers in all the securities.

The System's computers are also connected to the computers of data vendors who lease more than 150,000 quotation terminals displaying NASDAQ information to subscribers in the U.S. and 36 other countries. These terminals display "inside" quotations—the highest bids and the lowest offers—for all securities in this market.

When an investor places a buy or sell order for a security, a broker directs the order to his firm's trading room. If the firm is making a market in the security and is prepared to deal at the best bid or ask price on the screen, it executes the order as principal and, depending upon whether the customer is a buyer or a seller, the firm will charge the investor a mark-down from the best bid, or a mark-up over the best offer, in lieu of a commission. If the firm is not willing to deal at the best price or is not a market maker in the security, the trader consults his terminal to identify the market maker with the best price and telephones that market maker to execute the order. In this case, the investor pays a commission because the firm is acting in an agency capacity. Both principal and agency trades are completed in a few minutes.

For trades of 1,000 shares or less, the firm could also have completed the transaction through the NASD's Small Order Execution System (SOES). This system permits automatic execution of a customer's order at the best available price throughout the NASDAQ System at the time the order was placed, thereby eliminating the need for direct voice contact with a market maker. SOES directs orders to the market maker displaying the best bid or offer or to the market maker designated by the firm with the investor's order. Through SOES, an order can be executed in less than a minute.

The Mix of Companies

NASDAQ began February 5, 1971. It includes companies of all types and sizes, the new and the established.

- The high-tech area includes companies such as Apple Computer, Intel Corporation and MCI Communications Corporation.
- The bank and other finance sectors include Bank of New England, Citizens & Southern Corporation, First Union Corporation, Kemper Corporation, PNC Financial Corporation and Sovran Financial Corporation.
- In the insurance company group are American National Insurance, Farmers Group, Inc., First Executive Corporation, Ohio Casualty Corporation, Provident Life and Accident, SAFECO Corporation and St. Paul Companies.
- Transportation companies include Roadway Services and Yellow Freight System.
- Among the utility companies are Atlanta Gas Light Company, Citizens Utilities Company, El Paso Electric Company and Northwestern Public Service Company.

NASDAQ is also a leading market for foreign securities: Cadbury Schweppes, Jaguar and Reuters (U.K.), Gotaas-Larsen Shipping (Bermuda), Toyota (Japan), Waterford Glass Group plc (Ireland), Volvo (Sweden) and Broken Hill Proprietary (Australia). The 266 foreign securities and American Depositary Receipts (ADRs) trading in the NASDAQ market in 1986 were issued by 244 companies with headquarters in 27 foreign countries.

In 1986, the 178 foreign securities and 88 ADRs on NASDAQ accounted for 2.4 billion shares traded—or more than 8 percent of total share volume. Dollar volume amounted to nearly $24.9 billion, more than 6.5 percent of NASDAQ's total dollar volume. These 266 foreign shares and ADRs represent almost 2 1/2 times the number of overseas securities on the New York and American stock exchanges combined.

The Growth of the Market

As NASDAQ companies have grown in number and size, so too has their market. In 1975, its share volume was less than one third of the New York Stock Exchange (NYSE) and more than twice the share volume of the American Stock Exchange (Amex). By 1980, its share volume was almost 60 percent that of the NYSE and more than four times that of the Amex.

By 1986, NASDAQ share volume was 80 percent of the share volume of the NYSE and almost 10 times that of the Amex. From 1976 to 1986, the volume increased nearly 17 fold from 1.7 to 28.7 billion shares.

Equally significant are the changes in the numbers of companies in the three markets over the same 10-year period. The number of NASDAQ companies grew by 77 percent, while the number of NYSE companies declined by .2 percent. The number of companies on the Amex declined by 31 percent.

Not surprisingly, NASDAQ has dramatically increased its share of total U.S. stock trading. In 1976, NASDAQ represented 21.9 percent of the 7.7 billion shares traded in the three major U.S. markets. In 1986, its trading represented 42.6 percent of the 67.4 billion shares traded in the three markets.

From 1980 through 1986, the market grew faster than the other two exchanges in all five principal categories of market activity—share volume, dollar volume, market value, Composite Index and number of companies listed.

With increasing share volume and rising indices, the dollar volume of NASDAQ trading surged. In 1986, NASDAQ's dollar volume of equity trading—$378.2 billion—ranked it third among major world markets, exceeded only by the New York and Tokyo stock exchanges.

Share Volume/Number of Companies
NASDAQ, NYSE, AMEX Comparison Chart
1976-1986

	NASDAQ	NYSE	AMEX
1976	1,683,933,000	5,360,116,000	648,297,000
	2,495	1,576	1,161
1977	1,932,100,000	5,273,767,000	653,129,000
	2,456	1,575	1,098
1978	2,762,499,000	7,205,059,000	988,559,000
	2,475	1,581	1,004
1979	3,651,214,000	8,155,914,000	1,100,264,000
	2,543	1,565	931
1980	6,691,631,000	11,352,294,000	1,626,073,000
	2,894	1,570	892
1981	7,823,410,000	11,853,741,000	1,343,400,000
	3,353	1,565	867
1982	8,432,275,000	16,458,037,000	1,337,725,000
	3,264	1,526	834
1983	15,908,547,000	21,589,577,000	2,080,922,000
	3,901	1,550	822
1984	15,158,823,000	23,071,031,000	1,545,010,000
	4,097	1,543	792
1985	20,699,146,000	27,510,706,000	2,100,815,000
	4,136	1,540	783
1986	28,736,561,000	35,680,016,000	2,978,612,000
	4,417	1,573	796
Percentage Increase in Volume 1976-1986	1,607%	566%	359%
Percentage Change in Number of Companies 1976-1986	+77%	−0.2%	−31%
Actual Volume Increase 1985-1986	+8,037,415,000	+8,169,310,000	+877,797,000
Increase in Number of Companies 1985-1986	+281	+33	+31

Note: Share volume rounded to thousands.

Increase in Market Making

The unique strength of the NASDAQ market is the competitive, multiple market-maker system. In this

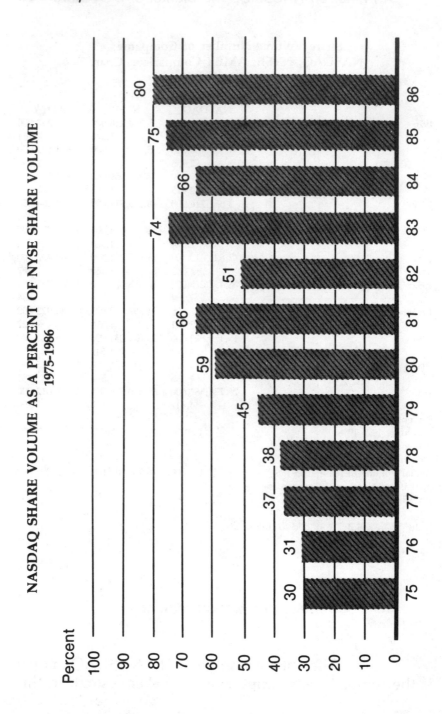

NASDAQ SHARE VOLUME AS A PERCENT OF NYSE SHARE VOLUME
1975-1986

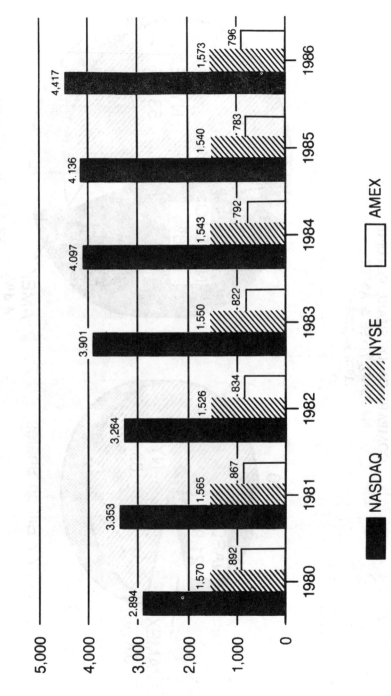

NUMBER OF COMPANIES LISTED ON NASDAQ, NYSE AND AMEX
1980-1986

NASDAQ ▓ NYSE ▒ AMEX □

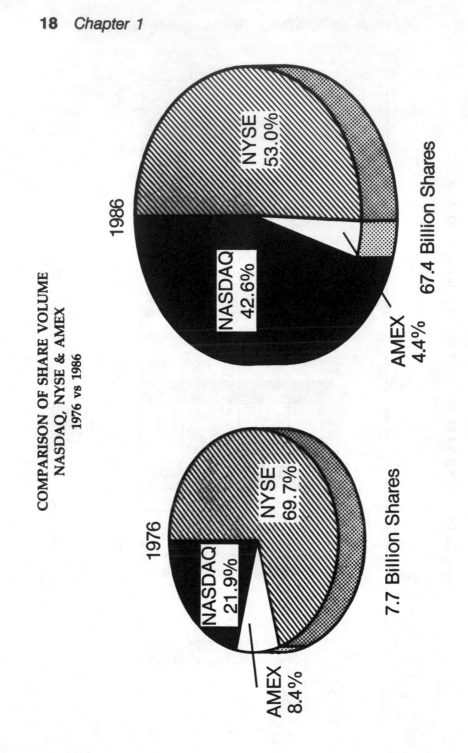

COMPARISON OF SHARE VOLUME
NASDAQ, NYSE & AMEX
1976 vs 1986

1986

NYSE
53.0%

NASDAQ
42.6%

AMEX
4.4%   67.4 Billion Shares

1976

NYSE
69.7%

NASDAQ
21.9%

AMEX
8.4%

7.7 Billion Shares

market, securities are traded by competing decentralized dealers located across the U.S. Very active securities may have in excess of 40 market makers; the average security has eight.

From 1980 to 1986, the number of participating market-making firms grew by 34 percent, from 394 to 526. These market makers include:

- The big national, full-service firms, each of which may make markets in more than 1,000 securities.
- Regional firms, making 200 to 400 markets.
- Firms with specialty areas such as banking, insurance and high technology.
- Local firms, making markets in the major business enterprises in their cities.
- Wholesalers, making markets in 1,000 securities or more, primarily to serve non-market-making firms.

The capital committed to NASDAQ and the level of activity in this market have also risen sharply. From 1980 to 1986, the number of market-maker positions almost doubled, from 22,300 to some 41,300.

The advantages of the competitive, multiple market-maker system are many:

- Competition among market makers gives the broker or dealer a clear choice among competing quotations by securities dealers. This affords investors the best price available.
- The capital commitment of competing, multiple market makers to NASDAQ stocks is generally greater than the capital commitment by exchange specialist firms to comparable listed stocks. Liquidity is enhanced.
- With operational capacity and risk distributed among several market makers rather than concentrated in a single specialist, NASDAQ trading is seldom delayed or interrupted due to an imbalance of orders. Quotation halts occur if material news is pending about the issuer

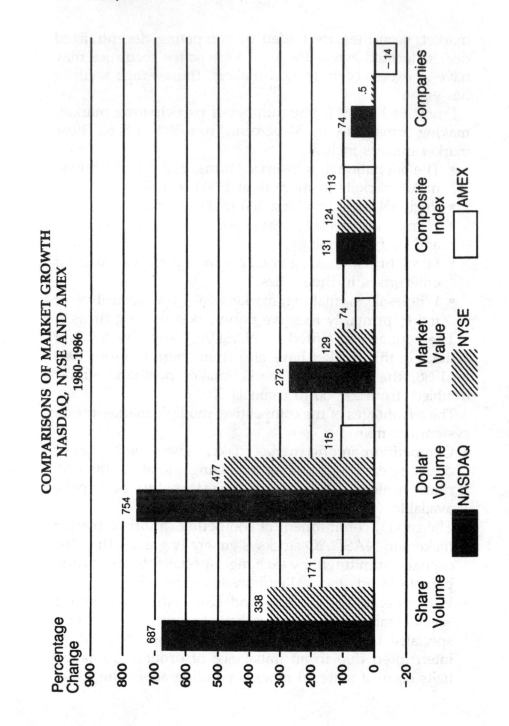

COMPARISONS OF MARKET GROWTH
NASDAQ, NYSE AND AMEX
1980-1986

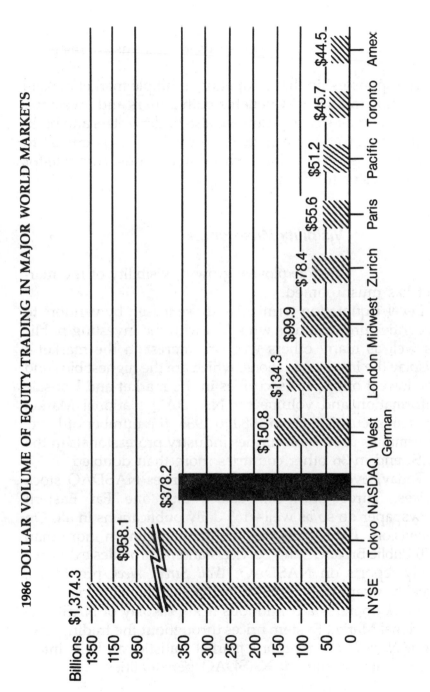

1986 DOLLAR VOLUME OF EQUITY TRADING IN MAJOR WORLD MARKETS

Billions

NYSE $1,374.3
Tokyo $958.1
NASDAQ $378.2
West German $150.8
London $134.3
Midwest $99.9
Zurich $78.4
Paris $55.6
Pacific $51.2
Toronto $45.7
Amex $44.5

that could affect its stock's price. Once the company makes the necessary disclosures, quotations are resumed promptly.

- The sponsorship that competing, multiple market makers provide to a security benefits both issuers and investors. Most market-making firms are also underwriters and brokers and provide investment research. This is crucial to thousands of companies whose stocks must compete for an investor following.

Visibility Mushrooms

With explosive growth, visibility of the market has mushroomed.

Level 1 quotation terminals—those leased by vendors to securities professionals who deal with the investing public as well as many others with an interest in the market—display the inside quotations, which are the highest bids and the lowest offers, for securities in the market and last-sale information and volume for NASDAQ National Market System securities. From 1980 to 1986, the number of Level 1 terminals used by securities industry professionals in the U.S. and in 36 other countries more than doubled.

Today, every major newspaper carries NASDAQ stock prices. Three European dailies and one Far Eastern newspaper do so as well—165 daily publications in all. On television, *The Nightly Business Report*, seen on more than 250 Public Broadcasting Service stations, provides extensive daily reports on NASDAQ; *Wall Street Week* provides a weekly wrap-up of activity in the market; *Financial News Network* operates a continuous ticker display of NASDAQ National Market System prices throughout the trading day; *Cable News Network* reports market statistics and airs interviews with prominent NASDAQ personalities.

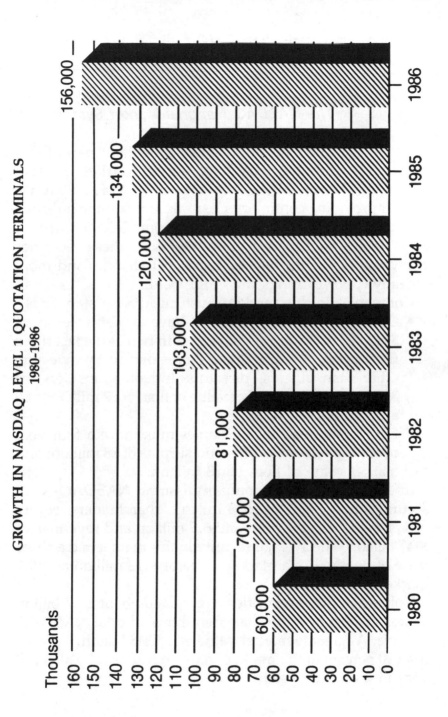

GROWTH IN NASDAQ LEVEL 1 QUOTATION TERMINALS
1980-1986

In addition, more than 2,500 radio stations broadcast market data during the trading day.

The NASDAQ National Market System

The largest and most prominent part of this market is the NASDAQ National Market System (NASDAQ/NMS). NASDAQ/NMS is a market within a market providing continuous last-sale and volume information throughout the trading day on some 3,000 securities. Stock tables published in newspapers on these securities show volume, high, low, last sale, net change, and more recently, price/earnings ratio and yield.

Companies in this market must meet these standards:
- Operating companies must have a net income of $300,000 in the last fiscal year or in two of the last three fiscal years; a public float (shares owned by investors other than officers, directors and other insiders) of 350,000 shares; a market value of float of $2 million; and a minimum bid of $3.
- Development-stage companies must have a four-year operating history; capital and surplus of $8 million; and market value of float of $8 million.

In 1986, the average company issuing NASDAQ/NMS securities had assets of $533 million, shareholders' equity of $71 million, net income of $6.5 million and revenues of $147 million. The average security in this market had a share price of nearly $16, a market value of $122 million and 9.2 market makers.

Volume in these securities aggregated about 19.7 billion shares in 1986 or more than two thirds of total NASDAQ volume. Aggregate market value was $318 billion, or more than 90 percent of the market value represented by all 5,200 securities on the System.

NASDAQ National Market System Companies and
Their Securities Profile Data,
December 1986

Securities Data
- Number of Securities*   2,613
- Average Share Price $ 15.82
- P/E Ratio   18.8
- Average Number of Market Makers   9.2
- Average Shares Outstanding - Per Issue   7,731,000
- Average Float   5,730,000
- Average Market Value $ 122,312,000

Company Data
- Number of Companies   2,600
- Average Assets $ 532,824,000
- Average Equity $ 71,325,000
- Average Revenue $ 146,880,000
- Average Net Income $ 6,491,000

*Domestic and foreign common stocks, ADRs and shares of beneficial interest.

At least 700 NASDAQ/NMS securities meet the financial requirements for listing on the New York Stock Exchange; more than 1,800 meet the requirements for listing on the Amex.

Individual Investors

About 10 million individual investors hold the bulk of NASDAQ securities by market value, some $341 billion. Individual investors account for nearly 60 percent of the trading in NASDAQ/NMS securities; the average individual trade in these securities is about 1,000 shares. Individual investors account for almost all of the share volume in the approximately 2,500 securities not in the NASDAQ National Market System. These securities have an aggregate market value of about $30 billion.

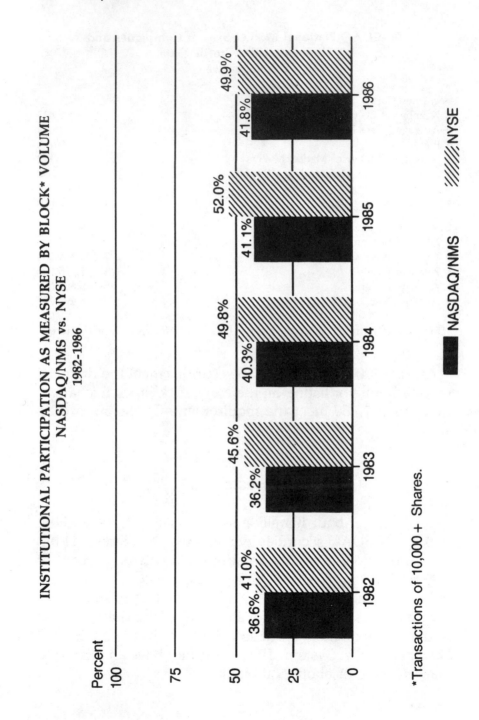

INSTITUTIONAL PARTICIPATION AS MEASURED BY BLOCK* VOLUME
NASDAQ/NMS vs. NYSE
1982-1986

Percent

*Transactions of 10,000 + Shares.

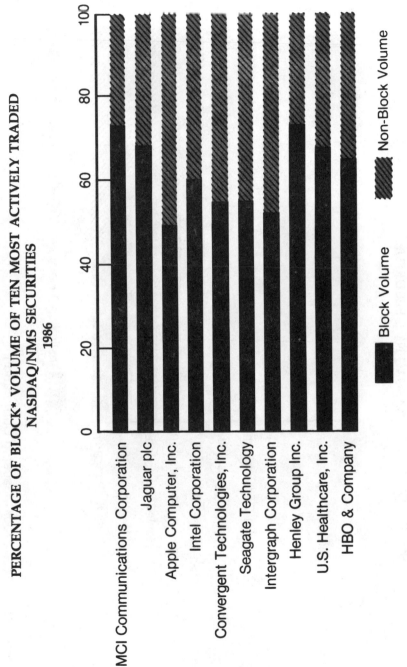

PERCENTAGE OF BLOCK* VOLUME OF TEN MOST ACTIVELY TRADED NASDAQ/NMS SECURITIES
1986

Block Volume

 Non-Block Volume

*Transactions of 10,000 + Shares.

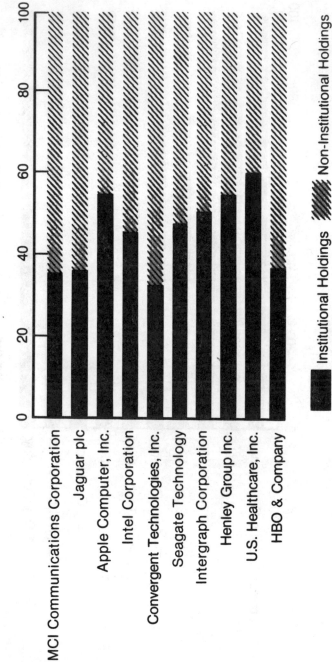

INSTITUTIONAL HOLDINGS IN TEN MOST ACTIVELY TRADED
NASDAQ/NMS SECURITIES
1986

Institutional Holdings   Non-Institutional Holdings

Source: Vickers Stock Research Corporation.

Institutional Trading

NASDAQ/NMS securities attract many financial institutions, both U.S. and foreign. More than 40 percent of their volume consists of blocks of 10,000 shares or more—with an average block size in excess of 20,000 shares.

In the 10 most actively traded NASDAQ/NMS securities, the percentage of block volume in 1986 ranged from 49 percent to more than 70 percent. Institutional holdings in these 10 securities ranged from 35 percent to more than 65 percent.

All told, U.S. and non-U.S. institutions in 1986 held $101 billion of NASDAQ/NMS common stocks. This was 32 percent of the aggregate market value of all such stocks. Institutions held positions in almost every NASDAQ/NMS stock. They had more than 53,000 positions in these stocks, with aggregate holdings of almost 4.6 billion shares. This brought the average position to over 85,000 shares.

As NASDAQ/NMS has grown, institutional participation in it has grown. According to a study by the Wharton School of the University of Pennsylvania (see Chapter 11), from the end of 1979 to the middle of 1985, the dollar value of NASDAQ stocks in institutional investors' portfolios more than tripled—from $20 billion to nearly $70 billion. The percentage of total NASDAQ market value held by institutions increased from 14.2 percent to 25.1 percent.

From the end of 1985 to the end of 1986, institutional holdings of NASDAQ/NMS stocks rose another $30 billion to $99 billion, or 33 percent of the aggregate market value of such stocks. Thus, in the last 7 years, institutional holdings have increased nearly 5 times.

The four principal types of institutions—banks, investment advisers, insurance companies and investment companies—all increased the percentages and dollar amounts of their holdings of NASDAQ stocks. Investment advisers accounted for the biggest dollar shift to this market as they increased

Institutional Holdings of NASDAQ Stocks
1979-1986*

Date	Market Value of NASDAQ Holdings by Institutions	Market Value of NASDAQ Holdings by All Investors	Percent of Total Market Value Held by Institutions
1979	$20.0 billion	$140.4 billion	14.2%
1985	$68.6 billion	$273.4 billion	25.1%
Percent Increase 1970-1985	+243%	+95%	—
1986	$108.0 billion	$335.7 billion	32.1%
Percent Increase 1979-1986	+440%	+139%	—

*As of June 30.
  Sources: Rodney L. White Center for Financial Research, University of Pennsylvania, The Wharton School; Vickers Stock Research, Inc.

Increases in NASDAQ Stock Holdings by Type
of Institutions,
1979-1985*

Type of Institution	Percent Increase
Banks	+35%
Investment Advisers	+75%
Insurance Companies	+55%
Investment Companies	+90%

*As of June 30.
  Source: Rodney L. White Center for Financial Research, University of Pennsylvania, The Wharton School.

their percentage of holdings by 75 percent. Investment companies made the biggest percentage increase, more than 90 percent. Insurance companies raised their holdings in these issues by 55 percent, and banks raised theirs by 35 percent.

According to data compiled by Vickers Stock Research, Inc., a total of 2,725 institutions held NASDAQ stocks in their portfolios. Of these 2,145 are in the U.S., while 580, more than 20 percent, are non-U.S. The five countries with the largest numbers of institutions participating in the market are: Canada (240), United Kingdom (175), France (70), Switzerland (26) and West Germany (25).

The World Market of the Future

The global equity market of tomorrow has begun to take shape and NASDAQ will play a prominent role in it. Fueled by technology, the emerging global stock market is a direct response to the worldwide needs of investors seeking global asset management, issuers looking to raise capital in overseas markets and securities firms exploring efficient means by which to participate in international trading.

Global trading, by definition, means the linking together of professionals from a wide variety of locations. To trade with one another, these professionals will need centralized market data provided through automated delivery systems such as NASDAQ. Consequently, a global network of stock trading will emerge, which will look very similar to a worldwide NASDAQ. This network will build on the foundation established by the linkage in 1986 of the NASDAQ market and the London Stock Exchange—a linkage facilitated by London's decision to model its new equity trading system after NASDAQ. The NASDAQ/London link was the first intercontinental step taken in the structuring of the global equity market. More international linkages for NASDAQ, on a larger scale, are ahead.

When we look at what is happening in London and the Eurobond market, as well as other signs in the markets throughout the world, we see the evidence building that trading is rapidly shifting from marble halls in fixed locations to flexible, decentralized global networks of screen-based automated systems modeled after NASDAQ.

George Hayter, the Director of Information Services at the London Stock Exchange, expressed it well when he said:

"Anyone looking down from heaven at our exchange in the year 1800 would have seen coffeehouses. By the beginning of the 20th century, a trading floor could be seen. In the year 2000, the exchange will be an electronic network connecting terminals all over the globe."

Chapter two

William G. McGowan, the Telecommunications Industry's Chief Executive of the Year in 1979, is the Chairman, MCI Communications Corporation. Mr. McGowan has guided his firm's progress over the past decade, building MCI into the nation's second largest, coast-to-coast telecommunications company, with a $5 billion investment in a worldwide communications network.

Why NASDAQ?

by William G. McGowan

In 1972, MCI made its initial public offering in the NASDAQ market. NASDAQ had been operating for all of one year, and our choice of market caused many investors to ask, "Why NASDAQ?" My answer then was the same as it is today: NASDAQ is perfect for MCI; perfect for MCI's stockholders; perfect for today's information-based economy.

The reasons are not surprising.

Reason Number 1: The Competitive, Multiple Market-Maker System

The heart of the NASDAQ market is its competitive, multiple market-maker system, which is a vast improvement over monopoly systems, where a single specialist has control over trading in a given stock. However, some people still think that a stock listed on an exchange has greater market strength. This just isn't true and hasn't been for years.

Two examples from MCI's experience concretely demonstrate the superiority of the multiple market-maker system.

At 12 noon, Friday, February 8, 1982, the Department of Justice announced AT&T's divestiture of the Bell operating companies. AT&T stock did not trade that day; the New York Stock Exchange (NYSE) called it a "regulatory halt."

Predictably, the media generated an outpouring of information about the divestiture over the weekend. Everybody had a chance to digest the news Friday, all day Saturday and all day Sunday. On Monday morning, however, AT&T stock still did not open. Something was said about "an imbalance of orders." Finally, late on Monday afternoon, some NYSE trading in AT&T occurred.

Meanwhile, MCI stock traded all day Friday and Monday. If MCI had been listed on the NYSE and it called a "regulatory halt," our shareholders might not have had the opportunity to buy or sell, which is, after all, what stock markets are all about.

A year and a half later, in August 1983, the Federal Communications Commission announced the charges that long-distance telecommunications companies would pay for access to local telephone companies' lines. Because these charges were exceptionally high, many in the securities industry believed they might have negative effect on our earnings.

With the access-charge news on the wire, MCI traded 16.5 million shares in a day. The turnover represented 14 percent of our total capitalization. No halt was called; investors bought and sold MCI at will, without interruption, during the entire time. MCI and the NASDAQ National Market System proved that we could handle such volume. On the New York Stock Exchange, trading probably would have been halted, as was the case with the stocks of two companies at that time.

One was Warner Communications. On the Friday that Warner Communications first released the bad news about Atari, its specialist on the New York Stock Exchange stopped trading. Trading did not resume until the following Monday afternoon. This was a protect-the-specialist halt, not a protect-the-public halt, because the news was already out. The specialist just needed to balance his books.

These contrasting examples demonstrate that the NASDAQ market lets people buy and sell when they want to, providing access and liquidity. And I will let the sophisticated issuer decide where his stock will receive greater continuity of trading: in the market dominated by a "specialist" or in the market made up of multiple market makers.

Reason Number 2: Liquidity

The competitive, multiple market-maker system also contributes to superior liquidity. Liquidity, of course, is measured by the dollar volume of trading that it takes to move the price of a stock. With high liquidity, it takes a lot of money to effect a small price change, a desirable effect.

NASDAQ's superior liquidity was first documented by an independent 1983 study, conducted at Texas A&M University, entitled *Liquidity, Exchange Listing and Common Stock Performance*. The study found that "...OTC liquidity tends to dominate Amex liquidity for stocks of the same size...Moreover, for most size ranges short of very large companies, NYSE listing may well imply a lower liquidity than had the firm remained OTC."

A second study, also conducted at Texas A&M in 1983, dealt more specifically with listing and the liquidity of bank stocks. It concluded that: "Listing [on the exchanges] does not appear to add to the liquidity of the stock of banking organizations...[and]... here is some surprising and reasonable evidence that listing actually significantly reduces the liquidity...for bank organizations."

Following these two studies, David A. Dubofsky and John C. Groth of the College of Business Administration, Department of Finance, at Texas A&M, published a paper entitled *Exchange Listing and Stock Liquidity* in the Winter 1984 volume of Georgetown University's *The Journal of Financial Research*. Dubofsky and Groth measured the liquidity of stocks, both before and after listing, of 112 companies that moved from NASDAQ to the American Stock Exchange, and 128 that moved from NASDAQ to the New York Stock Exchange, from 1975 to 1981.

Dubofsky and Groth summarized their findings as follows: "The results presented in this study indicate a marked decline in liquidity for securities moving from the [NASDAQ] market to either of the organized exchanges."

For securities moving from NASDAQ to the NYSE, the study reported a 24.4 percent decline in average liquidity 20 days after the listing and a further decline of 12.6 percent over the next 40 days. For stocks moving from NASDAQ to the Amex, liquidity increased slightly on NASDAQ—from 50 percent to 57.7 percent—as the moving day approached. Once a NASDAQ stock was listed on the Amex, however, liquidity declined by 26.4 percent.

Analyzing the cause, Dubofsky and Groth wrote: "The most logical reason for greater OTC liquidity is the different market-making mechanisms. Competing dealers in OTC securities may provide more continuous and liquid markets than the organized exchanges that employ monopolist specialists."

At MCI, our experience supports the findings of the Texas A&M studies. We measure the liquidity of our securities constantly, and we have found that our own securities are more liquid than comparable securities on the NYSE.

Reason Number 3: Cost of Capital

Just as we measure our liquidity, we constantly measure our net cost of capital. MCI has more than $5 billion invested in its domestic and international communications network. In March 1983, we raised $400 million in the public market; in August 1983, $1 billion; and in April 1986, $575 million. Obviously, the cost of capital is very important to us. Our experience has shown that capital costs are no more expensive for us than they would be if MCI's stock were listed on an exchange.

Once again, broader academic studies bear out MCI's findings. A 1982 study, *The Impact of Exchange Listing on the Cost of Equity Capital*, prepared at The American University by H. Kent Baker, Professor of Finance, and James Spitzfaden, Internal Auditor for Textron, concluded: "The cross-sectional and time-series analysis revealed that the cost of equity capital neither differed between matched pairs of NASDAQ-Amex and NASDAQ-NYSE firms nor changed significantly when a NASDAQ stock listed on either of these exchanges."

Another 1982 cost-of-capital study was published by the Securities and Exchange Commission and prepared under NASD sponsorship at the University of Iowa by Susan M. Phillips, now Chairman of the Commodity Futures Trading Commission, and J. Richard Zecher, now Senior Vice President and Treasurer of Chase Manhattan Bank. The study found that: ". . . listing does not affect risk or the cost of capital for companies of similar asset size, industry group, and trading volume. Further, the decision to list does not appear to have any predictable effect on risk or the cost of capital for the listing company."

Reason Number 4: International Visibility

From an issuer's point of view, the NASDAQ market affords excellent visibility. MCI usually has more than 40 securities firms making a market in its stock. The trading, research and sales departments of these firms all know MCI stock, follow it constantly and discuss it with their customers. At the same time, quotations and last-sale data on MCI stock are displayed on more than 150,000 securities salesmen's terminals in the U.S. and 36 other countries. More than 160 newspapers carry MCI statistics in the U.S., Europe and Asia. In fact, MCI has sold significant amounts of stock in Europe, mostly in England, Scotland and Switzerland.

In addition, the largest concentration of non-U.S. securities on a U.S. stock market is found on NASDAQ. At year-end 1986, 88 ADRs and 178 foreign securities from 27 countries traded in the NASDAQ market. This is substantially more than the 114 foreign issues listed on the New York and American stock exchanges.

There is no need to belabor the visibility issue. MCI stock traded in excess of 450 million shares in 1986.

Reason Number 5: It Doesn't Cost a Fortune

If MCI were to list on the NYSE, its first-year listing costs would be $877,860. Because of MCI's high capitalization, this is more than most companies would pay. But $877,860 still looks ridiculous when compared to the NASDAQ National Market System's cost of $7,500.

Another added cost of listing on the NYSE is for certificates; under NYSE rules, 100,000 certificates would cost MCI about $32,500, plus a $3,000 plate, versus about $13,000 for NASDAQ. The reason for this difference in cost is spelled out in the New York Stock Exchange Handbook, Section 502.01, "Certificates—Printing and Engraving Requirements."

"The face of a listed security in definitive form must be printed by the Intaglio plate process, to the extent prescribed below in this section for each particular type of security, from at least two engraved steel or nickel plates (unless the Split-Font Concept is utilized) which may be chromium plated, that is, one plate produced from original line engravings in steel from which a printing in color is made of the border and the tint underlying the face of the security; and a second plate produced from original hand cut engravings in steel from which a printing in black is made of the vignette, title and descriptive or promissory portion of the security."

All this for a piece of paper that is basically a receipt, which will languish for most of its existence in a fireproof vault and which contains information that is already stored electronically. Section 502.01 might be more appropriately called "a formula for the finest record-keeping system of the 19th century."

Reason Number 6: Advantage for Investors

The advantages of the NASDAQ market for MCI and its stock are advantages for investors, too. Continuity of trading, liquidity, reasonable cost of capital and visibility all make for an efficient NASDAQ market. Investors benefit from this efficiency, just as issuers and the securities industry do.

I think the following statistics are a testimonial to what investors think of this 16-year-old market:

NASDAQ is by far the largest stock market in the U.S. in the number of companies represented, and the second largest in terms of share and dollar volume.

NASDAQ's dollar volume of equity trading, $378 billion in 1986, secures its position as the world's third-largest equity market.

Over the past 10 years, the NASDAQ share volume has increased 16 times, compared to an increase of five times for the Big Board.

This immense growth says to me that the investing public sees NASDAQ as the future of global trading.

Reason Number 7: The Information Age

A final answer to "Why NASDAQ?" is simply this: NASDAQ is the prototype of future markets.

If we were just now starting a public market for trading securities in the United States, we would not even suggest, contemplate or discuss trading stocks the way it is done on the New York and American stock exchanges.

We all visit foreign countries, and we find that many still have markets for fruits and vegetables, where farmers and villagers meet each other. But why would we want to trade securities that way, in one building, in one place? Why would we want the melodramatic running-about and paper-waving of the exchanges? It's an exciting backdrop for stock market reports by television people, but for the rest of us, its inefficiency far outweighs any aesthetic benefit.

To trade years ago, it was necessary to bring people together. Today, we bring information together. Computers, linked by sophisticated networks, can do the job far better and far more efficiently.

Technology has even eliminated the need for the human voice in trading. In December 1984, the first fully automated trade in a NASDAQ security took place. It took only three seconds, nearly 10 times quicker than a manual transaction. A computer in Trumbull, Connecticut, bought 500 shares of Apple Computer common stock for an investor in California, with no voice communication between the investor's broker and the selling dealer in New York. Today, this automated execution system handles trades of up to 1,000 shares.

In short, computers and telecommunications—the information technologies—are changing the way we trade stocks. NASDAQ itself is an innovation of the information technologies. As such, it now finds itself in a position to participate in a 24-hour market. Already some 280 NASDAQ issues are displayed on the London Stock Exchange's new computerized system, and NASDAQ is carrying quotations on upwards of 300 London issues. The London exchange opens at 4:00 a.m. Eastern Standard Time, which gives these issues nearly 18 hours of trading time.

And the sun practically never sets on Broken Hill Proprietary, Australia's steel and mining company. The trading day for Broken Hill begins in Sydney and Melbourne. As the "down under" trading day comes to a close, the London exchange opens, and Broken Hill stock changes hands there. As the London market closes, NASDAQ market makers in the U.S. are still trading Broken Hill—for a total of 18 hours of trading time a day.

The British have recognized this potential. The London Stock Exchange Council has patterned its new equities trading system after NASDAQ, with its competing market makers and computerized quotations system. The London council liked the efficiencies that computer technology brings to the dealing environment. It liked placing all members on an equal basis irrespective of geographical location. Regional brokers, Channel Isle brokers and London brokers are all dealing under the same terms. It liked NASDAQ's ability to lend itself readily to a 24-hour international market. And the council absolutely and unequivocally refused to rely on the quality and state of mind of one individual specialist for the continuity of the market in any given stock.

As the London council has, many American companies have recognized the potential of NASDAQ. Since 1980, the number of companies listed by NASDAQ has grown from

2,894 to well over 4,400. More than 700 companies meeting the financial criteria for listing on the New York Stock Exchange prefer NASDAQ. Meanwhile, listings on the exchanges have been stable, or in the case of Amex, falling. And the public has recognized it—in 1986, NASDAQ traded more than 28.7 billion shares.

As usual, the redoubtable Peter Drucker has put his finger on it. He called the New York Stock Exchange "a smoke stack part of the financial services industry" and continued: "That is why NASDAQ is growing so quickly. The specialist system is a very poor substitute for communication. Such things hang on, but not forever."

The level of sophistication of computers and telecommunications, the speed of information, the diversity of this country, the desire of people to live where they want, and the sophistication of the investing public all demand a market exactly like the one in which MCI trades today—the NASDAQ market, a decentralized network of competing market makers, instantaneously and continuously linked by the automated NASDAQ System. I hope the New York and American stock exchanges will see the light and join the London exchange in following NASDAQ into the 21st century.

Chapter three

James M. Davin is a Managing Director of The First Boston Corporation and has been with the firm since 1969. He is a former chairman of the Corporate Bond Committee of the Securities Industry Association, a member of the Board of Governors of the NASD and the NASD's 1987 Vice Chairman-Finance.

From National to International

by James M. Davin

Some time ago an economist sent me a copy of "The Stock Exchange as an International Market." It is a fascinating study. Starting with the theory of "the inherent tendencies of markets to develop a closer intercommunication, and finally centralization in single great markets," the author enthusiastically traced the development of international markets.

"In the beginning, prices for the same American security in New York and London varied considerably and were established principally by local conditions," wrote the author, J. Edward Meeker, then an economist for the New York Stock Exchange. Soon, he explained, developments in arbitrage kept the domestic and foreign prices for American "international" securities much closer together than ever before, and these issues enjoyed a much broader market.

"Few features of Wall Street life so irresistibly appeal to the imagination as this extraordinary business, conducted in the various world markets over the flashing cables with a speed vastly more rapid than the roll of the earth... America today enters this future period of international financial pre-eminence with a confidence for the future grounded firmly in the achievements of the present,'' the author concluded.

The year of this study's publication was 1922. The growth and development in arbitrage refers to information transfer—at first by sailing packet ship, then steam navigation, and ultimately by the trans-Atlantic telegraph cable.

About a hundred years earlier, the House of Rothschild reportedly made a fortune by arranging for the results of the Battle of Waterloo to be sent to its trading rooms by carrier pigeon. Some 50 years later, a German named Reuter founded a great news (and ultimately information) network using the same technology—the carrier pigeon.

Have we been here before? For those of us who will listen, history does indeed teach lessons. International investing is more than a current fad; it has been going on for centuries. Mr. Meeker was right; markets do tend to centralize; there is simply no rule that this phenomenon has to occur in one physical location. And in general, the common wisdom of these visionaries is clear; the future has always blossomed from the technologies of the present.

The "If Theory" Is Tested

For years, those of us who believe in the concept of a dealer market have taken collective comfort in the ''If Theory'' (sometimes also known as the McGowan Theory). Namely, that if anyone were to build a modern marketplace from scratch, it would be far wiser to build a competitive, essentially portable network, capable of growing on a modular basis, expanding internationally using modern technology and 20th-century computer architecture—not the architecture of bricks and mortar. This opinion, while buttressed by logic, was for a long time still a laboratory theory and largely untested. In October 1986, all of that changed.

On October 27, 1986, "Big Bang" went off in London—
the dramatic restructuring of the venerable London Stock
Exchange (LSE). In responding to the directive of the British government to eliminate both fixed commission rates and
the single-capacity jobbing system, the London Stock
Exchange Council confronted the problem presumed in the
"If Theory"—how to structure a modern market in very real
terms. After literally years of study and consultation, the
council decided to restructure substantially along NASDAQ
lines, recommending a competitive, multiple market-maker
system and an automated quotations system to link its
market makers the way the NASDAQ System links U.S.
market makers.

When it originally announced its decision to pattern a new
equities marketplace after the NASDAQ System, the
London Stock Exchange Council cited a number of reasons
for preferring this type of market:

- It is a "quote chosen" system, as opposed to an "order
  driven" system, and as such is nearest to the present
  jobbing system.
- It preserves the practice of private negotiation between
  members.
- It recognizes and embraces the efficiencies that computer technology can bring to a dealing environment.
- It has the advantage of placing all members on an equal
  basis regardless of geographical location.
- It could grow modularly and would enable the London
  Stock Exchange to expand, capitalize on its time zone
  advantage and lend itself to the development of a
  24-hour international market.
- Unlike the specialist system, it does not rely on the
  quality and state of mind of one individual for the continuity of the market in any given share.
- It would likely require one set of rules and surveillance
  procedures.

- It would interface with the countrywide Talisman delivery system.

It was a short trip across this philosophical bridge to practical application. On April 22, 1986, the NASD and the London Stock Exchange initiated the first intercontinental market-to-market linkage. This link allows London traders to view NASDAQ securities via the 8,000 terminals of the new TOPIC system and allows U.S. traders to view quotes in a similar number of LSE-listed issues on 3,000 NASDAQ terminals in the U.S. This information exchange is clearly intended to be the first stage of a more comprehensive market linkage.

In my experience, the progression of markets is predictable: Visibility begets information flow, information flow begets investor curiosity, and investor curiosity begets research, market making and ultimately more volume and broader liquidity. Today, it is easy to foresee a worldwide computer-generated execution and information system on a wide variety of London-listed and NASDAQ-listed stocks through the technology windows of the NASDAQ and TOPIC systems.

NASDAQ Becomes Model for Debt Markets

NASDAQ modeling has gone beyond the international equity market and is having an impact on international debt markets as well. In July of 1986, the Association of International Bond Dealers (AIBD) announced the outline for a computerized communications system, which is similar in design to the NASDAQ System, for the massive Eurobond market.

Trading in Eurobonds, measured by settlement system volume, aggregated $2.2 trillion par value in 1985, making the Eurobond market the world's largest capital market after the U.S. Treasury market. Eurobonds are fixed-income securities largely denominated in U.S. dollars, but also in other major currencies including the Deutsche mark and the Japanese yen. Issuers are investment-quality corporations and governments worldwide, and liquidity is provided through a network of 800 dealers, most of which are AIBD members, in 39 countries, principally in Europe.

When studying the design of a computer communications system, the AIBD turned to NASDAQ for cooperation and assistance. "NASDAQ is recognized as a model for the international stock markets of the future, and we believe a similar system would lead to further expansion of the international bond market," said Stanley Ross, Managing Director of Deutsche Bank Capital Markets in London, who is heading the development effort. Such a system, he has said, "will streamline communication, improve liquidity and bring dramatic economies and efficiencies to matching for clearance and settlement."

The AIBD has approached this matter gradually. The beauty of the current technology is that it not only solves problems of time, distance, and custom in ways conventional systems cannot, but that it also allows for gradual progress in a modular format. And so, with cooperation from the London Stock Exchange and the AIBD, NASDAQ is making the transition from a national securities market to an international market model.

Internationalization — Accelerating Change

Change is as much a constant in modern securities markets as it was 50 or 60 years ago, but the key difference is its rate of speed. Certainly London markets accomplished more in 1986 than could have been imagined possible in a decade not too long ago. And it seems as if the modern media won't let us forget it.

The media have latched onto the topic of internationalization, daily publishing stories of "Big Bang," 'globalization" and "international capital markets" as if these were the most astounding and dramatic developments in security markets in the last 20 years. In fact, they very likely are.

While some find it fashionable to dismiss these current favorites of the financial press as a passing fad (like junk bonds, mortgage-backed securities and other multi-billion dollar trivia) and while still others deride them as latent interest in a process centuries old, the best evidence seems to suggest that we are seeing a unique confluence of investors, issuers and securities firms at a unique moment of time—the present. Like nuclear energy, it may not be easy to explain, but the effects are profound and the individual ingredients extremely powerful.

By the end of 1985, cross-border trading of equities was estimated to account for 10 percent to 12 percent of the $1.8 trillion traded that year in major world markets. Around that time, Arthur Anderson & Co. and the Securities Industry Association polled 600 leaders of the financial services industry for their views on the future of such trading. The consensus was that, as early as 1988, this cross-border share of world equity trading would amount to more than 16 percent. When the results for 1986 and early 1987 are tabulated, I suspect we will find these percentages were reached far ahead of schedule.

Investors, a Powerful Force

The worldwide tendency toward institutionalization of equity investment, coupled with a worldwide hunger for positive performance, has propelled investors into global markets. For example, some investors took note of a meeting of the *Group of Five*[1] at the Plaza Hotel in New York in the fall of 1985 and arranged their portfolios to profit from a soon falling dollar and more dramatic growth outside the U.S. These investors made some spectacular gains. Similarly, investors who shifted assets back to the U.S. after most of this effect was felt have been no less rewarded. These kinds of results gave birth, or at least popular recognition, to a new kind of global management in which asset allocation is not simply limited to standard sectors in one's own market but takes a broader (and more profitable) viewpoint.

Along with a desire for performance, investors have sought global markets for both currency and company diversification. Broader selection should, as the theory goes, produce less risk and better results. How can an investor ignore some of the world's largest food companies, defense contractors, chemical companies, technology or pharmaceutical companies? With less than a truly global perspective, an investor does. For example, as a fiduciary, would you encourage your funds manager to limit the stocks to be included in the automobile weighting of your portfolio to just Ford, General Motors and Chrysler...or to just Toyota, Honda and Nissan...or to just Jaguar or Volvo...or to just BMW and Mercedes? Or would you expect and encourage your funds manager to examine the *entire* universe before selecting those stocks that genuinely represent the best investments.

Particularly in the United States, investors have been driven to foreign markets by basic laws of supply and demand. Although pension assets in the U.S. have been growing at about 15 percent for the past five or six years,

---

[1]The Group of Five includes the Secretary of the Treasury of the United States, the Chancellor of the Exchequer of Great Britain and the Finance Ministers of France, West Germany and Japan.

the dollar denominated *base* into which they can be invested has actually been shrinking on a net basis. Mergers and acquisitions, leveraged buyouts and company stock repurchase programs have all taken their toll on the U.S. marketplace, which shrank $70 billion in 1986 alone. In fact, as you can see in the accompanying table, over the past seven years the net equity issues in the U.S. have declined by some $190 billion. And so, we have a basic economic phenomenon in which an increasing amount of money is chasing a decreasing amount of goods.

In practical application, an investor today has to decide to buy Dupont or Monsanto at 14 or 15 times earnings with the hope that earnings will grow or its multiple will grow to 25 or 30 times earnings; or he may conclude that ICI at 13 is a better growth avenue, or that Bayer, BASF and Hoechst are better values at eight times earnings.

Global management is finding willing support among many pension sponsors, who in 1986 controlled some $1.6 trillion of U.S. pension assets. In many cases, we are finding these funds increasingly controlled by a new kind of chief financial officer in the U.S.—in many cases, one with significant experience in the company's overseas operation and no small degree of sophistication in non-U.S. currencies and investments. For the new kind of CFO and others, this accelerating move into global equities is the next logical step in a diversification process that began with expanding from pure common stock investment into bonds in the 1960s; real estate and sometimes precious metals in the 1970s; and now to global markets for the 1980s and likely into the early 1990s.

Dedicated mutual funds with a global management perspective are also attracting a growing number of investors. There were 18 such funds totaling $3.82 billion in May of 1984; 32 such funds totaling $5.5 billion by May of 1985; just 20 selected global or international funds in September 1986 had total assets of $14.3 billion, according to a recent *Wall*

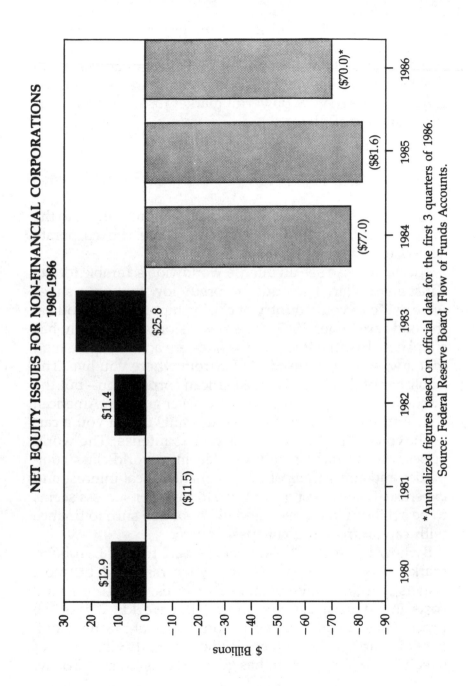

NET EQUITY ISSUES FOR NON-FINANCIAL CORPORATIONS
1980-1986

1980 $12.9
1981 ($11.5)
1982 $11.4
1983 $25.8
1984 ($77.0)
1985 ($81.6)
1986 ($70.0)*

$ Billions

*Annualized figures based on official data for the first 3 quarters of 1986.
Source: Federal Reserve Board, Flow of Funds Accounts.

Street Journal study. Add to this the growing involvement of the insurance industry, commercial bank trust departments, charitable institutions and investment advisers—all seeking competitive returns in modern markets—and you can see we have very powerful market forces in an important transitional phase.

Corporate Issuers Develop Global Plans

The second important force contributing to the internationalization of equity markets are the corporate issuers of securities worldwide.

Today, you can see an intense worldwide scramble for the consumer dollar. The odds are pretty low that your shoes were made in your country of citizenship; for your clothes, the odds are about 50/50. Your television set probably has a Japanese brand name, but the odds are actually quite high that it was manufactured not far from where you live. The publisher of this book is an American corporation—but the lumber for the paper pulp probably never grew on American soil. And today it seems everyone wants to sell you a car.

The competition for capital is no less intense. The world appears to be increasingly divided into world-class companies and companies of predominantly local interest and expertise. For the best of both, the formula for success seems to be similar: Find a need and fill it—but be sure to finance with capital from the cheapest source.

By now the recent lessons of the $2.2 trillion Eurobond market should be clear. Today, when raising debt, most issuers automatically compare structures, rates, size, and costs in financial centers around the world. This same process has already started in equity capital-raising activities. My partner, Hans-Joerg Rudloff, Deputy Chairman of Credit Suisse First Boston, has gone so far as to say, "Today, any company that does not search for capital worldwide is likely guilty of negligence.'' These sound like harsh words, but reality often is harsh. The reality is that in a highly competitive worldwide marketplace, no one can afford a structural disadvantage because of higher or less advantageous financing costs. People may be the key ingredient in the battle for the consumer's attention, but costs of capital can be the cutting edge.

In the bond markets, the concept of worldwide financial window shopping is relatively well established and few barriers to entry remain. Equity investment and equity markets worldwide are quite something else. Risks are higher, results are much more difficult to estimate, and the dependence on research and due diligence can be both admirable and infuriating. Various governments take a keen interest in what equity securities are sold on their shores, and the whole process is much more institutionalized, bureaucratic and time consuming.

Many of First Boston's clients are responding to this challenge with a fairly consistent global game plan. First, they deploy an investor relations effort in New York, London and their home market, and often in Tokyo as well. Second, they develop access—through broker relationships in London and a sponsored ADR program in the U.S., for example. Third, they list on the London exchange, NASDAQ and the Tokyo exchange, while maintaining local listings. Last, they mature through an ongoing company-sponsored information effort with research analysts, shareholders and potential investors in each geographical area.

If these efforts are well organized, their benefits can be lasting. In the U.S., for example, benefits can include a favorable blending of price/earnings ratios; the creation of additional currency for merger and acquisition activity; stock ownership programs for stateside employees; immediate access to the entire U.S. debt and equity capital market spectrum, including the U.S. commercial paper market; and a favorable impact on product recognition and sales.

For U.S. companies overseas, the benefits are no less compelling. When we manage an equity offering today, we almost always advise the client to set aside a portion of the offering for investors overseas. In the marketing process, roadshows to London, Switzerland and other European financial centers have become as important as trips to New York or Boston. By accessing the entire pool of equity capital worldwide, the issuer ultimately assures a better offering price and a broader shareholder base. And the next time equity capital is needed, the issuer is further along in its global game plan.

Securities Industry Recognizes Global Potential

The third force impelling the internationalization of markets is the securities industry. U.S. firms have over 250 branches in 30 countries. The president of Nomura Securities, arguably the largest securities firm in the world, estimates that under his successor, half of the firm's business will be international in nature. Much has been made of the firm's recent global alliance between Goldman Sachs and Sumitomo Trust. At First Boston, we have benefited from the wisdom of a unique partnership that dates from the late 1970s among First Boston Corporation, an American investment bank; Credit Suisse, one of the largest banks and investment managers in Switzerland; and CSFB, our jointly owned, London-based merchant bank. Today, no one organization raises more capital than this unique partnership, and no one knows better the extraordinary competition in and potential of global markets.

NASDAQ Is Well Positioned

The future is here and now—and no matter where you look, NASDAQ is especially well positioned. In the London laboratory in 1986, NASDAQ was repeatedly the choice of experts and practitioners. Global investors increasingly turn to NASDAQ for execution of trades in a wide variety of technology, telecommunication, bank and finance, and other world-class companies. For foreign issuers accessing the U.S. equity markets, NASDAQ is clearly the marketplace of choice, accounting for 88 of 116 listed ADRs or 76 percent of all ADR issues listed on U.S. exchanges. With almost 1.6 billion shares, NASDAQ trades about five times the share volume of ADRs on the NYSE and more than 12 times the share volume of ADRs on the Amex.

NASDAQ-style technology offers practical answers to the problems of 24-hour trading, global risk management, and fully automated dealing systems. The communications technology for the 24-hour world market exists or will be available very soon. The trading system—the competitive, multiple market-maker system—exists and is being expanded around the globe. The demand for the world market, from investors and issuers, is mounting. The construction of the full-fledged world equity market is therefore only a matter of economics, effort and time.

PART II
NASDAQ Companies: Who Are They?

Chapter four

Robert J. Flaherty is Editor of *OTC Review*, a monthly magazine covering over-the-counter companies. He is also the Chairman of the Over-the-Counter Securities Fund, whose total assets exceed $275 million.

The Panorama
of Companies
by Robert J. Flaherty

The NASDAQ market has attracted companies from every part of the broad spectrum of corporations that compose the U.S. and overseas economies. At year-end 1986, 4,417 companies had their securities quoted and traded there. Because many companies trade more than one type of security, the total number of NASDAQ issues was 5,189, including all categories of security issues of both domestic and foreign companies. Common stock issues of U.S. companies still comprise the majority of NASDAQ's securities and market value, with some 4,074 domestic common stock issues traded, accounting for a market value of $328.5 billion. An additional 266 foreign issuers' common stocks or ADRs are traded in the NASDAQ market, accounting for another $23.7 billion in market value. In addition, many companies have units, warrants, preferred shares, shares of beneficial interest, debentures and other securities in the market.

Market Growth

The extent to which companies have made NASDAQ their market of choice is reflected in the market's

DISTRIBUTION OF NUMBER OF ISSUES AND
MARKET VALUE BY ISSUE CLASSIFICATION
(December 31, 1986)

Issue Type	NASDAQ National Market System (NASDAQ/NMS)		Regular NASDAQ		Total NASDAQ	
	Number of Issues	Market Value ($ millions)	Number of Issues	Market Value ($ millions)	Number of Issues	Market Value ($ millions)
Domestic Common Stocks	2,513	$305,805	1,561	$22,721	4,074	$328,527
Foreign Securities	50	7,436	128	4,591	178	12,027
ADRs	26	4,964	62	6,695	88	11,659
Units	13	1,224	242	1,473	255	2,698
Warrants	29	70	313	558	342	629
Preferred Stocks	37	1,978	75	2,563	112	4,542
Shares of Beneficial Interest	27	1,445	13	210	40	1,655
Debentures	0	0	100	410	100	410
Totals	**2,695**	**$323,170**	**2,494**	**$39,407**	**5,189**	**$362,578**

exceptionally rapid growth relative to other stock markets.
NASDAQ was established in 1971 with 2,827 companies,
compared with 2,638 listed on the NYSE and Amex combined. By the end of 1986, the companies choosing NASDAQ
had grown to 4,417, an increase of 56 percent, while the
combined total of companies listed on both the NYSE and
Amex had declined to 2,370, a decrease of 10 percent.

The number of companies listed on the NYSE, which had
been increasing steadily for many years, peaked two or three
years after the introduction of the NASDAQ System. At the
end of 1986, the NYSE list was slightly smaller than it had
been a decade ago. The number of companies listed on the
Amex began to decline in 1973, a decline that has continued
almost without interruption.

NUMBER OF COMPANIES:
NASDAQ, NYSE, AMEX COMPARISON

	NASDAQ	NYSE	Amex
1971	2,827	1,426	1,232
1972	3,288	1,505	1,321
1973	2,761	1,560	1,292
1974	2,436	1,567	1,249
1975	2,467	1,557	1,215
1976	2,495	1,576	1,161
1977	2,456	1,575	1,098
1978	2,475	1,581	1,004
1979	2,543	1,565	931
1980	2,894	1,570	892
1981	3,353	1,565	867
1982	3,264	1,562	834
1983	3,901	1,550	822
1984	4,097	1,543	792
1985	4,136	1,540	783
1986	4,417	1,573	797

The widening gap between the number of companies choosing the NASDAQ System and those listing on an exchange is also reflected in NASDAQ's growth of volume compared with the traditional exchanges. In 1972, NASDAQ volume was 2.2 billion shares, equal to about 42 percent of the combined NYSE and Amex total. By 1986, NASDAQ share volume was 74 percent of combined NYSE and Amex activity. NASDAQ daily volume now frequently exceeds that of the NYSE and averages 10 times more than the Amex daily activity.

SHARE VOLUME:
NASDAQ, NYSE, AMEX COMPARISON

	NASDAQ	NYSE	Amex
1971	*	3,891,318,000	1,070,924,000
1972	2,220,925,000	4,138,188,000	1,117,989,000
1973	1,681,064,000	4,053,201,000	759,840,000
1974	1,179,723,000	3,517,743,000	482,173,000
1975	1,390,412,000	4,693,427,000	540,934,000
1976	1,683,933,000	5,360,116,000	648,297,000
1977	1,932,100,000	5,273,767,000	653,129,000
1978	2,762,499,000	7,205,059,000	988,559,000
1979	3,651,214,000	8,155,914,000	1,100,264,000
1980	6,691,631,000	11,352,294,000	1,626,073,000
1981	7,823,410,000	11,853,741,000	1,343,400,000
1982	8,432,275,000	16,458,037,000	1,337,725,000
1983	15,908,547,000	21,589,577,000	2,080,922,000
1984	15,158,823,000	23,071,031,000	1,544,335,000
1985	20,699,146,000	27,510,706,000	2,100,815,000
1986	28,736,561,000	35,680,016,000	2,978,612,000

*Share-volume reporting not initiated until October 1971.
Note: Share volume rounded to thousands.

Profile of NASDAQ Companies and Their Securities

Based upon year-end 1986 data, NASDAQ companies reported aggregate assets of $1.8 trillion, total equity of $292.4 billion, revenue of $606.2 billion and net income of $28.1 billion. The average company had $417.9 million in assets, $67.8 million in equity, $140.6 million in sales and $6.5 million in net income, placing it among the top 3,000 U.S. industrial corporations or top 2,000 U.S. service companies.

NASDAQ COMPANIES*
AND THEIR 1986 SECURITIES PROFILE DATA

Securities Data	NASDAQ/NMS	ALL NASDAQ
• Number of Securities	2,613	4,359
Average Share Price	$15.82	$9.95
Average Number of Market Makers	9.2	8.4
• Total Shares Outstanding (Aggregate)	20,201,103,000	35,499,696,000
Average Shares Outstanding (Per Issue)	7,731,000	8,144,000
• Total Float	14,972,490,000	24,593,478,000
Average Float	5,730,000	5,642,000
• Total Market Value	$319,601,256,000	$353,554,131,000
Average Market Value	$122,312,000	$81,109,000

Company Data		
• Number of Companies	2,600	4,312
• Total Assets	$1,385,342,400,000	$1,801,989,112,000
Average Assets	$532,824,000	$417,901,000
• Total Equity	$185,445,000,000	$292,392,408,000
Average Equity	$71,325,000	$67,809,000
• Total Revenue	$381,888,000,000	$606,232,704,000
Average Revenue	$146,880,000	$140,592,000
• Total Net Income	$16,876,600,000	$28,114,240,000
Average Net Income	$6,491,000	$6,520,000
Average Price/Earnings Ratio**	18.8	21.2

*Domestic common and foreign stocks, ADRs and shares of beneficial interest only.
**Domestic common stocks and shares of beneficial interest only.

The average price/earnings ratio of the companies' shares was 21.2 with an average share price of $9.95. The average security had 8.1 million shares outstanding and a public float of 5.6 million shares; the market for individual securities is served by an average of 8.4 market-making firms. The aggregate market value of equity shares (including foreign and domestic common stocks, ADRs, and shares of beneficial interest) was $353.6 billion at the end of 1986.

Broad Industry Representation

NASDAQ companies fall into approximately 73 two-digit and 316 three-digit standard industry classification (SIC) codes. They run the gamut of the U.S. economy with broad representation in the agricultural, mining, construction, food products, manufacturing, transportation and retail industries as well as in the advanced technology sectors.

1986 INDUSTRY CLASSIFICATION
OF NASDAQ COMPANIES

Industry	Number of Companies	Market Value ($ millions)
Agricultural Products-Crops	8	1,513.5
Agricultural Products-Livestock	5	39.2
Agricultural Services	7	216.5
Fishing, Hunting and Trapping	1	23.3
Metal Mining	110	5,928.8
Anthracite Mining	2	422.9
Bituminous Coal and Lignite Mining	7	408.8
Oil and Gas Extraction	232	3,388.2
Mining and Quarrying	9	641.1
Building Construction	16	525.4
Construction-General Contractors	10	410.2
Construction-Special Trade Contractors	10	170.8
Food and Tobacco Kindred Products	56	5,520.4
Tobacco Manufacturers	1	2.9
Textile Mill Products	19	897.6
Apparel	21	3,543.5
Lumber and Wood Products	24	2,391.6
Furniture and Fixtures	26	3,124.9
Paper and Allied Products	29	4,937.9
Printing and Publishing	54	5,716.1
Chemicals and Allied Products	189	19,630.0
Petroleum Refining & Related Industry	8	365.9
Rubber and Miscellaneous Plastic Products	49	1,604.5

1986 INDUSTRY CLASSIFICATION
OF NASDAQ COMPANIES
(Continued)

Industry	Number of Companies	Market Value ($ millions)
Leather and Leather Products	11	267.4
Stone, Clay, Glass & Concrete Products	20	1,003.5
Primary Metal Industries	27	2,104.8
Fabricated Metal Products	67	2,448.1
Machinery, Except Electrical	311	22,699.6
Electrical and Electronic Machinery	350	17,110.9
Transportation Equipment	47	6,614.6
Measuring Instruments	262	13,450.7
Miscellaneous Manufacturing Industries	35	1,267.7
Railroad Transportation	3	141.1
Local and Suburban Transit	1	520.0
Motor Freight Transportation	32	4,557.3
Water Transportation	12	1,839.9
Transportation by Air	31	1,486.6
Pipe Lines, Except Natural Gas	1	1,121.9
Transportation Services	12	413.0
Communication	88	11,637.8
Electric, Gas and Sanitary Services	73	7,125.4
Wholesale Trade-Durable Goods	119	5,179.4
Wholesale Trade-Nondurable Goods	48	5,833.8
Building Materials	5	353.9
General Merchandise Stores	22	1,837.5
Food Stores	30	3,523.1
Automotive Dealers	10	301.0
Apparel and Accessory Stores	32	4,863.6
Furniture Stores	27	2,138.7
Eating and Drinking Places	86	5,275.3
Miscellaneous Retail	73	5,104.2
Banking	206	10,341.9
Credit Agencies Other Than Banks	138	5,913.5
Security and Commodity Brokers	35	2,160.1
Insurance	119	18,486.4
Insurance Agents, Brokers and Service	13	4,601.7
Real Estate	35	1,773.7
Combinations of Real Estate, Insurance	40	8,487.9

1986 INDUSTRY CLASSIFICATION
OF NASDAQ COMPANIES
(Continued)

Industry	Number of Companies	Market Value ($ millions)
Financial Holding and Other Investment Offices	479	74,860.3
Hotels and Other Lodging Places	20	805.0
Personal Services	11	895.8
Business Services	357	21,471.9
Automotive Repair Services and Garages	12	865.2
Miscellaneous	3	98.3
Motion Pictures	40	1,215.9
Amusement and Recreation Services	24	532.9
Health Services	103	4,663.3
Legal Services	3	74.4
Educational Services	14	391.6
Social Services	6	897.6
Membership Organizations	2	6.7
Miscellaneous Services	30	1,231.7
Nonclassifiable Establishments	5	285.9

The NASDAQ list is not dominated by concentrations of companies in particular industries. For example, 55 of the 73 basic industry categories are represented by 10 or more companies, and some major industries include hundreds of companies: financial holding and investment companies (479); business services (357); electrical and electronic machinery (350); machinery (excluding electrical) (311); measuring instruments (262); oil and gas extraction (232); banking (206); chemicals and allied products (189); credit agencies other than banks (138); insurance companies (119); wholesale trade (119); metal mining (110); and health services (103).

Moreover, the market value and the number of issues traded in the various industry groups suggest a distribution of securities across SIC categories that is consistent with the distribution of public companies throughout the economy. In each of 45 of the 73 two-digit SIC industry categories represented by NASDAQ companies, the combined market value of the companies' stocks exceed $1 billion.

The industrial component is the largest in terms of market value of underlying securities—totaling $188.4 billion—while the financial sector is $123.7 billion (including banks, insurance and other finance). Similarly, the utility and transportation segments, with market values of shares of $18.0 billion and $10.9 billion, respectively, illustrate the economic breadth and depth of the NASDAQ market. The market value of issues included in the NASDAQ indices* as of December 31, 1986, are as follows:

Industrial	$188,351,374,000
Other Finance	$89,964,166,000
Insurance	$23,619,794,000
Utility	$17,976,138,000
Transportation	$10,888,767,000
Bank	$10,114,426,000
Composite	$340,914,665,000

A Market for All Sizes

NASDAQ has also emerged as the market of choice for very large as well as smaller companies. Companies valued at $1 billion or more (the *OTC Review* Billionaires Club) had 39 NASDAQ members at year-end 1986.

---

*NASDAQ issues not included in NASDAQ indices have a total market value of $21.7 billion.

MARKET VALUE OF LARGEST AND SMALLEST COMPANIES

Industry	SIC Code	NASDAQ/NMS		All NASDAQ	
		Largest	Smallest	Largest	Smallest
			— In Thousands —		
Agricultural Products-Crops	01	$957,750	$73,766	$957,750	$1,870
Agricultural Services	07	153,171	20,024	153,171	1,195
Metal Mining	10	814,129	4,226	814,129	44
Bituminous Coal and Lignite Mining	12	179,118	169,125	179,118	2,141
Oil and Gas Extraction	13	361,750	1,199	361,750	101
Mining and Quarrying	14	48,760	12,868	398,745	1,454
Building Construction	15	141,680	8,270	141,680	1,806
Construction-General Contractors	16	90,856	4,958	90,856	4,985
Construction-Special Trade Contractors	17	50,408	9,180	50,408	450
Food and Tobacco Kindred Products	20	1,160,468	3,903	1,160,468	1,068
Textile Mill Products	22	147,075	12,782	147,075	1,750
Apparel	23	1,849,108	4,758	1,849,108	826
Lumber and Wood Products	24	919,161	5,312	919,161	971
Furniture and Fixtures	25	515,400	4,879	515,400	3,612
Paper and Allied Products	26	1,121,773	635	1,121,773	277
Printing & Publishing	27	1,098,000	5,924	1,098,000	743
Chemicals and Allied Products	28	2,818,005	3,388	2,818,005	3,388
Petroleum Refining & Related Industries	29	251,384	10,451	251,384	173
Rubber and Miscellaneous Plastics Products	30	215,250	4,866	215,250	345
Leather and Leather Products	31	129,536	8,228	129,536	1,713
Stone, Clay, Glass & Concrete Products	32	194,066	4,938	194,066	2,371
Primary Metal Industries	33	684,255	6,159	684,255	1,253
Fabricated Metal Products	34	294,442	2,980	294,442	760
Machinery, Except Electrical	35	2,600,019	1,558	2,600,019	166
Electrical and Electronic Machinery	36	2,469,243	1,719	2,469,243	45
Transportation Equipment	37	1,435,893	4,261	1,435,893	383
Measuring Instruments	38	886,378	3,726	886,378	257
Miscellaneous Manufacturing Industries	39	206,070	5,721	206,070	590
Motor Freight Transportation	42	1,379,103	4,600	1,379,103	861
Water Transportation	44	1,260,720	7,218	1,260,720	304

MARKET VALUE OF LARGEST AND SMALLEST COMPANIES
(Continued)

Industry	SIC Code	NASDAQ/NMS		All NASDAQ	
		Largest	Smallest	Largest	Smallest
		In Thousands			
Transportation by Air	45	318,448	4,460	318,448	2,342
Transportation Services	47	153,375	9,160	153,375	633
Communication	48	1,787,521	4,389	1,787,521	475
Electric, Gas and Sanitary Services	49	870,817	6,951	870,817	1,426
Wholesale Trade-Durable Goods	50	933,201	4,387	933,201	598
Wholesale Trade-Nondurable Goods	51	1,601,016	8,263	1,601,016	1,170
Building Materials	52	273,309	10,155	273,309	385
General Merchandise Stores	53	287,415	3,904	287,415	218
Food Stores	54	974,940	10,723	974,940	2,601
Automotive Dealers	55	80,959	3,474	90,993	695
Apparel and Accessory Stores	56	1,690,040	9,780	1,690,040	1,055
Furniture Stores	57	359,766	2,344	359,766	2,344
Eating and Drinking Places	58	901,196	4,032	901,196	375
Miscellaneous Retail	59	709,656	4,873	709,656	149
Banking	60	406,453	2,990	406,453	405
Credit Agencies Other Than Banks	61	729,720	1,140	729,720	876
Security and Commodity Brokers	62	256,069	4,268	256,069	3,092
Insurance	63	1,860,797	1,700	1,860,797	503
Insurance Agents, Brokers and Service	64	2,694,016	64,741	2,694,016	3,485
Real Estate	65	977,676	4,880	977,676	378
Combinations of Real Estate, Insurance	66	3,234,540	7,646	3,234,540	356
Holding and Other Investment Offices	67	2,650,830	3,111	2,650,830	330
Hotels and Other Lodging Places	70	200,049	27,000	200,049	915
Personal Services	72	316,268	29,520	316,268	1,616
Business Services	73	1,242,920	2,082	1,242,920	47
Automotive Repair Services and Garages	75	474,815	9,868	474,815	1,742
Motion Pictures	78	383,819	6,235	383,819	1,297
Amusement and Recreation Services	79	111,647	2,503	111,647	256
Health Services	80	531,006	4,278	531,006	325
Educational Services	82	98,410	14,741	98,410	1,581
Miscellaneous Services	89	249,184	8,006	249,184	628

1986 MARKET VALUE OF NASDAQ COMPANIES

Market Value	NASDAQ/NMS		OTHER NASDAQ		ALL NASDAQ	
	Number of Companies	Market Value ($ billions)	Number of Companies	Market Value ($ billions)	Number of Companies	Market Value ($ billions)
$1 Billion or more	37	$60.9	2	$2.7	39	$63.6
$500 M to less than $1 B	82	58.7	3	2.1	85	60.8
$250 M to less than $500 M	188	64.9	9	2.7	197	67.6
$125 M to less than $250 M	294	53.2	21	3.4	315	56.5
$75 M to less than $125 M	314	30.4	30	2.9	344	33.3
$50 M to less than $75 M	297	18.2	49	3.1	346	21.3
$25 M to less than $50 M	528	18.8	151	5.2	679	24.0
Less than $25 Million	860	11.6	1,552	10.6	2,412	22.3
Total	**2,600**	**$316.7**	**1,817**	**$32.7**	**4,417**	**$349.4**

NASDAQ "BILLIONAIRES"
1986

Company Name	Closing Price Per Share	Market Value ($000s)
Berkshire Hathaway, Inc.	$2,820.000	$3,234,540
Genentech, Inc.	85.000	2,818,005
Farmers Group, Inc.	38.750	2,694,016
First Union Corporation	24.125	2,650,830
Apple Computer, Inc.	40.500	2,600,019
Intel Corporation	21.000	2,469,243
Henley Group, Inc. (The)	22.625	2,381,960
PNC Financial Corp.	41.250	2,019,311
St. Paul Companies, Inc. (The)	40.250	1,860,797
Liz Claiborne, Inc.	42.750	1,849,108
Safeco Corporation	53.500	1,804,983
Tele-Communications, Inc.	22.875	1,787,521
MCI Communications Corporation	6.250	1,768,706
Nordstrom, Inc.	41.750	1,690,040
Glaxo Holdings (PLC)	15.375	1,674,798
Price Company (The)	32.750	1,601,016
Kemper Corporation	25.000	1,507,500
Tandem Computers Incorporated	34.250	1,486,861
LIN Broadcasting Corporation	55.375	1,475,522
Jaguar plc	7.937	1,435,893
Citizens & Southern Corp.	24.500	1,432,196
Bank of New England	29.750	1,427,583
Sovran Financial Corporation	33.750	1,425,093
Corestates Financial	35.750	1,403,866
Roadway Services, Inc.	34.500	1,379,103
Alexander & Baldwin, Inc.	45.000	1,260,720
National City Corporation	45.875	1,248,534
Microsoft Corporation	48.250	1,242,920
American National Insurance	41.000	1,187,934
Tyson Foods, Inc.	27.250	1,160,468
Interprovincial Pipe Line	28.375	1,121,862
Consolidated Papers, Inc.	51.500	1,121,773
Commerce Clearing House, Inc.	61.000	1,098,000
First Executive Corporation	15.000	1,055,640
Yellow Freight System, Inc.	36.875	1,055,251
Wacoal Corp.	37.750	1,046,430
Reuters Holdings PLC	49.875	1,045,429
Willamette Industries, Inc.	40.750	1,035,294
Shared Medical Systems	40.500	1,018,170

Geographical Diversity

NASDAQ companies are headquartered in every state and 27 foreign countries. At year-end 1986, there were 4,173 domestic companies with headquarters in the U.S. (including Puerto Rico) and 244 with headquarters in foreign countries. The greatest numbers of NASDAQ companies are headquartered in California and New York, and 44 different states contain the headquarters of 10 or more NASDAQ companies.

Most of NASDAQ's 244 foreign issuers are Canadian companies. Seventeen are domiciled in England, 16 in Japan, 17 in South Africa and 11 in Australia. Foreign companies traded in NASDAQ include internationally known names such as Biogen, Cadbury Schweppes, De Beers Consolidated Mines, Ericsson Telephone Company, Fuji Photo, Glaxo Holdings, Gotaas-Larsen Shipping, Jaguar, Morgan Products, Philips Gloeilampen, Reuters, Toyota, and Volvo.

Domestic NASDAQ companies include industry leaders such as Adolph Coors, American Greetings, Apple Computer, Berkshire Hathaway, Citizens Utilities, Crazy Eddie's Inc., Farmers Group, First Union Corporation, Genentech, Intel Corporation, Liz Claiborne, MCI Communications Corporation, PNC Financial Corporation, Subaru of America, and United Artists Communications.

Many NASDAQ companies, especially those listed on the NASDAQ National Market System, have market values exceeding $100 million. At year-end 1986, 748 companies were valued at $100 million or more.

Diversity in Company Age and Stock Activity

NASDAQ listings include many mature corporations, some as venerable as Alex. Brown & Sons Incor-

1986 NATIONWIDE DISTRIBUTION OF NASDAQ AND NASDAQ/NMS COMPANIES

State	No. of Companies		State	No. of Companies	
	NASDAQ	NASDAQ/NMS		NASDAQ	NASDAQ/NMS
California	624	402	Nevada	35	13
New York	469	210	Kansas	31	19
Texas	242	122	Iowa	28	21
New Jersey	239	129	South Carolina	25	19
Massachusetts	227	165	Kentucky	23	12
Florida	198	103	New Hampshire	22	17
Pennsylvania	157	101	Nebraska	21	16
Colorado	145	50	New Mexico	20	7
Illinois	143	101	Mississippi	18	11
Minnesota	143	90	Louisiana	18	11
Ohio	135	103	District of		
Connecticut	132	74	Columbia	15	11
Michigan	99	72	West Virginia	14	9
Georgia	89	64	West Virginia	14	9
Virginia	88	66	Wyoming	12	3
Maryland	78	55	Vermont	12	11
Washington	74	52	Delaware	11	8
North Carolina	74	49	Arkansas	10	9
Indiana	59	43	Idaho	10	7
Wisconsin	59	47	Rhode Island	9	5
Missouri	57	40	Maine	9	8
Utah	53	19	Alaska	7	7
Oklahoma	49	18	Hawaii	7	6
Tennessee	46	34	Montana	7	6
Arizona	42	15	Puerto Rico	6	6
Alabama	38	34	North Dakota	4	0
Oregon	38	24	South Dakota	2	2

1986 WORLDWIDE DISTRIBUTION OF NASDAQ
FOREIGN COMPANIES

Countries	ADR Issuers	Foreign Securities Issuers	Countries	ADR Issuers	Foreign Securities Issuers
Aruba	0	1	Israel	3	13
Australia	11	0	Japan	13	3
Bahamas	0	2	Liechtenstein	0	1
Bermuda	2	6	Luxembourg	0	1
Bolivia	0	1	Mexico	2	0
Canada	0	119	Netherlands	4	4
Cayman Islands	0	3	New Zealand	1	0
El Salvador	1	0	Norway	1	0
England	15	2	Scotland	1	0
Finland	1	0	South Africa	17	0
France	2	0	Sweden	7	0
Germany (West)	1	0	Switzerland	0	1
Hong Kong	0	1	Virgin Islands	0	1
Ireland	3	0			
			Total	**85**	**159**

porated, founded in 1800, and Constellation Bancorp of New Jersey, incorporated in 1812. Now, more than 15 years after the NASDAQ System debuted in 1971 with 2,318 companies, over 400 companies remain as charter members. More than 1,000 NASDAQ companies have been incorporated for at least 25 years; 102 are over 100 years old. On the other hand, nearly 20 percent of NASDAQ companies are less than five years old.

Diversity is also reflected in NASDAQ stock activity. Some of the least active NASDAQ securities trade fewer than 50,000 shares per year—100 to 200 shares per day. In contrast, the most active securities trade more than 100 million shares per year—400,000-plus per day. Many factors such as industry, size and institutional interest determine the market for a company's securities, particularly the level of activity. The volume of trading for the most active company in a particular industry in 1986 was frequently 100 times the comparable share volume of the most inactive company.

1986 YEARS OF INCORPORATION OF NASDAQ COMPANIES
(December 31, 1986)

Years of Incorporation	Number of Companies*
100 years or more	102
75 to less than 100 years	136
50 to less than 75 years	267
25 to less than 50 years	552
15 to less than 25 years	888
10 to less than 15 years	408
5 to less than 10 years	814
Less than 5 years	852
Total	**4,081**

* Companies include issuers of domestic common stocks and shares of beneficial interest. Dates of incorporation were not available for 62 companies.

NASDAQ National Market System

The NASDAQ National Market System (NASDAQ/NMS), which was introduced in April 1982, established real-time, last-sale reporting of transactions in qualified NASDAQ securities. Inclusion in NASDAQ/NMS, provides for automatic marginability of all qualified securities and, in an expanding number of states, an exemption from state blue-sky restrictions. In November 1984, the Federal Reserve Board amended its Regulation T to enable

1986 SHARE VOLUME FOR MOST ACTIVE AND LEAST ACTIVE NASDAQ AND NASDAQ/NMS COMPANIES BY INDUSTRY

Industry	SIC Code	NASDAQ/NMS		All NASDAQ	
		Largest	Smallest	Largest	Smallest
			In Thousands		
Agricultural Products-Crops	01	26,357	200	26,357	31
Agricultural Services	07	17,119	2,977	17,119	319
Metal Mining	10	66,322	870	66,322	3
Bituminous Coal and Lignite Mining	12	6,043	1,173	25,934	65
Oil and Gas Extraction	13	23,823	89	71,218	8
Mining and Quarrying	14	16,122	1,180	75,367	512
Building Construction	15	10,397	207	10,397	181
Construction-General Contractors	16	14,157	982	14,157	352
Construction-Special Trade Contractors	17	10,937	125	10,937	41
Food and Tobacco Kindred Products	20	37,523	126	100,806	15
Textile Mill Products	22	22,933	365	22,933	60
Apparel	23	57,077	625	57,077	34
Lumber and Wood Products	24	7,512	89	7,512	14
Furniture and Fixtures	25	24,255	97	24,255	42
Paper and Allied Products	26	11,537	298	11,656	40
Printing & Publishing	27	49,223	345	49,223	22
Chemicals and Allied Products	28	121,273	257	121,273	257
Petroleum Refining & Related Industries	29	5,182	1,664	5,182	112
Rubber and Miscellaneous Plastics Products	30	22,551	200	22,551	200
Leather and Leather Products	31	11,211	82	11,211	68
Stone, Clay, Glass & Concrete Products	32	14,460	374	14,460	37
Primary Metal Industries	33	17,360	951	17,360	12
Fabricated Metal Products	34	13,723	230	28,264	157
Machinery, Except Electrical	35	238,228	69	238,228	18
Electrical and Electronic Machinery	36	193,545	112	193,545	4
Transportation Equipment	37	257,662	140	257,662	53
Measuring Instruments	38	78,414	142	78,414	1
Miscellaneous Manufacturing Industries	39	56,089	432	76,862	29
Motor Freight Transportation	42	36,234	75	36,234	63
Water Transportation	44	22,444	1,197	22,444	91

1986 SHARE VOLUME FOR MOST ACTIVE AND LEAST ACTIVE NASDAQ AND NASDAQ/NMS COMPANIES BY INDUSTRY
(Continued)

Industry	SIC Code	NASDAQ/NMS Largest	NASDAQ/NMS Smallest	All NASDAQ Largest	All NASDAQ Smallest
			In Thousands		
Transportation by Air	45	33,102	505	105,314	263
Transportation Services	47	7,346	1,265	7,346	68
Communication	48	448,379	142	448,379	24
Electric, Gas and Sanitary Services	49	29,811	81	51,340	40
Wholesale Trade-Durable Goods	50	60,843	9	117,214	5
Wholesale Trade-Nondurable Goods	51	47,626	165	61,337	7
Building Materials	52	5,493	500	5,493	6
General Merchandise Stores	53	33,220	291	33,220	93
Food Stores	54	23,607	375	23,607	46
Automotive Dealers	55	2,964	513	34,668	83
Apparel and Accessory Stores	56	81,663	417	81,663	69
Furniture Stores	57	85,739	624	85,739	138
Eating and Drinking Places	58	85,270	340	85,270	6
Miscellaneous Retail	59	54,426	111	54,426	7
Banking	60	41,835	40	41,835	2
Credit Agencies Other Than Banks	61	26,796	19	26,796	6
Security and Commodity Brokers	62	22,541	119	36,125	34
Insurance	63	96,883	111	96,883	2
Insurance Agents, Brokers and Service	64	36,525	341	36,525	240
Real Estate	65	17,468	43	17,468	22
Combinations of Real Estate, Insurance	66	33,830	79	33,830	1
Holding and Other Investment Offices	67	69,710	14	69,710	2
Hotels and Other Lodging Places	70	18,723	213	18,723	61
Personal Services	72	10,368	875	10,368	59
Business Services	73	112,555	142	112,555	1
Automotive Repair Services and Garages	75	9,379	318	16,788	40
Motion Pictures	78	31,355	451	45,435	94
Amusement and Recreation Services	79	51,649	276	82,088	44
Health Services	80	114,395	736	122,779	17
Educational Services	82	12,604	884	12,604	37
Miscellaneous Services	89	12,709	233	12,709	106

broker-dealers to purchase any NASDAQ/NMS security on margin. Similar regulatory reform is occurring at the state level, where many states have amended their securities statutes to exempt NASDAQ/NMS (and, in some states, all NASDAQ) securities from the merit review (blue-sky) provisions of state securities laws.

NASDAQ/NMS includes nearly all the larger NASDAQ companies. At the end of 1986, the 2,600 NASDAQ/NMS companies had average assets of $532.8 million, average equity of $71.3 million, average revenue of $146.9 million and average net income of $6.5 million. The average share price of NASDAQ/NMS issues is $15.82; the average number of market makers is 9.2; and, although the average float is about the same and the average number of shares outstanding for NASDAQ/NMS stocks is actually below the norm for NASDAQ as a whole, the average market value ($122.3 million) is nearly double that of the typical NASDAQ company. As a result, the aggregate market value of NASDAQ/NMS equity shares accounts for 93 percent of the total market value of all NASDAQ stocks.

Qualification Standards and Fees for NASDAQ Companies

The basic requirement for all NASDAQ issuers is that they be registered with the Securities and Exchange Commission and make the disclosures required under Section 12(g) of the Securities Exchange Act of 1934 or its equivalent. Section 12(g), which was enacted in the mid-1960s, extended to many over-the-counter companies the requirements of Section 12(b)(1) of the Securities Exchange Act of 1934, which contains the disclosure requirements applicable to exchange-listed companies. This means that the same disclosure obligations that apply to securities listed on exchanges also apply to NASDAQ issuers.

QUALIFICATION STANDARDS FOR NASDAQ AND NASDAQ NATIONAL MARKET SYSTEM

Standard	For Initial NASDAQ Inclusion (domestic common stocks)*	For Continued NASDAQ Inclusion (domestic common stocks)*	Criteria for NASDAQ/NMS Inclusion**	
			Alternative 1	Alternative 2
Registration Under Section 12(g) of the Securities Exchange Act of 1934 or Equivalent	Yes	Yes	Yes	Yes
Total Assets	$2 M	$750,000	$2 M	$8 M
Tangible Assets	—	—	—	—
Capital and Surplus	$1 M	$375,000	$1 M	$8 M
Net Income	—	—	$300,000 in latest or 2 of 3 last fiscal years	—
Operating History	—	—	—	4 years
Public Float (Shares)	100,000	100,000	350,000	800,000
Market Value of Float	—	—	$2 M	$8 M
Minimum Bid	—	—	$3	—
Trading Volume	—	—	—	—
Shareholders of Record	300	300	300	300
Number of Market Makers	2	1	2	2

---

* Qualification standards for other types of securities are available upon request from the NASDAQ Company Operations Department in Washington, D.C.

** In addition to the quantitative standards for NASDAQ/NMS inclusion, companies must also meet certain corporate governance requirements.

The standards for entering the NASDAQ System are deliberately modest to permit small companies to avail themselves of efficient trading mechanisms and to encourage venture capital investments. To qualify, a company must have $2 million or more in total assets, $1 million or more in capital and surplus, a public float of 100,000 shares or greater, at least 300 shareholders of record, and at least two market makers.

The standards for entering NASDAQ/NMS are more stringent and are generally comparable to the requirements for listing on the Amex.

The relatively nominal fees charged to issuers facilitate entry into the NASDAQ System. Company fees, which are substantially less than similar charges on exchange markets, are as follows:

Initial Fee Per Share:	$.001
Minimum Initial Fee:	$1,000 (maximum initial fee is $5,000 per issuer during any 24-month period)
Continuing Annual Fee Per Share:	$.0005
Minimum Continuing Fee:	$250 (maximum continuing fee is $4,000 per issuer)

Summary

NASDAQ is a very broad and diverse market, structured to serve the entire spectrum of U.S. and overseas business.

*Chapter
five*

Morris A. Schapiro, who has nearly 60 years of experience in the securities business, is President of M. A. Schapiro & Co., Inc. The firm specializes in bank securities.

Gene L. Finn is Chief Economist for the National Association of Securities Dealers, Inc. Before joining the NASD, Dr. Finn was the Chief Economist for the Securities and Exchange Commission.

The Integration of Financial Companies Into the Global Market

Part I: by Morris A. Schapiro

Part II: by Gene L. Finn

Part I
NASDAQ in London

Creative technological developments in the field of electronic communications have set the stage for a global network of world financial markets. London, New York and Tokyo are the three major centers. London's "Big Bang" on October 27, 1986, brought radical deregulatory changes—ending fixed commissions, inviting competition and promoting fair dealing. With their new computer system, traders are doing business at their desks and not on the floor of the London Stock Exchange

The U.S. NASDAQ market now enjoys electronic presence in London and is open for trading with clearance and settlement facilities in place. NASDAQ market information is available through a cooperative arrangement with the London Stock Exchange. A full montage of market-maker quotations displays the high, low and last-sale prices and share volume on each of the 100 largest NASDAQ-listed U.S. financial companies, as well as the 100 largest non-financial and 68 international issues—a total of 268.

All the information is available on the 8,000 TOPIC

terminals operated by the London Stock Exchange. International trading in these issues is facilitated by a pilot linkage between the International Securities Clearing Corporation based in New York City and the Stock Exchange Clearing Corporation in London.

Of the 100 largest NASDAQ financial companies whose shares are now quoted and traded in London, 73 are banking institutions. Whether in New York or in London, the competition is evident by the number of competing market makers. In each of 15 issues, at least 20 or more dealers are in active competition. In each of 19 issues, the range is 15 to 19 market makers. Participants vary in number from 3 to 14 in the remaining 39 issues.

NASDAQ-FINANCIAL INDEX® COMPONENT STOCKS
(As of December 31, 1986)

Company Name	NASDAQ Symbol
20th Century Industries	TWEN
A. L. Williams Corporation	ALWC
* Allied Bancshares, Inc.	ALBN
* American Fletcher Corporation	AFLT
American National Insurance Company	ANAT
* American Security Corporation	ASEC
* AmeriTrust Corporation	AMTR
* Banco Popular de Puerto Rico	BPOP
* Bancorp Hawaii, Inc.	BNHI
* Bank of New England Corporation	BKNE
* Bank South Corporation	BKSO
* Baybanks, Inc.	BBNK
Berkley (W.R.) Corporation	BKLY
* Boatmen's Bancshares, Inc.	BOAT
* Branch Corporation	BNCH
Business Men's Assurance Company of America	BMAC
* C B & T Bancshares, Inc.	CBTB
* Centerre Bancorporation	CTBC
* Central Bancorporation, Inc. (The)	CBAN
* Central Bancshares of the South	CBSS

NASDAQ-FINANCIAL INDEX® COMPONENT STOCKS
(Continued)

Company Name	NASDAQ Symbol
* Central Fidelity Banks, Inc.	CFBS
Cincinnati Financial Corporation	CINF
* Citizens Fidelity Corporation	CFDY
* Citizens and Southern Corporation	CSOU
* City National Corp.	CTYN
* Comerica, Inc.	CMCA
* Commerce Bancshares, Inc.	CBSH
* Corestates Financial Corporation	CSFN
* Dime Savings Bank of New York	DIME
* Dominion Bankshares Corporation	DMBK
Durham Corporation	DUCO
Farmers Group, Inc.	FGRP
* Fidelcor, Inc.	FICR
* Fifth Third Bancorp	FITB
* First Alabama Bancshares Inc.	FABC
* First American Corporation	FATN
* First Commerce Corporation	FCOM
First Executive Corporation	FEXC
* First Florida Banks, Inc.	FFBK
* First Kentucky National Corporation	FKYN
* First Maryland Bancorp	FMDB
* First National Cincinnati Corporation	FNAC
* First Security Corporation	FSCO
* First Tennessee National Corporation	FTEN
* First Union Corporation	FUNC
* First of America Bank Corporation	FABK
* Florida National Banks of Florida, Inc.	FNBF
Foremost Corporation of America	FCOA
Fremont General Corporation	FRMT
Hanover Insurance Company (The)	HINS
* Hartford National Corporation	HNAT
* Hartford Steam Boiler Inspection and Insurance Co. (The)	HBOL
* Huntington Bancshares Incorporated	HBAN
* Indiana National Corporation	INAT
Kemper Corporation	KEMC
Life Investors Inc.	LINV
* Louisiana Bancshares, Inc.	LABS
* Manufacturers National Corporation	MNTL
* Marshall & Isley Corporation	MRIS

NASDAQ-FINANCIAL INDEX® COMPONENT STOCKS
(Continued)

Company Name	NASDAQ Symbol
* Maryland National Corporation	MDNT
* Mercantile Bancorporation, Inc.	MTRC
* Mercantile Bankshares Corporation	MRBK
* Meridian Bancorp, Inc.	MRDN
* Meritor Savings Bank	MTOR
* Michigan National Corporation	MNCO
* Midlantic Banks, Inc.	MIDL
* National City Corporation	NCTY
* Northern Trust Corporation	NTRS
Northwestern National Life Insurance Company	NWNL
Ohio Casualty Corporation	OCAS
* Old Kent Financial Corporation	OKEN
Old Republic International Corporation	OLDR
* PNC Financial Corp.	PNCF
* Pennbancorp	PNBA
* Perpetual American Bank, F.S.B.	PASB
Progressive Corporation (The)	PROG
Protective Life Corporation	PROT
Provident Life and Accident Insurance Company	PACC
* Rainier Bancorporation	RBAN
Republic American Corp.	RAWC
* Riggs National Corporation	RIGS
Safeco Corporation	SAFC
* Shawmut Corporation	SHAS
* Society Corporation	SOCI
* South Carolina National Corporation	SCNC
* SouthTrust Corporation	SOTR
Southland Financial Corporation	SFIN
* Sovran Financial Corporation	SOVN
St. Paul Companies, Inc. (The)	STPL
* State Street Boston Corporation	STBK
* U.S. Bancorp	USBC
USLICO Corporation	USVC
* United Banks of Colorado, Inc.	UBKS
* United Missouri Bancshares, Inc.	UMSB
* United Virginia Bankshares, Incorporated	UVBK
* Valley National Bancorp	VNBP
* Valley National Corporation	VNCP

NASDAQ-FINANCIAL INDEX® COMPONENT STOCKS
(Continued)

Company Name	NASDAQ Symbol
* Wilmington Trust Co.	WILM
Zenith National Insurance Corp.	ZNAT
* Zions Utah Bancorporation	ZION

* Banking Institution

Of the 73 banking companies, First Union Corporation of North Carolina leads with 31 market makers, followed by Bank of New England Corporation in Massachusetts with 29, and PNC Financial Corp. in Pennsylvania with 27.

NASDAQ has traditionally been a major market for bank, bank holding company and insurance company securities. Of the 816 bank and insurance companies in NASDAQ, 376 are more than 25 years old and two thirds were operating prior to the start of NASDAQ in 1971.

NASDAQ BANKS AND INSURANCE COMPANIES'
YEARS OF OPERATION*
(As of December 31, 1986)

Years in Operation	Commercial Banks	Savings Banks	Savings & Loan Associations	Bank Holding Companies	Insurance Companies	Total
100 or more	23	37	4	16	5	85
50-99	46	26	58	46	16	192
25-49	16	6	16	34	27	99
10-24	11	2	6	145	41	205
5-9	2	5	5	51	21	84
Less than 5	11	2	7	69	22	111
Totals	109	78	96	361	132	776

* Data were not available for 40 companies.

Many banks from all regions of the country are among NASDAQ's charter members. The ability to accommodate trading in regional and local stocks, as well as national stocks, makes the NASDAQ System ideally suited to provide efficient and liquid markets in stocks across the banking spectrum.

NASDAQ CHARTER-MEMBER BANKING COMPANIES

Northeast

Bank of Delaware Corporation
Bank of New England Corporation
Baybanks, Inc.
Capitol Bancorporation
Central Jersey Bancorp
Citytrust Bancorp, Inc.
Constellation Bancorp
Continental Bancorp, Inc.
Corestates Financial Corporation
Fidelcor, Inc.
First Jersey National Corporation
First Maryland Bancorp
IDB Bankholding Corporation
Hartford National Corporation
Maryland National Corporation
Mercantile Bankshares Corporation
Meridian Bancorp, Inc.
Midlantic Banks, Inc.
National Community Bank of
   New Jersey
Northeast Bancorp, Inc.
PNC Financial Corp.
Ramapo Financial Corporation
Riggs National Corporation
State Street Boston Corporation
U. S. Trust Corporation
Union National Corporation
Wilmington Trust Company

Great Lakes

American Fletcher Corporation
AmeriTrust Corporation
Central Bancorporation, Inc. (The)
Comerica, Inc.
Fifth Third Bancorp
First National Cincinnati Corporation
Huntington Bancshares Incorporated
Indiana National Corporation
Manufacturers National Corporation
Marine Corporation (The)
Michigan National Corporation
Northern Trust Corporation
Society Corporation

Midwest

Affiliated Bankshares of Colorado, Inc.
Banks of Iowa, Inc.
Boatmen's Bancshares, Inc.
Centerre Bancorporation
Commerce Bancshares, Inc.
Firstier, Inc.
Fourth Financial Corporation
IntraWest Financial Corporation
Mark Twain Bancshares, Inc.
Mercantile Bancorporation, Inc.
United Banks of Colorado, Inc.

NASDAQ CHARTER-MEMBER BANKING COMPANIES
(Continued)

South

American Pioneer Savings Bank
Banco Popular de Puerto Rico
Bank South Corporation
Banponce Corporation
Central Fidelity Banks, Inc.
Citizens & Southern Corporation
Commerce Union Corporation
Dominion Bankshares Corporation
First American Corporation
First Florida Banks, Inc.
First Kentucky National Corporation
First Tennessee National Corporation
First Union Corporation
Florida Commercial Banks, Inc.
Southern National Corporation
Sovran Financial Corporation
United Virginia Bankshares, Inc.

Southwest

BancOklahoma Corp.
United Bancorp of Arizona
Valley National Corporation

West

California First Bank
Central Banking System, Inc.
City National Corp.
First Hawaiian, Inc.
First Security Corporation
First Western Financial Corporation
Hawthorne Financial Corporation
Nevada National Bancorporation
Orbanco Financial Services Corporation
Rainier Bancorporation
Santa Monica Bank
Sumitomo Bank of California
U. S. Bancorp
Zions Utah Bancorporation

Part II
How NASDAQ Provides A Market for Financial Companies' Securities

NASDAQ has been the market of choice for all types of banks, including trust companies and establishments performing functions closely related to banking, such as check-cashing agencies, currency exchanges, safe-deposit companies and corporations for banking abroad. Similarly, all types of insurance companies choose to have their securities traded on NASDAQ, including insurance brokers, agents and related services. Other types of financial companies included in NASDAQ are non-bank credit agencies, savings and loan associations, real-estate investment trusts and securities brokers.

In some ways, the market for financial companies in NASDAQ is larger than most of the world's exchanges. In 1986, more than 1,000 financial companies' securities were traded in the NASDAQ market—more than all of the companies listed on the American Stock Exchange and more than double the number of financial companies traded in the NASDAQ market when the System began operating in 1971.

The total market value of financial companies' securities in NASDAQ aggregates $130 billion dollars. This market-value figure is comprised of: banks and bank holding companies—$82 billion; savings and loan companies—$4 billion; insurance companies—$24 billion; other financial companies—$20 billion. The list of large banks, savings and loans, and insurance companies in NASDAQ reads like a "Who's Who" of the financial industry in most U.S. cities. Moreover, a perusal of the firms in these groups evidences the wide geographical representation of financial companies in the NASDAQ market.

The dispersed NASDAQ System provides an efficient, optimum trading environment for a range of companies in the financial industry, including small regional and local banks. For example, the market value of the smallest 20 companies in the banking, savings and loan, and insurance groups is generally less than one tenth the size of the largest companies. Large and small companies are equally well served, as are national, regional and local companies. This explains NASDAQ's growth.

Market-Maker Support and Sponsorship

When a company joins NASDAQ, an extensive network of market makers, market-maker support and

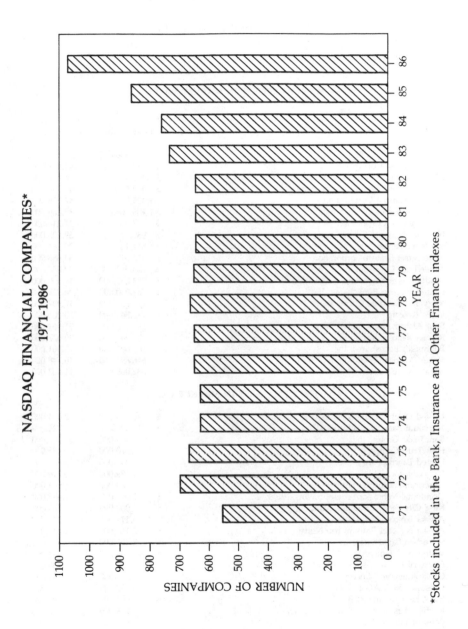

NASDAQ FINANCIAL COMPANIES*
1971-1986

*Stocks included in the Bank, Insurance and Other Finance indexes

LARGEST AND SMALLEST NASDAQ
BANK AND BANK HOLDING COMPANIES
(As of December 31, 1986)

—TWENTY LARGEST IN MARKET VALUE—

Company Name	Market Value	Total Shares Outstanding
First Union Corporation	$ 2,650,830,000	109,879,000
PNC Financial Corp.	$ 2,019,311,000	48,953,000
Citizens & Southern Corporation	$ 1,432,196,000	58,457,000
Bank of New England Corporation	$ 1,427,583,000	47,986,000
Sovran Financial Corporation	$ 1,425,093,000	42,225,000
Corestates Financial Corporation	$ 1,403,866,000	39,269,000
National City Corporation	$ 1,248,534,000	27,216,000
Hartford National Corporation	$ 985,545,000	39,820,000
Midlantic Banks, Inc.	$ 814,121,000	20,164,000
State Street Boston Corporation	$ 810,645,000	34,680,000
AmeriTrust Corporation	$ 783,992,000	20,837,000
Student Loan Marketing Association	$ 783,000,000	14,500,000
United Virginia Bankshares, Inc.	$ 765,060,000	26,727,000
Maryland National Corporation	$ 719,880,000	17,997,000
U. S. Bancorp	$ 713,545,000	30,203,000
First Alabama Bancshares, Inc.	$ 691,156,000	31,961,000
Rainier Bancorporation	$ 682,341,000	20,677,000
Boatmen's Bancshares, Inc.	$ 666,005,000	18,961,000
Valley National Corporation	$ 646,891,000	16,748,000
Society Corporation	$ 632,065,000	11,187,000

—TWENTY SMALLEST IN MARKET VALUE—

Company Name	Market Value	Total Shares Outstanding
United Oklahoma Bankshares, Inc.	$ 330,000	2,644,000
Merchant Bank of California (The)	$ 405,000	721,000
BancTexas Group, Inc.	$ 568,000	909,000
First Trust Company	$ 970,000	485,000
United Bancorp, Inc.	$ 1,048,000	932,000
Firstcorp, Inc.	$ 1,589,000	16,000
American Bancorporation	$ 2,169,000	964,000
Occidental Nebraska Federal Savings Bank	$ 2,990,000	1,495,000
King City Federal Savings Bank	$ 3,000,000	500,000
Alaska Bancorporation	$ 3,111,000	922,000
Alaska National Bank of the North	$ 3,115,000	1,246,000
Suburban Bankshares, Inc.	$ 3,302,000	518,000
Valley West Bancorp	$ 3,603,000	1,201,000
Financial Federal Savings Bank	$ 3,720,000	480,000
Great American Bancorp	$ 3,771,000	2,155,000
Dresdner Bank AG (ADR)	$ 3,990,000	19,000
Bank Leumi Le-Israel B. M. (ADR)	$ 4,063,000	189,000
Fairfield First Bank & Trust Company	$ 4,288,000	512,000
Bank of Darien (The)	$ 4,658,000	548,000
First Savings Bank, F.S.B.	$ 5,005,000	455,000

LARGEST AND SMALLEST NASDAQ
SAVINGS AND LOAN COMPANIES
(As of December 31, 1986)

—TWENTY LARGEST IN MARKET VALUE—

Company Name	Market Value	Total Shares Outstanding
Washington Federal Savings & Loan Association of Seattle	$ 270,663,000	7,571,000
First Federal of Michigan	$ 250,366,000	10,945,000
Farm & Home Savings Association	$ 153,670,000	6,985,000
Home Owners Federal Savings and Loan Association	$ 123,039,000	5,859,000
Florida Federal Savings and Loan Association	$ 118,586,000	9,393,000
Columbia Savings and Loan Association	$ 118,218,000	8,153,000
Talman Home Federal Savings and Loan Assoc. of Illinois	$ 83,125,000	9,500,000
Dominion Federal Savings and Loan Association	$ 79,462,000	4,890,000
Great Lakes Federal Savings and Loan Association	$ 76,302,000	3,888,000
Bay View Federal Savings and Loan Association	$ 74,212,000	5,997,000
Bayamon Federal Savings & Loan Association of Puerto Rico	$ 74,088,000	4,704,000
Loyola Capital Corporation	$ 68,125,000	5,000,000
First Southern Federal Savings and Loan Association	$ 67,816,000	4,844,000
Valley Federal Savings and Loan Association	$ 67,586,000	2,876,000
First Federal Savings and Loan Association of Fort Myers	$ 67,505,000	2,348,000
Metropolitan Federal Savings and Loan Association	$ 66,808,000	3,686,000
San Francisco Federal Savings and Loan Association	$ 65,495,000	5,634,000
Western Federal Savings and Loan Association	$ 58,971,000	3,574,000
Fidelity Federal Savings and Loan Association of Tennessee	$ 58,603,000	3,525,000
Union Federal Savings and Loan Association	$ 58,093,000	3,250,000

—TWENTY SMALLEST IN MARKET VALUE—

Company Name	Market Value	Total Shares Outstanding
Financial Security Savings and Loan Association	$ 1,140,000	912,000
Lincoln Savings and Loan Association	$ 1,607,000	1,429,000
Savers, Inc.	$ 2,359,000	2,696,000
Star Savings and Loan Association	$ 2,636,000	285,000
Cypress Savings Association	$ 3,502,000	824,000
Bloomfield Savings & Loan Association, F.A.	$ 3,599,000	2,215,000
United Savings Association	$ 3,857,000	417,000
Summit Savings Association	$ 4,641,000	952,000
Century Federal Savings and Loan Association	$ 5,152,000	322,000
East Texas Savings and Loan Association	$ 5,715,000	635,000
Southern Federal Savings and Loan Assoc. of Thomas County	$ 5,906,000	675,000
North Land Savings and Loan Association	$ 6,279,000	483,000
Continental Federal Savings and Loan Association	$ 6,286,000	1,397,000
Franklin Savings and Loan Association	$ 6,446,000	573,000
Seaboard Savings and Loan Association	$ 6,666,000	808,000
Suncoast Savings and Loan Association	$ 6,893,000	707,000
Home Federal Savings and Loan Association of the Rockies	$ 7,350,000	525,000
Railroad Savings and Loan Association	$ 7,480,000	748,000
North Carolina Federal Savings and Loan Association	$ 7,566,000	1,261,000
Frontier Savings Association	$ 7,608,000	2,341,000

LARGEST AND SMALLEST NASDAQ
INSURANCE COMPANIES
(As of December 31, 1986)

—TWENTY LARGEST IN MARKET VALUE—

Company Name	Market Value	Total Shares Outstanding
Farmers Group, Inc.	$ 2,694,016,000	69,523,000
St. Paul Companies, Inc. (The)	$ 1,860,797,000	46,231,000
Safeco Corporation	$ 1,804,983,000	33,738,000
American National Insurance Company	$ 1,187,934,000	28,974,000
First Executive Corporation	$ 1,055,640,000	70,376,000
Provident Life and Accident Insurance Company	$ 920,384,000	37,376,000
Ohio Casualty Corporation	$ 878,963,000	11,305,000
Progressive Corporation (The)	$ 866,295,000	27,945,000
Hanover Insurance Company (The)	$ 654,685,000	10,310,000
Zenith National Insurance Corp.	$ 554,698,000	20,932,000
Hartford Steam Boiler Inspection and Insurance Co. (The)	$ 499,949,000	10,609,000
Life Investors Inc.	$ 449,707,000	9,085,000
20th Century Industries	$ 441,600,000	25,600,000
A. L. Williams Corporation (The)	$ 432,635,000	24,722,000
Northwestern National Life Insurance Company	$ 346,580,000	11,180,000
Republic American Corporation	$ 341,600,000	22,400,000
Employers Casualty Company	$ 330,120,000	10,080,000
Crawford & Company	$ 293,581,000	11,627,000
Arthur J. Gallagher & Co.	$ 277,803,000	10,583,000
USLICO Corporation	$ 268,187,000	11,233,000

—TWENTY SMALLEST IN MARKET VALUE—

Company Name	Market Value	Total Shares Outstanding
Acap Corporation	$ 503,000	2,686,000
American Underwriters Group, Inc.	$ 1,041,000	463,000
Equities International Life Insurance Company	$ 1,168,000	935,000
Unilife Corporation	$ 1,356,000	1,808,000
Integrity Financial Group, Inc. (The)	$ 1,700,000	6,800,000
Windsor Life Insurance Company of America	$ 1,766,000	1,663,000
Kentucky Medical Insurance Company	$ 2,192,000	137,000
North East Insurance Company	$ 2,673,000	1,944,000
Conseco, Inc.	$ 2,738,000	25,000
MoNAT Capital Corporation	$ 2,760,000	690,000
First Centennial Corporation	$ 2,825,000	1,507,000
American Investors Corporation	$ 2,992,000	11,966,000
Citizens Insurance Company of America	$ 3,336,000	785,000
Liberty American Corporation	$ 3,388,000	9,037,000
Celina Financial Corporation	$ 3,485,000	1,549,000
Lifesurance Corporation	$ 3,591,000	756,000
United Securities Financial Corporation of Illinois	$ 3,930,000	1,310,000
American Claims Evaluation, Inc.	$ 3,952,000	930,000
Aneco Reinsurance Company Limited	$ 4,400,000	2,071,000
Southern Security Life Insurance Company	$ 4,418,000	1,537,000

market-maker sponsorship develops for its securities. The market for bank stocks illustrates the quality, depth and broad reach of services that naturally evolve when state-of-the-art technology combines with an openly competitive environment.

Of the 526 NASDAQ market-maker firms, 276 made markets in one or more bank stocks during 1986. About half of these market makers make markets in one to five bank stocks; but more than 50 firms make markets in 20 or more bank stocks.

DISTRIBUTION OF THE NUMBER OF MARKETS MADE IN NASDAQ BANK* STOCKS BY NASDAQ MARKET MAKERS

Number of Market Makers	Number of Markets Made
3	More than 200
7	101–200
13	51–100
6	41–50
11	31–40
14	21–30
16	16–20
24	11–15
44	6–10
138	1–5

Note: Of the 526 NASDAQ market makers, 276 make markets in NASDAQ bank stocks.
*675 commercial banks, savings and loans, and bank holding companies.

The list of leading market makers in almost any industry group includes the national full-line broker-dealers that have become household names. These firms, such as Merrill Lynch, Dean Witter, Shearson Lehman and Paine Webber, have extensive retail networks with hundreds of domestic and foreign branch offices through which they provide integrated services including investment banking, retail brokerage, market making and research for retail clients. Their retail clients include both individual public customers as well as institutional customers.

LEADING NASD MARKET MAKERS IN NASDAQ BANK STOCKS

Market Maker	Number of Stocks
Merrill Lynch, Pierce, Fenner & Smith Incorporated	238
Dean Witter Reynolds Inc.	208
Shearson Lehman Brothers Inc.	202
Keefe, Bruyette & Woods, Inc.	169
PaineWebber Inc.	168
Kidder, Peabody & Co. Incorporated	136
Moseley Securities Corporation	125
Thomson McKinnon Securities	119
E.F. Hutton & Company, Inc.	110
Herzog, Heine, Geduld, Inc.	104
Ryan, Beck & Co., Inc.	88
Bear, Stearns & Co., Inc.	76
Robinson Humphrey/American Express, Inc.	74
Salomon Brothers, Inc.	70
Tucker, Anthony & R.L. Day, Inc.	69
Prudential-Bache Securities, Inc.	65
Smith Barney, Harris Upham & Co., Inc.	64
Drexel Burnham Lambert, Inc.	63
M.A. Schapiro & Co., Inc.	63
Williams Securities Group, Inc.	55
Goldman, Sachs & Co.	53
Advest, Inc.	52
F.J. Morrissey & Co., Inc.	51

Also included in this network are market makers that specialize in investment banking, serving institutional clients. Such firms include Salomon Brothers and Goldman

Sachs, among others. The presence of these firms as market makers in NASDAQ securities reflects the growing presence of institutional investors in NASDAQ securities and these firms' desire to be registered market makers in companies with which they have an underwriting or corporate-financing relationship.

Some firms specialize in making markets in the securities of particular companies or particular industries. In our bank-stock illustration, M. A. Schapiro & Company and Keefe, Bruyette & Woods make wholesale and institutional markets in bank stocks. They provide specialized research and information support in bank and bank holding company securities. The degree of their specialization in bank stocks is reflected in the ratio of bank stocks to the total number of stocks in which they make markets—M. A. Schapiro & Company with 95 percent; Keefe, Bruyette & Woods with 89 percent.

Regional and local broker-dealers provide market-making services by closely following and sponsoring companies' stocks. For example, in the case of banking stocks, 138 firms make markets in one to five stocks. Many are local broker-dealers that make markets in very few stocks. Major regional firms, such as Alex. Brown & Sons in Baltimore, McDonald & Company in Cleveland and Robinson Humphrey in Atlanta are also bank-stock market makers. The locations of these firms illustrates the regional and local fabric of the NASDAQ network for a particular industry.

Information, Research and Stock Pricing

The multiple market-maker system also provides an extensive information and research/communications system that leads to efficient pricing of NASDAQ securities.

GEOGRAPHIC LOCATION OF NASDAQ MEMBERS
MAKING MARKETS IN ONE TO FIVE BANK STOCKS

City	State	Number of Market Makers
New York	NY	50
Salt Lake City	UT	7
Chicago	IL	6
San Francisco	CA	5
Los Angeles	CA	5
Rochester	NY	3
Portland	OR	3
St. Louis	MO	3
Seattle	WA	3
Minneapolis	MN	3
Cincinnati	OH	3
Birmingham	AL	2
Beverly Hills	CA	2
Kansas City	MO	2
Oklahoma City	OK	2
Houston	TX	2
Philadelphia	PA	2
Indianapolis	IN	2
Detroit	MI	2
Dallas	TX	2
Jersey City	NJ	2
Washington	DC	2
Tulsa	OK	2
Little Rock	AR	2
Denver	CO	2
Spokane	WA	2
Grand Rapids	MI	2
Great Falls	MT	1
Greensboro	NC	1
Clifton	NJ	1
Fort Lauderdale	FL	1
Boston	MA	1
Miami	FL	1
Falls Church	VA	1
East Hartford	CT	1
Encino	CA	1
Baltimore	MD	1

GEOGRAPHIC LOCATIONS OF NASD MEMBERS
MAKING MARKETS IN ONE TO FIVE BANK STOCKS
(Continued)

City	State	Number of Market Makers
Des Moines	IA	1
Boca Raton	FL	1
Aurora	IL	1
Phoenix	AZ	1
Rockville	MD	1
Pittsburgh	PA	1
Pompton Plains	NJ	1
Atlanta	GA	1
San Diego	CA	1
Allentown	PA	1
Albuquerque	NM	1
Southfield	MI	1
Nashville	TN	1
Albany	NY	1
Toluca Lake	CA	1
New Orleans	LA	1
Costa Mesa	CA	1
Whitestone	NY	1
Williamsport	PA	1
Worcester	MA	1
Youngstown	OH	1

Some market makers simply obtain information disclosed by companies in their regular financial reports. These firms respond to bids and offers in securities, with their primary focus on the equilibration of supply and demand and the constant rebalancing of their own long or short positions in particular stocks. They do not employ research analysts or other special information-gathering analyses to support their market-making endeavors. Nevertheless, through their pricing activities and their agile responses to new information, they serve an information function—they help accelerate the process through which new information is incorporated into the price of the underlying security.

However, many market-making firms undertake specialized research into the stocks in which they make markets. These activities may be broad, ranging over many stocks in numerous industries, or they may be highly specialized, focusing on a particular industry or a single stock. In the case of the banking industry, many of the 276 market makers that make one or more markets in NASDAQ bank stocks perform bank-stock analyses and bank-stock research.

RESEARCH COVERAGE BY MARKET MAKERS FOR THE LARGEST NASDAQ BANK IN EACH REGION

	Allied Bancshares (Southwest)	U.S. Bancorp of Portland (West)	Boatmen's Bancshares (Midwest)	National City Corporation (Great Lakes)	PNC Financial (Northeast)	First Union Corporation (South)
Alex. Brown & Sons, Inc.						X
Bear, Stearns & Co., Inc.	X	X				
Boettcher & Co., Inc.		X				
J. C. Bradford & Co., Incorporated						X
Burns Pauli & Co., Inc.			X			
Dean Witter Reynolds Inc.	X	X			X	X
Drexel Burnham Lambert Incorporated		X		X	X	X
A. G. Edwards & Sons, Inc.			X			
The First Boston Corporation		X				
Goldman, Sachs & Co.	X			X		X
E. F. Hutton & Co., Inc.	X	X				
Interstate Securities Corporation						X
Johnson, Lane, Space, Smith & Co., Inc.						X
Keefe, Bruyette & Woods	X	X		X	X	X
Legg Mason Masten Inc.					X	
Mabon, Nugent & Co.				X	X	
McDonald & Company Securities, Inc.				X	X	
Merrill Lynch, Pierce, Fenner & Smith Incorporated	X	X		X	X	X
Montgomery Securities, Inc.	X	X				
Morgan Stanley & Co. Incorporated		X		X	X	
The Ohio Company				X		
Piper, Jaffray & Hopwood Incorporated		X				
Prescott, Ball & Turben, Inc.				X		

RESEARCH COVERAGE BY MARKET MAKERS
FOR THE LARGEST NASDAQ BANK IN EACH REGION
(Continued)

	Allied Bancshares (Southwest)	U.S. Bancorp of Portland (West)	Boatmen's Bancshares (Midwest)	National City Corporation (Great Lakes)	PNC Financial (Northeast)	First Union Corporation (South)
Rauscher Pierce Refsnes, Inc.	X					
Robinson Humphrey/ American Express Inc.						X
Salomon Brothers Inc.				X	X	X
Scott & Stringfellow, Inc.						X
M. A. Schapiro & Co., Inc.					X	
Shearson Lehman Brothers, Inc.	X				X	X
Smith Barney, Harris Upham & Co. Incorporated		X			X	X
Weber, Hall, Sale & Associates	X					
Wheat, First Securities, Inc.						X
Williams Securities Group, Inc.						X

Source: Nelson's Directory of Wall Street Research, 1986.

Research departments in the major wirehouses generate general market, industry and research reports about particular companies and stocks. Also, the regional firms provide research and market making in the stocks of companies located in their geographic areas.

NASDAQ Financial Indexes

NASDAQ and the over-the-counter market were historically considered to be the primary markets for bank and insurance company stocks. Consequently, component price indexes have been calculated for banks, insurance companies and other financial companies since the inception of the NASDAQ market in 1971. The number and market value of companies in other component industries could also support separate indexes.

Bank and other financial securities performed exceptionally well from 1980 to 1986, a period of declining inflation, major deregulation of banking activities and extensive merger-and-acquisition activity. This environment also led to a surge of initial public offerings, particularly by savings and loan companies.

A Market for Newly Public Companies

The NASDAQ market was chosen by 283 newly public banks and savings and loans during the industry's period of rapid growth between 1980 and 1986. The market value of the initial public offerings of these companies totaled $6.2 billion. By moving immediately into the NASDAQ market, these companies assured that their securities had liquid, deep secondary markets for investors from the outset.

The investment banking firm that brings a company public generally continues to sponsor the security by registering on a continuing basis as a market maker. Such sponsorship is a reflection of the economic realities of the new securities offerings (primary market) and secondary trading processes. It reflects the interdependence of the various activities in which securities firms engage. The various profit centers in a securities firm, including underwriting, market making and retail commission business, are interrelated and interdependent. Therefore, NASDAQ market-making firms that bring new companies public generally find it is also in their economic interest to act as market makers in the companies' stocks.

Bank Stock Ownership and Public Float

The mix of shareownership of bank stocks is not unlike that of NASDAQ generally. While institutional

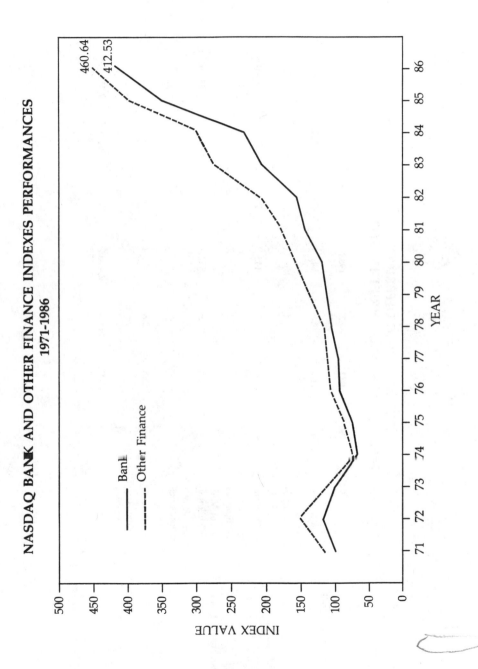

NASDAQ BANK AND OTHER FINANCE INDEXES PERFORMANCES
1971-1986

INITIAL PUBLIC OFFERINGS
OF NASDAQ BANK AND THRIFT INSTITUTIONS

		1980	1981	1982	1983	1984	1985	1986	Totals
Commercial Banks	Market Value ($ Millions)	—	1.6	4.8	547.4	135.5	275.5	825.2	1,790.0
	Number of Companies	—	1	1	12	13	17	27	71
Savings Banks	Market Value ($ Millions)	—	—	29.1	143.2	79.0	143.3	706.0	1,110.6
	Number of Companies	—	—	1	7	8	7	30	53
Savings & Loans	Market Value ($ Millions)	—	55.6	96.6	1,552.7	153.4	207.1	282.9	2,348.3
	Number of Companies	—	5	4	43	15	13	16	96
Bank Holding Companies	Market Value ($ Millions)	26.4	2.8	13.8	177.4	218.2	235.9	336.6	1,011.1
	Number of Companies	1	1	2	10	10	9	30	63
	Totals	**26.4**	**60.0**	**144.3**	**2,420.7**	**586.1**	**861.8**	**2,150.7**	**6,250.0**
		1	**7**	**8**	**72**	**46**	**46**	**103**	**283**

holdings of NASDAQ stocks have been growing sharply, nearly three quarters of the market value of NASDAQ shares is still held by individual investors. The breakdown for banks shows that institutions hold stock in 420 of the 586 bank stocks on NASDAQ. By year-end 1986, these institutional holdings accounted for nearly 28 percent of the market value of those companies and 25 percent of the market value of all bank stocks listed on NASDAQ.

SUMMARY OF INSTITUTIONAL HOLDINGS
OF NASDAQ BANK AND BANK HOLDING COMPANIES
(As of December 31, 1986)

	NASDAQ/NMS	NASDAQ
Number of stocks with at least one institutional position	369	420
Number of stocks with no reported institutional positions	90	166
Total number of stocks	459	586
Number of institutional positions	9,063	9,299
Total shares held by institutions (millions)	765.7	773.9
Total shares outstanding of stocks with institutional positions (millions)	2,952.1	3,058.0
Total shares outstanding of all stocks (millions)	3,245.4	3,471.3
Market value of shares held by institutions (millions)	$20,303.2	$20,430.7
Total market value of stocks with institutional positions (millions)	$72,028.4	$73,754.8
Total market value of all stocks (millions)	$77,134.7	$80,530.3
Percent of market value held by institutions for stocks with at least one institutional position	28.2%	27.7%
Percent of market value held by institutions for all stocks	26.3%	25.4%

Data source: Vickers Stock Research Corporation.

In most industries, companies vary widely in size, business mix and portions of shares that are retained by officers, directors and principal stockholders as compared to the portions that are in public hands. Because of NASDAQ's electronic market and its multiple market-maker system, optimum markets are economically feasible even if a company has a public float that is substantially less than the total stock outstanding. In banks, particularly small ones, the officers, directors and founding stockholders often retain substantial percentages of the shares outstanding. For example, the public float in the 20 smallest bank stocks in NASDAQ is equivalent to 76 percent of the shares outstanding of those companies. By contrast, the public float in the 20 largest banks accounts for 94 percent of the shares outstanding in those companies. For NASDAQ as a whole, public float is 68 percent of the total shares outstanding.

The wide diversity of investor mix and the composition of shareownership in NASDAQ issues is reflective of a market that can provide an optimum trading environment for securities with widely differing shareholder-population characteristics. At the same time, this market can offer issuers the opportunity to develop the kind of investor mix that they find most desirable.

Chapter six

*F*or more than 20 years, Charles Allmon has been editor of *Growth Stock Outlook*, an investment advisory service. He manages individual accounts aggregating $270 million and is investment adviser to Growth Stock Outlook Trust, Inc., a closed-end investment company with assets of some $137 million.

Emerging Growth Companies

by Charles Allmon

Big capitalization stocks leave me cold. I call them the "blue gyps." Over the years, the big gainers have been in the NASDAQ/OTC market. The performance of rapidly growing smaller companies over the past five to 10 years clearly establishes them as superior investment values when compared to most giant corporations.

When I use the term "growth stocks," I do not mean the glamour stocks that resemble Roman candles—burn brightly for two, three or four years and then snuff out. They have names like "Kentucky Fried Computers." Such "go-go" stocks are hot on the gossip circuit and cold in an early grave.

Growth Companies Defined

To me, a genuine growth company is one that produces a truly necessary product or service and produces it efficiently through good management. One such NASDAQ company makes industrial coatings, which are always in demand, and it makes them so well that revenues and earnings have been up for 39 consecutive years. That is a real growth company.

115

Companies like this—and the NASDAQ market has many of them—can grow during good times and bad. They are not tied to national or industry business cycles because they have products that are in demand even during periods of economic decline. They keep growing, even under adverse business conditions, for three reasons: They are among the lowest cost producers in their fields, or actually are the lowest cost producers; they demonstrate a high degree of pricing flexibility; and they generally have a very low ratio of debt to equity. These characteristics are the result of top-notch management.

How do we find such genuine growth stocks? Let me first point out how we do *not* find them.

Inexperienced investors make two mistakes. The first is that they try to hit a home run in one or two stocks. This is the worst thing they could possibly do. They must diversify. Investors who try to hit home runs in one or two stocks are probably going to lose their shirts—and they deserve to—because that approach flies in the face of all rational investment logic.

The second biggest mistake that inexperienced investors make is listening to the latest tip or rumor on the grapevine. They go to the office or a cocktail party and some friend says, ''I've got a red hot tip for you—this stock is the best thing since scrambled eggs,'' and they listen to it. Inexperienced people never look at the numbers; they just listen to the baloney. I can tell you from long experience that most often the numbers never appear.

Five Tests of a Growth Company

I have five basic tests to determine a legitimate growth company.

1. Earnings should have increased by at least 15 percent

a year over the last three or four years. I don't go back any farther because I don't want to factor in the exaggerated earnings growth rates of a then much smaller company.

2. Sales should also have increased by at least 15 percent annually. Revenues are much more important than earnings; revenues are the lifeblood of companies. When it comes right down to it, no company can grow faster than its revenue in the long run. If revenue growth doesn't keep pace with earnings growth, profit margins are being stretched. Earnings may go up, and profit margins may go up for three, four or five years, but revenues create an absolute limit to the expansion of profit margin. They are the most important indication of how fast a company is growing and how consistently.

   Besides looking at the last three or four years' revenues, we look very carefully at the most recent one or two quarters. This short-term view avoids surprises. We would not recommend a company whose revenues were up only 1 or 2 percent in the last quarter, even though earnings might be up. Such a company is currently not doing well enough to justify the term "growth company."

3. The company usually should have a return on equity of 16 to 25 percent. Occasionally, a lower return on equity is acceptable, but only when it has increased substantially in the last year or two.

4. Ideally there should be no long-term debt and little leverage in general. A highly leveraged company will have an inflated return on equity, which can disguise a deteriorating balance sheet.

5. Current assets should be at least double current liabilities. I don't use book value as the only asset measurement. I take a company apart and make my own asset

evaluation. Sometimes I find pleasant surprises, like valuable real estate being carried on book at cost. Other times I find negatives, such as obsolete manufacturing facilities being carried at an inflated value.

NASDAQ—A Gold Mine of Growth Stocks

The NASDAQ market is a gold mine of the growth stocks that meet some or all of these tests. In one of my recent advisory letters, I listed 58 NASDAQ companies.

- *Thirty of them had four-year growth rates that were higher than 15 percent*—American Greetings, Ampad, Andros Analyzers, Bel Fuse, Clear Channel Communications, Continental Health Affiliates, Dow B. Hickam, Dress Barn, Dynatech, Food Lion, Graphic Industries, Interface Systems, Knape & Vogt Manufacturing, Laidlaw Industries, LIN Broadcasting, Modern Controls, Noxell, Nuclear Support Services, Par Pharmaceutical, Pic 'N' Save, Plenum Publishing, Powertec, ServiceMaster Industries, Shared Medical Systems, Shelby Williams Industries, Sigma-Aldrich, Standard Register, Stryker Corporation, Technalysis Corporation and Worthington Industries.
- *Thirty three of them had revenue growth of more than 15 percent in the latest year*—Ampad, Andros Analyzers, Clear Channel Communications, Comprehensive Care, Continental Health Affiliates, Crawford & Co., Dress Barn, Durr-Fillauer Medical, Dynatech, Food Lion, Graphic Industries, Gray Communications Systems, Interface Systems, Laidlaw Industries, LIN Broadcasting, Modern Controls, Nuclear Support Services, Ocilla Industries, Par Pharmaceutical, Pic 'N' Save, Rocky Mount Undergarment, RPM, Inc., ServiceMaster Industries, Shared Medical Systems, Shelby Williams Industries, Sigma-

Aldrich, Stocker & Yale, Stryker Corporation, Technalysis Corporation, TSI Inc., Vallen Corporation, WD-40 and Western Waste Industries.

* *Sixteen companies had 10 or more consecutive years of uninterrupted growth in sales and earnings:*

Company	Sales (years)	Earnings (years)
American Greetings	80	12
Citizens Utilities	41	41
Durr-Fillauer Medical	31	26
Dynatech	15	15
Food Lion	18	18
Graphic Industries	12	12
LIN Broadcasting	17	11
Noxell	30	10
Pic 'N' Save	18	18
Plenum Publishing	15	12
RPM, Inc.	39	39
ServiceMaster Industries	20	15
Shared Medical Systems	15	13
Shelby Williams Industries	11	11
Sigma-Aldrich	21	21
Stryker Corporation	16	10

Other funds have also produced impressive results. One fund investing in NASDAQ growth companies has shown better than a 20 percent return on equity over a five-year period. This represented a 40 to 45 percent premium over traditional larger companies, such as those in the Standard & Poor's 500.

In another instance, a group of investment advisers looked for companies with earnings growth of at least 30 percent, or three times the average earnings growth of companies in the Standard & Poor's 500. Those advisers found that 80 percent of the securities on their approved list were NASDAQ securities.

How to Find the NASDAQ Winners

How can the investor—individual or institutional—find the NASDAQ growth stock winners?

Since I am in the investment adviser business, I would recommend buying an advisory service—but with great caution. Nobody should buy an advisory service unless it has been around for five years, and preferably longer. If the advisory has been around 15 or 20 years, it presumably has been doing something right or people wouldn't keep buying it.

Better still, buy an advisory service that also manages money. If people entrust millions of dollars to an investment adviser over the years and the adviser has a solid track record of making money for them, that says a lot more than if they only spend $150 a year for a newsletter. (Yes, I manage money, too.)

To evaluate advisory letters, read the *Hulbert Financial Digest*—it keeps a running box score on how well advisers' stock recommendations turn out. If you want to evaluate advisories that also manage money, plenty of services measure the performances of funds.

For someone who has absolutely no stock market experience, my suggestion would be to start in mutual funds that specialize in growth stocks. Suppose you are a new investor and have $5,000 to invest. I would suggest that the $5,000 be placed in five separate funds. It's just as difficult to pick the individual fund that with do well as it is to pick an individual stock that will do well. Therefore, you must diversify in growth funds, just as you would in growth stocks.

The Basic Prospects of Growth Stocks

While picking the winning growth stocks or growth funds takes work, brains and judgment, the

NASDAQ market offers a wealth of potentially good choices, and those good choices keep coming along.

Small businesses account for better than half of all industrial inventions and innovations in the U.S. Not only that, a National Science Foundation study found that small firms produce about four times as many innovations per research-and-development dollar as medium-sized firms and about 24 times as many as the largest firms. Profit margins are made of such efficiency in innovation.

Growth companies are also the nation's job creators. Studies by the Massachusetts Institute of Technology show that the rate of employment growth in small technology companies is nearly nine times that in other sectors of the economy. A report by a House Subcommittee indicates that this greater rate of employment growth in small businesses is not limited to the technology sector but cuts across the entire spectrum of the economy. Such a multiplier in employment in growth companies is only possible if their sales and revenues are multiplying. And, as I said earlier, revenue increases are the lifeblood of companies—and the essentials of appreciation in their stock prices.

Of course, this dynamic environment entails risks—risks for the entrepreneurs and risks for the investors. The bottom line, however, is that NASDAQ can be the most rewarding market for the intelligent investor.

Chapter
seven

William R. Hambrecht is President & CEO of Hambrecht & Quist Group, a venture capital and investment banking firm that specializes in financing high technology and emerging growth companies. He was a co-founder of the firm in 1968 and currently serves as director for numerous privately held companies and the following public companies: ADAC Laboratories, Inc., Auto-trol Technology Corporation, Adobe Systems Incorporated, Chalone Incorporated, Massachusetts Computer Corporation, MiniScribe Corporation, NBI Corporation, Rexon Incorporated, Silicon General Inc., and Xidex Corporation.

Standish O'Grady, an assistant to Mr. Hambrecht, has been associated with the firm since 1984. Previously, he was a Process Engineer at Intel Corporation.

Nancy Pfund joined Hambrecht & Quist in 1985 and is currently the firm's Chemical Technology Analyst. She formerly worked at Intel Corporation in new product marketing and government affairs.

High-Tech Stocks in a High-Tech Market

by William R. Hambrecht
Standish H. O'Grady
Nancy E. Pfund

Since the close of World War II, the capital markets of the United States have been the envy of the world. Investors from all over the globe view the U.S. markets as one of the most effective places to achieve liquidity. While in other nations a growing company that needs more capital often has to sell out to a larger one, in the United States the securities markets provide a growth path that allows young, low-capitalization companies to mature on their own.

In addition to creating a strong economic and employment base, the securities markets provide an attractive vehicle making liquid the investments of early-stage investors. In many ways, the strength of venture capital in this country owes much of its success to this system. NASDAQ, as the market best suited to young, high-growth companies, has played a key role in the development of the high-technology sector. As a highly efficient, computer-based and competitive system, NASDAQ allows the stocks of high-technology companies to be traded in an environment that suits their entrepreneurial flavor and their bias toward automation.

The High-Tech Opportunity

Thirty years ago, high-technology stocks formed a pretty slim portfolio. The major companies were IBM, Burroughs, National Cash Register, RCA and Sperry-Rand, and few investment banking firms devoted significant resources to the sector. Today, "high tech" has become the rule and not the exception. Our economy has moved from a reliance on traditional heavy manufacturing to one whose core is knowledge-intensive industries. Because of the fundamental nature of this shift, high-tech companies, in different shapes and sizes, are likely to become even more dominant in the next 25 years, and their presence will truly be a global phenomenon.

The definition of high-tech companies has evolved over the years to reflect the changes that have been made in high-tech products and the new markets they have created. "High-tech" development was once only the province of lab-coated engineers in cool rooms. Today, many children are exposed to computers before they attend school, and microprocessors have become ubiquitous. This evolution can be attributed to the dramatic reduction in the price of computing power that has occurred steadily since the late 1960s. Without microprocessors, the move toward localized intelligence, which in turn created the need for printers, disk drives and software programs, could not have been made.

The increased capability brought about by the microprocessor helps explain why technology companies reflect a different set of operating principles than more mature industries. The first microprocessor, for example, measured 1/8" x 1/6" and contained 2,300 transistors. Its computing power equaled the first electronic computer, ENIAC, built in 1946, which occupied 3,000 cubic feet and included 18,000 vacuum tubes. The first ad for a microprocessor, in fact, stood four rectangular chips on end around two computer programmers to evoke the more commonly known image of a mainframe and hailed "a new era in integrated electronics: a microprogrammable computer on a chip."

Today's microprocessors, of course, make this early attempt appear primitive by comparison. New products routinely pack close to 300,000 transistors on a chip, and computing architectures now allow processing so rapid and efficient that software developers are challenged to use all of the power resident in the hardware.

Revolutionary products like microprocessors do not come around very often. But when they do, they create a cascade of revolutionary market changes as old solutions become obsolete and as entirely new markets are created. This, in turn, creates the opportunity for new companies to be formed. For example, in 1977, Santa Clara County, California, had about 900 high-tech companies in manufacturing, software/service and distribution. By 1984, that number had jumped to 2,500.

Biotechnology is another classic case of this phenomenon at work. As this transformation progresses, the rate of change may slack off as incremental upgrades and improvements tend to replace giant leaps forward. Still, looked at over a longer period of time, even incremental changes can have dramatic implications. For example, the automotive market now uses microelectronic products for fairly rudimentary dashboard controls. During the next decade, it is estimated that the total automotive electronics market will be larger than the *entire* 1985 semiconductor market. Similarly, the office automation market for very powerful 32-bit microprocessors was only one third of the total market in 1985; it is expected to be close to 85 percent by 1990.

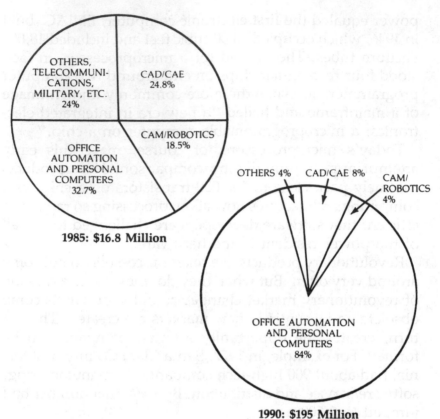

OTHERS,
TELECOMMUNI-
CATIONS,
MILITARY, ETC.
24%

CAD/CAE
24.8%

CAM/ROBOTICS
18.5%

OFFICE
AUTOMATION
AND PERSONAL
COMPUTERS
32.7%

1985: $16.8 Million

OTHERS 4%   CAD/CAE 8%   CAM/ROBOTICS 4%

OFFICE AUTOMATION
AND PERSONAL
COMPUTERS
84%

1990: $195 Million

Technology Alters Industrial Landscapes

High technology can severely alter existing industrial landscapes. Although this is a great source of high-tech's attraction, it can lead to turbulence in the growth cycles of both markets and companies. Market size estimates may contain more fiction than fact, as happened in the early 1980s when the predictions for the personal computer market turned out to be too great. This led to a considerable surplus in capacity and overfunding of several computer-related companies, and the digestion/consolidation period is still underway.

NUMBER OF COMPETITORS
IN SELECTED INDUSTRIES

	1981	1985
5¼" Winchester Disk Drives	11	54
Microcomputer Software	34	280
Microcomputer Hardware	8	47
32-bit Engineering Workstations	0	32
Local-Area Networks	9	61

Still, this market continues to show healthy growth (in the range of 20 percent per year by unit) as personal computers become more powerful and find other uses.

For these reasons, high-tech investments can carry considerable risk and much more volatility than investments in other sectors. Any combination of capital intensiveness, technological hurdles, unknown market sizes, competing technical standards, unseasoned management and poorly conceived distribution channels can quickly transform a high flyer into a dinosaur. And, even if a company controls these variables, a decision by a giant like IBM to go after its particular market can upset the playing field and doom its chances of survival. The selection process then becomes key to maximizing the return on investment.

Investing in High Tech

Venture capitalists look at four factors before investing in high-technology companies.

1. **The presence of strong management.** This is the number one criterion those providing venture capital cite in their decision to finance a high-tech company. Too often, the most compelling company plan can collapse under the weight of inexperienced or inadequate management. The problem is particularly intense in high technology for four reasons: technologists often lack managerial training; technologists rarely stay in one place long enough to go through the various cycles of a company's growth; companies often grow so fast that both balance sheet and management can burn out before anyone notices; and market size predictions may prove illusory. Entrepreneurs, in general, tend to be very optimistic, a trait that can mask and compound all of these problems.

2. **A company's size and growth rate.** Investors in high-tech companies are growth oriented. If a company carves out a market that is too small or slow-paced, it will find it hard to sustain attractive return on earnings. It will also suffer when compared to the high-tech norm of 25 percent growth. Under-performance will lead to underattention, which will adversely affect the liquidity of a company's stock—another key attribute that high-tech entrepreneurs and investors consider.

3. **A company's proprietary technology.** This is the best barrier to entry by would-be competitors. Without proprietary technology, a company does not have the pricing freedom to create an attractive return structure. Proprietary technology can come through patents, trade secrets, manufacturing expertise, key technical people or any combination of these.

   The current ceding of much of the semiconductor market to low-cost suppliers in Japan and Korea indicates what can happen when the proprietary component decreases and what was once a high value-added product becomes a commodity. Only those U.S. manufacturers which are pursuing particularly advanced or specialized semiconductors, such as application-specific integrated circuits and high-speed microprocessors, are able to sustain earlier periods of rapid growth. VLSI Technology and Linear Technology Corporation are two examples.

4. **Balance sheet strength.** This final point, balance sheet strength, is not unique to high-technology companies but is a cornerstone of sound investing. Healthy cash positions, manageable debt and other balance sheet variables are often the most important clues to a company's financial strength. Very high accounts receivable, for example, could mean that the new product introduced with so much fanfare at a trade show last spring may have turned out to be this winter's discontent for the customer.

Although venture capitalists consider these four factors in making their decision about a particular high-tech company, in reality there is no hard, fast rule and even the most experienced investor can get burned. The Hambrecht & Quist Growth Index, which tracks 100 high-tech stocks with market valuations under $200 million, has been a roller coaster, both in terms of the swings in value in the index (in November 1986, it was down 46 percent from its high in June 1983) and in the price/earnings multiples assigned to the sector. The bad news is that the downward slope represents considerable losses because too many "me-too" companies entered the high-tech market at inflated valuations. The good news is that the underlying strong growth in technology remains and that investors now attach more realistic multiples to this growth.

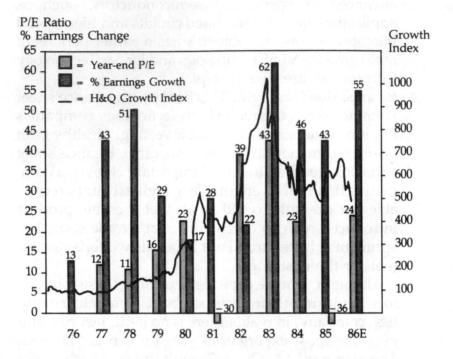

HAMBRECHT & QUIST GROWTH INDEX
P/E RATIOS vs. EARNINGS GROWTH

Companies Begin to Specialize

Many of the big names in high technology had positions across our four variables that were solid enough to withstand the shock of the 1983 aftermath. Genentech, Apple, and Lotus, for example, made some of the fundamental advances in their field and, to date, have weathered and have been improved through their various management changes. Often, although not always, these changes have included a diminished role for the original entrepreneurs who founded the company.

Today, most new companies pursue a particular piece of a market rather than seeking out the more dramatic breakthroughs. One example is Adobe Systems, a company that makes software for desktop publishing. This company was founded by people out of Xerox Research Center and Hewlett-Packard with considerable experience in technology and management. The desktop publishing market is growing at about 35 percent to 40 percent per year and is only at the beginning of its life cycle, with a market size of $500 million. The core of the Adobe product, the Postscript Interpreter, executes page descriptions to produce documents with multiple typefaces and graphics. It is protected by a combination of trade secrets, copyright and trademark laws, license agreements and technical blocks designed into the product. The company went public in August 1986; four months later, its stock had jumped to $24, a 118 percent appreciation.

Desktop publishing is a revolutionary concept because it transfers quality printing from the expensive and time-consuming realm of typesetters and printers to the owner of a personal computer with a laser printer. It will allow rapid text development not only in the Western world, but in Kanji characters, which have historically proven very difficult to adapt to computer-generated printing. These kinds of breakthroughs, while not as broad in scope as the first microprocessor or biotechnology-derived drug, will, in the right hands, create the exceptional investment values of tomorrow.

Financial Factors

While today we take for granted the well-established capital market for high-technology stocks, it has not always been this way. In the mid-1970s for example,

high-tech stocks went through a down cycle that lasted most
of the rest of the decade. The situation began to change in
the late 1970s as technology's successes became more widely
known and specialty investment banking firms began to
sponsor these types of companies. Terrain that Hambrecht
& Quist had occupied with very few other firms since 1968
began to receive more attention. The reduction in the capital
gains tax rate and the more relaxed interpretation of ERISA
"prudent investor" rules, which spurred more pension fund
investment in venture capital, drew more money into the
front end of technology investing and caused a necessary
expansion at the public market level in order to achieve
liquidity and finance more growth.

	HAMBRECHT & QUIST
Year	Total Raised Capital ($ millions)
1969	13.6
1970	12.1
1971	12.3
1972	52.8
1973	20.6
1974	11.3
1975	0.0
1976	38.4
1977	16.0
1978	47.9
1979	122.0
1980	556.7
1981	10.2
1982	94.3
1983	2,165.8
1984	352.3
1985	652.5
1986	1,222.6
TOTAL	**$6,601.4**

As described, the high-tech market tends to be quite volatile and its stocks tend to have a high beta factor, especially relative to the Dow Jones and Standard & Poor's 400.

HAMBRECHT & QUIST GROWTH INDEX
HAMBRECHT & QUIST TECHNOLOGY INDEX
STANDARD & POOR'S 400
1970-Present*

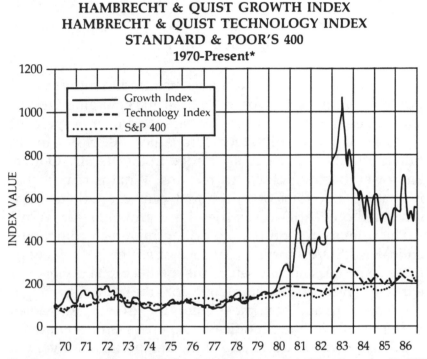

*For the purpose of comparison, all indexes have been set at 100 at December 31, 1978. Chart reflects month-end values. Latest values are for November 28, 1986.

Thus, when these stocks react, the magnitude of the swing up or down tends to be swift and strong. On the upside, this can mean significant appreciation for investors, which is the lifeblood of high-tech investing. Those with a more dividend-and-yield orientation do not usually last long in this sector. From the beginning, in fact, high technology has attracted a strong institutional following, a presence that has enabled a greater amount of risk taking to occur than is possible in retail-dominated sectors.

With high betas, historic volatility and a penchant for risk, high-tech stocks must be traded in an environment that has sufficient volume and speed to be able to react quickly to information. It is also crucial that this information be widely accessible and rapidly transmitted.

The Role of NASDAQ

Hambrecht & Quist has underwritten initial public offerings (IPOs) for more than 100 emerging growth companies during the past 18 years, and over 90 percent of these have been high-tech companies. All of our initial public offerings have initially traded in the NASDAQ market for fairly straightforward reasons. What is remarkable is that all but four of our initial public offerings have remained on NASDAQ as they have grown larger. Why?

The primary reason that emerging high-tech companies choose NASDAQ for initial public offerings is that few of these companies initially satisfy the market capitalization and earnings history requirements for the other principal exchanges. In addition, most emerging growth companies prefer to avoid the significant expenses and somewhat burdensome procedural and filing requirements involved with listing on other exchanges.

Hambrecht & Quist specializes in taking emerging high-tech companies public because of the expectation that these companies will enjoy long and prosperous growth paths toward becoming larger, well-established businesses. Those high-tech companies that achieve such growth are then more capable of fulfilling the trading requirements of any principal exchange within a very short time. For example, Apple and Genentech, which have been two of our more successful NASDAQ IPOs, have each developed market capitalizations in excess of $2.5 billion since 1980.

Similarly, some very well-established high-tech companies have gone public recently. As NASDAQ trading volumes have approached those of the New York Stock Exchange, greater numbers of these well-established high-tech IPOs—including Microsoft and Sun Microsystems—have initially chosen the NASDAQ route. These kinds of companies initially choose and remain with NASDAQ for two reasons:

1. **NASDAQ's competitive market-making system offers greater liquidity.** In contrast with single specialists who make markets in other principal exchanges, the multiple market makers for each NASDAQ company compete to balance buy and sell orders in each stock with orders from their clients and with their own capital. The result is a more orderly market with less volatile price fluctuations in periods of heavy buying and selling. Consequently, investors can hold larger positions of high-tech NASDAQ stocks with greater confidence of liquidity in a particular price range.

2. **Entrepreneurs prefer a competitive environment.** The individuals who started and built these companies are more comfortable in NASDAQ's competitive environment; they find monopolies conceptually displeasing. These individuals and their teams are drawn toward the idea of many market makers trading their stocks, versus a single specialist.

Similarly, these entrepreneurs are more comfortable with the computer communication technologies that form the basis of this multiple market-maker system than with the specialist, pit and trading floor auction infrastructures of the exchanges. More than one computer executive has remarked, upon viewing the floors of the other major exchanges, that their entire activity could be replaced with a single large computer program and communications network. This is exactly what NASDAQ has done and other exchanges, such as the London Stock Exchange, are currently in the process of doing.

Conclusion

The high-tech companies that have developed and grown in the United States over the past 30 years collectively constitute one of the healthiest sectors of the U.S. economy. The private and public U.S. capital markets have been the single force most responsible for the commercialization of the technological break-throughs of these companies. Indeed, it is markets such as NASDAQ, with its promise of liquidity and capability of supporting larger numbers of high-quality emerging growth companies, that have attracted the venture capital to spawn the growth of new technologies and the companies that deliver them.

Chapter eight

Jack Petersen, President of Kirkpatrick, Pettis, Smith, Polian Inc., has been in the securities business in Omaha for more than 25 years. In 1981, he was Chairman of the Board of Governors of the NASD.

Traditional Stocks in a Not-So-Traditional Market

by L. C. (Jack) Petersen

The NASDAQ market provides issues for all types of investors, and each of us can decide which type we are. My firm and our clients prefer what some might call the traditional NASDAQ stocks—and we find them very rewarding indeed.

The Biggest NASDAQ Stock

The largest NASDAQ security by market capitalization is Berkshire Hathaway, with a current market value of about $3.3 billion. Berkshire Hathaway is run by the legendary money manager Warren Buffett, a fundamentalist in investment philosophy if there ever was one. Warren resides in Omaha, and it has been his home all his life. The Berkshire Hathaway story is not as well known as Warren's own. The stock is not actively traded, and this is not a disappointment to Warren because he believes in investing for the long term.

Berkshire Hathaway is currently trading at approximately $3,100 per share, and that price alone inhibits many potential investors from buying shares in the company. However, the clients who bought the stock at approximately $20 a share in the 1960s are content to sit back and watch its price continue to increase. It has been as high as $3,250 per share, but Warren is the first to admit he cannot continue to compound earnings at the rate of the recent past. His public statement to that effect has not discouraged current shareholders in the least.

Some Traditional Winners

Not the size of Berkshire Hathaway, but as impressive in its own field is Valmont Industries of Valley, Nebraska, whose NASDAQ symbol is VALM. Valmont is the largest manufacturer of center-pivot irrigation systems. We have watched this company grow from a small, privately held manufacturer to a firm recognized around the world as a leader in the irrigation business.

The W. A. Krueger Company, a printing firm, was located in New Berlin, Wisconsin, when I first became acquainted with it about 23 years ago. The company did not make a great deal of progress for the next several years, but in the early 1970s it grew rapidly. A friend of mine, now living in Florida, has shares of W. A. Krueger with an adjusted cost of 66 cents per share, and the stock is currently trading at $15.50. I also have a client whose 100 shares purchased in May, 1976, at a cost of $875 now have, through splits, a market value of about $23,000. The company is now located in Scottsdale, Arizona.

The friend in Florida also purchased stock in George Banta, another printing company, in Menasha, Wisconsin, at $2.27 a share (now $20.50) and in H. B. Fuller, an adhesives manufacturer in St. Paul at $8.25 per share (now $29.50).

Her top-five core holdings are all over-the-counter companies.

The Stocks We Quote

When NASDAQ came into being in 1971, we were making markets in 24 issues. Seven were industrials, seven financials (banks and insurance companies) and 10 were utilities. Currently, we are quoting 46 issues, of which 35 are on NASDAQ and 11 are traded in the pink sheets. Of the 46 issues, 17 are industrials, 18 financials (banks, insurance companies and savings and loans) and 11 are utilities. The ratio of financials to the total has changed primarily because of the inclusion of savings and loan issues. Of the 24 we quoted in 1971, we still actively trade 13. Eight no longer exist because of mergers, sellouts and the like. We have dropped only three because of a lack of interest or for other reasons.

Good Companies for Our Clients

The primary purpose of our quoting a security that we recommend is to make it readily available for purchase by our clients. Once we have a substantial number of shares of a security in the hands of clients, we will continue to quote the security so that clients who choose to sell can receive a good execution. Many of the securities we trade today are quoted because of the substantial holdings by our clients.

When I started in the securities business, my first client, needless to say, was my mother. She was quite skeptical about the stock market but thought she could take a chance because her son was now involved. Although my mother has made charitable contributions of some of her stock and has given some to her grandchildren, the market value of her stocks today is nine times the original cost, and her dividend income, although modest, provides a return of more than 20 percent on her original investment. Had she given no shares to charity and family, I would guess the market value would be about 15 times the original purchase and her dividend income would be 30 to 40 percent of the original cost.

Another client, a friend of mine, in June 1978 purchased 1,000 shares of UB Financial at a cost of $16,750. Through stock splits, my friend's shares increased to 4,500. This NASDAQ company, now known as United Bancorp of Arizona, was bought out for $33 a share in 1987, giving the 4,500 shares a total value of more than $148,000. We have all heard of the problems plaguing banks throughout the country, but this is one that has fared very well. I am sure the visit to Omaha by the senior officers of the bank will be long remembered by the holders of their shares. We commenced market-making activities in the issue on April 21, 1978, and we are sorry to see them leave our list.

Serving Issuers, Too

In addition to market making to serve our clients, we also are interested in serving issuer companies. We are not bothered if the stock is thinly traded. I recall having lunch with the president of a small savings and loan who asked if we would consider making a market in his S&L's shares. In fact, he thought he would have to pay us for that service. I told him we would consider quoting his shares and if we did, there would be no charge. However,

I did strongly suggest that he channel buyers or sellers to us. We have been fortunate since that time in trading several thousand shares of his company's stock and have made both sellers and buyers happy. It goes without saying that the president of the S&L is also pleased with our market-making activity.

The Investment Banking Connection

The third reason for making markets is because of investment banking relationships. We have four companies on our market-making list that we have continuously quoted for nearly 50 years. Three of the four companies remain investment banking clients. In addition, our retail clients—and in some cases, institutional clients—hold substantial amounts of those issuers' securities.

We believe such long-standing relationships benefit everyone, including the issuer, the shareholders and certainly our firm. We believe it is our responsibility to get to know well the management of smaller companies that we may recommend to our clients for purchase. Because this requires a commitment of our time, we stay with companies for as long as we are convinced the fundamentals are still in place.

To expose our clients and prospects to some of the lesser-known, smaller companies, we bring the management personnel of the companies to Omaha. Most often we invite the chief executive officer, chief operating officer and chief financial officer. Our clients and prospects appreciate the opportunity to shake the hands of senior management personnel of the companies in which they own or may be purchasing securities. The managements also appreciate our efforts to help them broaden the ownership of their shares. Experience has taught us the negative impact of having highly concentrated ownership in any particular issue.

Long-Term Relationships

Our market-making list reflects our long-term relationships with clients and companies.

Three utilities in which we have made markets for more than 40 years are Washington Energy Company, Seattle (formerly Washington Natural Gas); Southern California Water Company, Los Angeles; and Edison Sault Electric Company, Sault Ste. Marie, Michigan. We still have an investment banking relationship with two of them and, in fact, have representation on their boards through Omaha residents. Our clients hold a substantial amount of the shares in each of the three issues.

In addition to those three utilities, we make a market in Iowa Southern Utilities, Centerville, Iowa; Madison Gas and Electric, Madison, Wisconsin; Northwestern Public Service Company, Huron, South Dakota; Otter Tail Power Company, Fergus Falls, Minnesota; and Lincoln Telecommunications Company of Lincoln, Nebraska.

Justin Industries, Inc., of Ft. Worth, Texas, manufactures boots, leather goods, ceramic cooling towers and bricks. Surprisingly, although it is the nation's largest face brick manufacturer, Justin Industries is not known outside of its territories for that business. We have had a relationship of nearly 20 years with Justin and its predecessor company. Although the economy is depressed in the areas served by Justin, we feel it has long-term potential and therefore we continue to quote the shares of the company. Management personnel have visited Omaha a number of times and we expect another visit very soon.

Our firm had its start in 1933, when two of the founders of our firm left the Omaha National Bank Trust Department to strike out on their own. The Omaha National Bank later became a part of the Omaha National Corp. holding company. Subsequently, the Omaha National Corp. tendered

for the First National Bank of Lincoln, which was successful, and now the name is FirsTier, which is a holding
company for the largest banks in Omaha and Lincoln. We
acted as the soliciting dealer when Omaha National made
a tender offer for the First National Bank of Lincoln.
Obviously, our relationship with the bank has continued
for more than 50 years. On January 8, 1987, we handled the
buy and sell sides of a 478,000-share block of FirsTier.

We make markets in a variety of companies in the financial services industry. For many years, we have been a
market maker in Fremont General Corporation, an insurance company in Los Angeles. The shares of Fremont
General are widely held by individuals and institutions.
Also, we were the sole market maker for years in Continental
General Insurance Company of Omaha, which has grown
and is now on the NASDAQ National Market System.
Although other market makers participate today, we believe
we are closest to the company because of our long relationship.

The largest financial institution in Nebraska is the Conservative Savings Bank, a holding company for Conservative Savings & Loan. We commenced our market-making
activities in this issue just two years ago and today enjoy
substantial trading volume in this issue. Because of its rapid
growth and expansion in other states, we expect to see the
activity increase even more.

Some Investors Own Yachts

Relatively recent additions to our market-
making list are Atcor, Inc., a producer of steel conduit,
located in Harvey, Illinois; Occidental Nebraska Federal
Savings Bank, Omaha, Nebraska; Pentair, Inc., a manufacturer of paper and power tools, located in St. Paul, Min-

nesota; and Werner Enterprises, a trucking company, located in Omaha, Nebraska.

We know that many non-glamorous growth companies are traded in the NASDAQ market and that many of them have prospered handsomely. We also know that the quiet companies of this great country of ours provide jobs today and will provide even more jobs as they grow and prosper. In fact, it is a published statistic that the major, mature firms on balance are eliminating jobs.

Investing in traditional and sometimes thinly traded companies has risks as well as great rewards. Just ask the investors who now own yachts.

PART III
The Investors

Chapter
nine

A research practitioner for more than 25 years, Eugene E. Heaton, Jr., is Senior Vice President and Division Manager at Opinion Research Corporation.

The Individual Investor in the NASDAQ Market

by Eugene E. Heaton, Jr.

Opinion Research Corporation conducted a study of individual investors in the NASDAQ market in late 1985. The results of the study are based upon interviews with the financial decision makers in 1,628 households: 1,328 shareholding households and 300 non-shareholding households. To complete the survey for the NASD, Opinion Research did the following:

- Used a national probability sample to randomly select the households.
- Collected detailed information about the equities held by the financial decision maker and each household member.
- Verified all of the stocks reported to be held to classify the market in which they traded.
- Mailed a questionnaire to households holding five or more issues to further check the accuracy of reported holdings.
- Carefully weighted and projected to U.S. household and population estimates the final data.

153

- Conducted interviewing from November 7 to December 16, 1985.

In this chapter, we first present a summary of our findings, and then we provide a more detailed report.

Summary of Survey Findings

An estimated 45.8 million Americans owned shares in at least one publicly traded company at the end of 1985. Of the 36.6 million shareowners whose stock ownership can be accurately classified by trading market, 24 percent hold OTC shares, 20 percent hold NASDAQ stocks and 16 percent (or 5.9 million individual shareowners) hold NASDAQ/NMS stocks. Nearly 9 million individual shareowners own at least one OTC security, and 7.3 million of them own at least one NASDAQ security. More than 6.6 million shareowners hold equity mutual funds.

Slightly more than half, or 56 percent, of all OTC shareowners hold listed securities or equity mutual funds as well; 3.9 million shareowners hold OTC stocks exclusively. Another 4 million shareowners hold stocks exclusively through equity mutual funds, and most of these funds include OTC stocks in their portfolios.

The results can also be stated in terms of households. Of the 21 million shareowning households whose holdings could be classified by trading market, 24 percent, or over 5 million households, own OTC stocks. NASDAQ stocks are held by 20 percent.

The survey provides an in-depth profile of financial decision makers for households that own OTC and NASDAQ stocks. These decision makers are generally older and, compared to shareowning households overall and those holding equity mutual funds, they are more likely to be male and married. The median age for all U.S. household decision

NASDAQ INDIVIDUAL SHAREOWNERSHIP SURVEY
Profile of Shareowning Households and Decision Makers

	NASDAQ/OTC*	Equity Mutual Funds (Total)	All Shareowners
Number of Shareowners	8,795,000	6,606,000	45,755,000
• **Characteristics of Decision Makers**			
Sex: Male	65%	65%	60%
Female	35%	35%	40%
Median Age (years)	43	46	44
Married	70%	58%	63%
Education:			
Completed College	54%	59%	47%
Occupation:			
Professional or Management	54%	51%	44%
• **Characteristics of Households**			
Homeowners	82%	78%	76%
1984 Household Income	$44,000	$42,000	$41,000
Median Total Assets	$70,000	$74,000	$55,000
Market Value of Household Stock Portfolio (including Mutual Funds)	$12,000	$15,000	$9,000

*NASDAQ/OTC includes NASDAQ and all other OTC.

NASDAQ INDIVIDUAL SHAREOWNERSHIP SURVEY
Profile of Shareowning Households and Decision Makers
(Continued)

	NASDAQ/OTC*	Equity Mutual Funds (Total)	All Shareowners
• **Securities Investment Behavior**			
Shareowners per Household	2.0	2.0	1.9
Diversified Portfolio (More than one holding per household)	67%	63%	46%
Acquired Stock:			
Employee Stock Plan	37%	29%	45%
Stockbroker or Dealer	67%	66%	53%
Households With:			
Trading Accounts	53%	50%	37%
Margin Accounts	13%	8%	9%
Will Be Financially Better Off One Year From Now	61%	52%	55%
• **Investment Philosophy**			
Future Price Appreciation Very Important	74%	70%	70%
Level of Risk Rate Very Important	59%	67%	66%
Willing to Take at Least a Moderate Risk	51%	55%	42%
Market Where Security Is Traded Very Important	15%	16%	24%
Liquidity Very Important	45%	46%	50%
Institutional Interest Very Important	24%	18%	29%

makers is 41. Shareowning decision makers overall have a median age of 44; the median age of OTC decision makers is 43, and the median age of equity mutual funds decision makers is 46. Sixty-five percent of OTC household decision makers are men, compared with 49 percent of all decision makers and 60 percent of all shareowning decision makers. Seventy percent of OTC household decision makers are married, compared with 57 percent of all household decision makers and 60 percent of decision makers who own non-OTC stocks.

Decision makers who own OTC stocks tend to be better educated and are more likely to be employed in a professional or managerial capacity than the total shareowner population. Fifty-four percent of these decision makers have completed college, and the same percentage classified themselves as professionals or managers. These proportions are higher than comparable figures for the total shareowner population, which are 47 and 44 percent, respectively.

OTC households also tend to be financially better off and more optimistic about their financial futures. Eighty-two percent of OTC shareowners are homeowners, versus 76 percent of all shareowners. The median household value of total assets, stock portfolios and 1984 income for OTC shareowning households is $70,000, $12,000 and $44,000, respectively, compared to $55,000, $9,000 and $41,000, respectively, for shareowners overall. Sixty-one percent of decision makers owning OTC stocks said they expected to be financially better off next year, compared to an overall shareowner proportion of 55 percent.

In general, NASDAQ and OTC households are more active in and familiar with securities markets. Over two thirds of NASDAQ and OTC households own more than one stock, and 53 percent have a securities account with a broker. Two thirds of OTC shareowners acquired stock through a broker at least once, while one third obtained stock through an employee stock-purchase plan. Overall, 37 percent of shareowning households have an account with a securities broker, and over four in 10 own more than one stock. About half of all non-OTC shareowning households acquired stock through employee stock-purchase plans, and about half purchased stock from a broker at least once.

The investment habits and philosophies of decision makers who own OTC stocks were also surveyed. Twenty-six percent of OTC decision makers entered the market for the first time during or after 1983. Fifty-three percent of these households have a current trading account with a securities broker, but only 13 percent have established a margin account. The financial decision makers reported they made, on average, six individual transactions in their trading accounts during the last 12 months.

OTC decision makers are more likely to rate price appreciation over risk as an important consideration when choosing a stock. Fifty-nine percent said the risk associated with a stock is very important, but 74 percent rated price appreciation as very important. Most OTC decision makers agree that market liquidity and institutional participation are at least somewhat important.

Detailed Report on Individual Shareownership in the NASDAQ Market

The Shareowners

Overall Ownership. Our studies show that individuals held about 72 percent of the market value of NASDAQ securities at year-end 1985, with institutions holding 28 percent.

DISTRIBUTION OF NASDAQ SHAREOWNERSHIP
1985

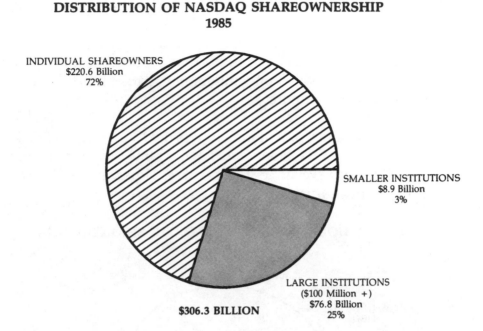

INDIVIDUAL SHAREOWNERS
$220.6 Billion
72%

SMALLER INSTITUTIONS
$8.9 Billion
3%

LARGE INSTITUTIONS
($100 Million +)
$76.8 Billion
25%

$306.3 BILLION

Information on the precise breakdown of the NASDAQ shareowning public is incomplete, primarily because small institutions and foreign institutions are not required to report holdings. The result: Some institutional holdings are unavoidably included in the individual category. However, a recent study of institutional stock holdings by the University of Pennsylvania, Wharton School, revealed a growing institutional presence in the NASDAQ market. Our estimates are based upon and consistent with the findings of that study.

Based on extrapolation of findings, individual shareownership in the contiguous United States at year-end 1985 was estimated at 45,755,000—nearly one third of all adult Americans.[1] Of the 36,613,000 individuals whose stock

---

[1]Alaska and Hawaii are not included in the ownership projections.

ownership can be accurately classified by trading markets, 24 percent, or almost 8.8 million, hold at least one over-the-counter (OTC) stock. Eight shareholders in 10 own exchange-listed issues, and 18 percent report that they own stock mutual funds. (Bond and money market funds are not included in this figure.)

OTC Ownership. Among owners of OTC shares, 44 percent own only OTC shares. About the same proportion own both OTC and exchange-listed shares; 11 percent own OTC shares and mutual funds.

EQUITY HOLDINGS OF NASDAQ/OTC SHAREOWNERS
1985

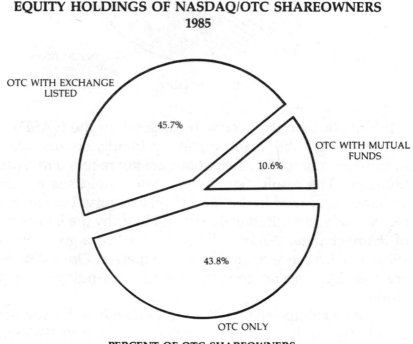

PERCENT OF OTC SHAREOWNERS

A more detailed analysis of OTC shareownership reveals that holders of NASDAQ-listed stocks in total account for

83 percent of OTC holders. Nearly three quarters of OTC shareholders own NASDAQ issues exclusively. Ownership of NASDAQ/NMS issues accounts for 67 percent of the OTC holders, and 62 percent of these shareholders own NASDAQ/NMS issues exclusively.

Only 17 percent of OTC shareowners hold non-NASDAQ stocks in general. Shareowners whose investments are limited to NASDAQ stocks not included in NASDAQ/NMS constitute only 8 percent of the total OTC shareowner population.

NASDAQ/OTC SHAREHOLDER GROUPS
1985

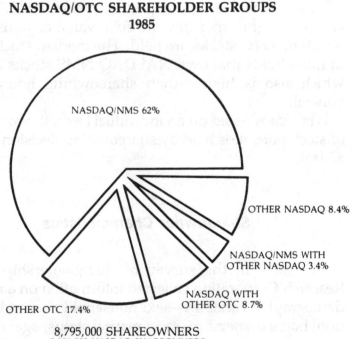

NASDAQ/NMS 62%

OTHER NASDAQ 8.4%

NASDAQ/NMS WITH
OTHER NASDAQ 3.4%

NASDAQ WITH
OTHER OTC 8.7%

OTHER OTC 17.4%

8,795,000 SHAREOWNERS
7,254,000 NASDAQ SHAREOWNERS

Household Ownership of Shares. Shareownership can also be analyzed on a household basis. Of the estimated 21 million shareowning households whose holdings can be classified by trading market, over 5 million hold OTC stocks.

This is nearly one quarter of the shareowning households. Over 4 million of the households, or 20 percent, hold NASDAQ stocks. The largest proportion of these households—16 percent—own NASDAQ/NMS issues.

The total number of stock issues (on a duplicated basis) held by the shareowning population is 68,907,000. Households owning NASDAQ/NMS stocks have an average of 1.8 issues. The figure is virtually the same for households that own other NASDAQ stocks or other OTC issues.

Portfolio Values. The median stock portfolio value for U.S. *households* is $9,000. Households in which a member owns OTC stocks have a median portfolio value of $12,000, which is $4,000 higher than the portfolio value of households in which no OTC stocks are held. The median stock portfolio in households that own NASDAQ/NMS stocks is $13,000, which also is higher than shareowning households in general.

When considered on an individual basis, the median value of stock portfolios held by shareowning decision makers is $7,000.

Shareowner Characteristics

In the survey of shareownership, Opinion Research Corporation collected information on a number of demographic variables—sex; household size and composition; home ownership; race; marital status; age; education; employment status; total assets; and household income. Opinion Research Corporation collected this information for all of the financial decision makers contacted, whether they represented shareowning or nonshareowning households.

A review of this information generates the following basic profile of NASDAQ shareholders:

Sex. The proportions of male and female decision makers in U.S. households are about evenly divided (49 percent vs. 51 percent). Decision makers who own stock, however, are more frequently men than women (60 percent vs. 40 percent). Males are also the more active investors. Holders of five or more stocks are more likely to be men than women (74 percent vs. 26 percent), and men describe themselves as more willing to take some financial risk (68 percent vs. 32 percent).

Ownership of over-the-counter stocks in general is more prevalent among men than women (65 percent vs. 35 percent), as is ownership of NASDAQ (64 percent vs. 36 percent) and NASDAQ/NMS stocks (63 percent vs. 37 percent). Consequently, 75 percent of the men indicate that they are at least somewhat familiar with NASDAQ, compared with 25 percent of the women.

Household Size and Composition. A median of two people regularly live in households in which OTC stocks are held. The same is true for households in which NASDAQ and NASDAQ/NMS shares are held. (The median number of people living in shareowning households generally is comparable.) Almost two thirds of American households owning OTC, NASDAQ and NASDAQ/NMS issues, have no children living at home. This figure is comparable for all shareowning households (64 percent).

Of the shareowning population, 95 percent are adults; only 5 percent of shareowners are minors.

Home Ownership. Homeowners are more prevalent in the U.S. than are renters (63 percent vs. 37 percent). As would be expected, considerably more shareowning households own a home than non-shareowning households (76 percent vs. 58 percent). Approximately eight decision makers in 10 who own OTC, NASDAQ or NASDAQ/NMS issues own their own homes.

A higher proportion of shareowners who hold five or more issues own a home (5 to 9 issues—89 percent; 10 or more issues—90 percent) than those holding fewer than five issues (2 to 4 issues—75 percent; 1 issue—72 percent).

Race. The great majority of financial decision makers are white, and the proportion of white shareowners is greater than non-white shareowners (94 percent vs. 85 percent). Blacks make up 4 percent of the shareowner group.

Focusing on the shareowners group only, 97 percent of all decision makers who own OTC stocks are white, as are owners of NASDAQ (97 percent) and NASDAQ/NMS stocks (98 percent).

Only a very small proportion of decision makers—2 percent of the shareowning and 6 percent of the non-shareowning decision makers—are of Hispanic origin or background. Two percent of the decision makers who own OTC stocks and 1 percent of the decision makers who own NASDAQ/NMS stocks are Hispanic.

Marital Status. Of all decision makers in U.S. households, 57 percent are married, 20 percent are single, 8 percent are divorced and 11 percent are widowed. A higher proportion of decision makers who personally own stock are married (63 percent), compared with those who are non-shareowners (55 percent). Of the married decision makers, 70 percent hold OTC stocks, 68 percent hold NASDAQ issues, 70 percent hold NASDAQ/NMS issues and 60 percent hold non-OTC issues, illustrating that married decision makers hold more OTC stocks than non-OTC stocks.

Age. The median age of all decision makers in U.S. households is 41 years. Those owning stock are slightly older than those who do not (44 vs. 40). The median age of decision makers holding OTC issues or NASDAQ/NMS issues is 43, and the median age for shareowning decision makers in general is 44.

The effect of age on investment behavior is evident in the number of stocks held and the inclination to take investment risks. Decision makers who own one stock have a median age of 41 years. This figure increases to 46 years among owners of two to four issues and to 57 years among those who hold five or more issues. Although older investors appear to have accumulated more stock, they are less likely to take risks with their portfolios. The median age of those willing to take some risk when investing is 33 years; the median age of those willing to take little risk is 43 years.

Education. Nearly half of all decision makers in U.S. households have attained more than a high school education. About two in 10 have some college education, about one sixth completed college, and one decision maker in 10 has some postgraduate training. More than one third of decision makers have a high school diploma, while only 17 percent have not finished high school.

The educational attainments of decision makers who own stock are considerably higher than those who do not. Of the former group, 47 percent have a college education or beyond, while only 19 percent of those who do not own stock have similar educational levels.

Furthermore, decision makers who own OTC stock in general and NASDAQ and NASDAQ/NMS issues in particular, have a higher educational level (54 percent in each group have a college education or beyond) than do those who do not own OTC stocks (44 percent have a college education or beyond). It is also notable that the educational level of decision makers willing to take investment risks is also higher than those who are not (31 percent vs. 21 percent completed college or beyond).

Employment Status. About three quarters of financial decision makers in U.S. households are employed, and almost all of them work on a full-time basis. White-collar workers are by far the dominant career group represented

(63 percent). Blue-collar workers comprise 14 percent of the decision-making group, and the proportion of housewives, retired and unemployed decision makers is 24 percent.

Eighty percent of decision makers who hold OTC stock are employed, again reflecting statistics for financial decision makers in general. The same is true for those who own NASDAQ (79 percent) and NASDAQ/NMS stock (80 percent). Only 74 percent of decision makers holding only listed stocks are currently employed on either a full-time or part-time basis.

Of all shareowning decision makers, 44 percent have a spouse who is employed outside the home on either a part-time or full-time basis. Similar proportions of decision makers who own OTC issues (44 percent), as well as NASDAQ (45 percent) and NASDAQ/NMS issues (47 percent), also have working spouses.

Household income increases in proportion to households composed of two wage earners (under $25,000—13 percent have two wage earners; $25,000 to $50,000—42 percent have two wage earners; $50,000 or more—52 percent have two wage earners).

Total Assets. The median combined market value of total assets owned by U.S. households is $55,000. Again, households in which someone owns OTC stocks have higher median assets than those that do not ($70,000 vs. $51,000). Households holding NASDAQ stocks, and more specifically NASDAQ/NMS issues only, also have higher-valued assets ($71,000 and $67,000, respectively).

Household Income. Shareowning households in the U.S. have a median household income of $41,000 before taxes, with stock ownership increasing proportionately with income (1 stock—$36,000; 2 to 4 stocks—$42,000; 5 to 9 stocks—$63,000). A correlation between household income and the value of these stock investments and household assets is also evident; as household income increases, so does the value as well as the scope of investments and assets.

Individual Shareowners' Investment Activities

Financial decision makers who own OTC stocks have been involved in the market for a number of years; 77 percent acquired stocks or stock mutual fund shares during 1982 or before. A similar proportion—75 percent—of decision makers who own NASDAQ/NMS issues entered the market during this period; owners of stock mutual funds show the same lengthy history of investment activity—75 percent first acquired shares in 1982 or before.

Decision makers who hold *only* OTC stocks, however, have generally acquired their shares more recently than those who may own more than one type of stock—42 percent entered the market in 1983 or later, while 56 percent acquired stocks in 1982 or before. In fact, more than one decision maker in 10 who owns OTC stocks exclusively first obtained shares in 1985—within a year of this survey.

The value of stock investments increases with the number of issues held and the years of investment activity. Predictably, decision makers with stock investments under $5,000 generally acquired their shares more recently than those with investments of $20,000 or more; 32 percent with investments of under $5,000 first acquired stocks during or after 1983 vs. 6 percent with investments of $20,000 or more.

It is also not surprising that decision makers owning only one issue have entered the market more recently (30 percent—1983 or later) than those holding a number of issues (5 or more issues—only 4 percent entered the market during 1983 or later).

Methods of Acquiring Shares

Of OTC shareowners, 67 percent acquired their stock through a stock broker or dealer, 37 percent by employee stock-purchase plans and 25 percent through stock splits or dividends. Decision makers who hold NASDAQ/NMS stocks show the same pattern of stock acquisition: 67 percent acquired their stocks through a stock broker, 36 percent through employee stock-purchase plans and 27 percent through stock splits or dividends.

However, those decision makers holding OTC stock exclusively are much less likely to have acquired their shares through a stock broker or dealer (39 percent). In fact, they are as likely to have acquired stock through an employee stock-purchase plan (40 percent) as through a broker.

The majority of decision makers holding stock mutual funds also acquired their shares through a stock broker or dealer (66 percent). They are less likely than those owning over-the-counter issues to have obtained stocks through an employee stock-purchase plan (29 percent) and much more likely than that group to have acquired shares through an IRA (32 percent).

As can be expected, decision makers holding only one issue are much more likely than those owning two or more issues to have acquired their stock through an employee stock-purchase plan (1 issue—54 percent; 2 to 4 issues—38 percent; 5 or more issues—34 percent).

Stock gifts, although not a prevalent means of stock acquisition on an overall basis, are particularly important in accounting for the presence of women in the market. Almost one quarter of women acquired stocks through a gift or inheritance, compared with 14 percent of men. In addition, a greater proportion of men obtain stocks through stock brokers or dealers than do women (60 percent vs. 44 percent).

Investment Decision Making

Regardless of the type of stock they own, 69 percent of the decision makers discuss their investments with someone else before making their decisions. Only 27 percent say they make decisions without additional input.

Decision makers holding numerous issues—five or more—are more likely to say they make investment decisions alone (38 percent) than are those holding fewer stocks (2 to 4 issues—29 percent; 1 issue—25 percent). Similarly, those with a highly valued stock portfolio are more likely to make investment decisions by themselves ($20,000 or more—37 percent; under $5,000—23 percent). In addition, more males make investment decisions alone than do females (32 percent vs. 20 percent).

Securities Trading Accounts

Fifty-three percent of households owning over-the-counter issues have securities trading accounts, with the decision maker usually having a personal or a joint account (29 percent and 21 percent, respectively). In 3 percent of the cases, another household member has an account. Of the households in which members hold NASDAQ/NMS stocks, 54 percent have securities trading accounts.

Securities trading accounts are found far more often in households owning OTC stocks (53 percent) than in households owning listed stocks only (31 percent).

The presence of securities trading accounts in a household also increases in relation to the number of issues owned by household members. Eighty-six percent of households with 10 or more issues have securities trading accounts, while only 16 percent of households holding only one stock have their own trading accounts.

Predictably, securities trading accounts are more prevalent in households with more valuable stock portfolios ($20,000 or more—64 percent; $5,000 to $20,000—37 percent; under $5,000—21 percent).

The number of stock brokerage accounts in a household does not vary according to the type of stock owned, and approximately two stock brokerage accounts are held in households that have such accounts. The average number of different brokerage firms with whom household members have securities is 1.4.

Trading Activity

Decision makers who own OTC stocks, including NASDAQ and NASDAQ/NMS securities, made an average of six trades (separate buy and sell transactions) in the past six months. Individuals holding stock mutual funds made an average of five trades.

When making stock transactions, 9 percent of household decision makers who have securities trading accounts and own OTC issues say they "usually" buy or sell as many as 500 or more shares. The majority—60 percent—trade between 100 and 500 shares, but a sizable minority—28 percent—usually trade fewer than 100 shares. This pattern of trading activity is similar in households owning NASDAQ and NASDAQ/NMS issues.

Roughly seven out of 10 households that have stock brokerage accounts and own over-the-counter issues leave their stocks on deposit with the securities firm; 26 percent of the households have their stock delivered to them. Of households in which mutual funds are held, 80 percent prefer to leave their securities on deposit.

Margin Accounts

Margin accounts are not widely held; only 9 percent of the shareowning households have a margin account with a brokerage firm or bank. However, 16 percent of households owning NASDAQ/NMS stocks have margin accounts. Ownership of margin accounts is also higher in households in which some form of OTC issue is held (13 percent). However, of those owning OTC stocks exclusively, only 5 percent have a margin account. The presence of margin accounts in households that own mutual funds mirrors shareowning households in general (8 percent).

Margin accounts are also more prevalent in households that own a number of stocks (10 or more stock issues—25 percent), have a high income level ($50,000 or more—17 percent), large total assets ($100,000 or more—19 percent) or high stock portfolio value ($20,000 or more—20 percent).

Willingness to Take Risks

Decision makers owning OTC stocks are more willing to take investment risks than those owning only listed stocks. About half of decision makers who own OTC stocks are willing to take at least a moderate amount of risk when making their investment decisions. The same is true for those who own NASDAQ/NMS issues. Only 35 percent of decision makers who own only listed stocks are willing to take a moderate amount of risk.

Factors in the Decision-Making Process

When making stock investment decisions, 70 percent of the decision makers who own mutual funds and

69 percent of the decision makers who own listed issues perceive the potential for future price appreciation to be *very* important. This factor is also paramount for decision makers who own OTC stocks (74 percent) and NASDAQ/NMS issues (77 percent).

The level of risk associated with a stock is the second most important criteria considered by decision makers—66 percent rate risk as an important factor. This factor, however, is considered to be somewhat less important by decision makers who hold NASDAQ/NMS issues (59 percent) and OTC stocks in general (59 percent) than it is for those holding mutual funds (67 percent) and listed issues only (69 percent).

Market liquidity of a stock is considered to be very important by 45 percent of decision makers who own OTC issues and 42 percent of decision makers who own NASDAQ/NMS issues. This factor is somewhat more important for shareowners holding only listed stocks; 52 percent of them rate market liquidity as very important.

The importance of market liquidity when making investment decisions, however, appears to be related to stock portfolio value. As the value of shares owned increases, so does the importance of market liquidity (under $5,000—46 percent; $5,000 to $20,000—50 percent; $20,000 or more—57 percent).

Only about one quarter of decision makers holding OTC issues consider institutional shareownership to be very important when making stock investment decisions. A comparably small proportion of those holding NASDAQ/NMS issues rate this factor as very important. Decision makers holding stock mutual funds attach even less importance to this matter (18 percent). Despite the extensive institutional ownership of listed stocks, only 31 percent of decision makers who own only listed stocks attribute much importance to institutional ownership.

Finally, the market on which a company's stock is traded is not an overriding concern to shareholders when making investment decisions. Only 15 percent of decision makers who own OTC stocks say they give this issue a great deal of consideration; 29 percent say they give it a fair amount of consideration. In fact, over half say they give the market on which the company's stock is traded very little consideration or no consideration at all. This same distribution holds true for decision makers who hold NASDAQ/NMS issues and mutual funds. Decision makers holding only listed stocks give somewhat more consideration to the subject of marketplace—51 percent give the issue at least a fair amount of consideration.

Chapter
ten

James B. Cloonan is President of the
American Association of Individual
Investors (AAII), a non-profit organization
that he formed in 1979 and that now has
more than 100,000 members and 37
chapters. From 1974 to 1978, Dr. Cloonan
helped found and served as CEO of
Heinold Securities, a stock brokerage firm.
From 1965 to 1982, Dr. Cloonan taught at
the University of Missouri, Loyola
University of Chicago and DePaul
University.

Individual Strategies in the NASDAQ Market

by James B. Cloonan

Over the past 70 or 80 years for which detailed records are available, the stock market appears fairly efficient. In an efficient market, stocks are priced very close to where they should be, based on information that is publicly available. Few people would say the market is perfectly efficient, but its degree of efficiency makes it difficult to find general strategies that will beat the averages consistently.

The returns on some stocks will be higher than on others, but most of this can be attributed to higher risk. Riskier stocks are supposed to have higher average returns to make up for the additional risk. The risk/return relationship theoretically looks like the illustration on page 178.

Point (A) indicates the yield for riskless T-bills; points on the line run from government bonds, blue-chip stocks and aggressive stocks to futures contracts (B). In practice, the risk/return relationship holds very closely, and very few investment approaches consistently give results above the AB line. This line is called the Capital Market Line, and it is basic to the efficient-market theory.

RISK/RETURN RELATIONSHIP

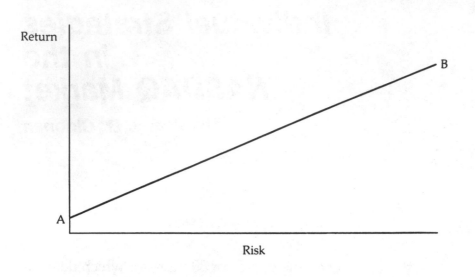

The Small-Stock Effect

Some exceptions, however, have been well documented. The most famous of these is the small-stock effect. "Small" in this case means low capitalization (the number of shares outstanding times share price). These stocks have market values between $20 million and $100 million. While some of these stocks are exchange-listed, most of them are traded over the counter, primarily through NASDAQ.

The original extensive study of small stocks by Rolf Banz has been followed by many other studies. R. G. Ibbotson Associates, Inc., chronicled the results over time as shown in the accompanying table, "Sixty Years of Returns: 1926-1985."

SIXTY YEARS OF RETURNS: 1926 to 1985
Average Annual Compound Rates of Return

	Small Stocks	S&P 500	Long-Term Government Bonds	Long-Term Corporate Bonds	Treasury Bills	Inflation
Last 10 Years	27.8	14.3	9.0	9.8	9.0	7.0
Last 20 Years	15.3	8.7	6.0	6.7	7.3	6.4
Last 30 Years	15.3	9.5	4.6	5.3	5.8	4.8
Last 40 Years	14.3	11.2	3.8	4.4	4.6	4.6
Last 50 Years	15.2	10.7	3.9	4.3	3.7	4.2
Last 60 Years	12.6	9.8	4.1	4.8	3.4	3.1

Growth of a Dollar

	Small Stocks	S&P 500	Long-Term Government Bonds	Long-Term Corporate Bonds	Treasury Bills	Inflation
Last 10 Years	$ 11.57	$ 3.81	$ 2.36	$ 2.55	$2.37	$1.96
Last 20 Years	17.10	5.26	3.18	3.63	4.09	3.43
Last 30 Years	71.20	15.03	3.84	4.69	5.41	4.07
Last 40 Years	207.46	70.39	4.38	5.64	6.06	6.00
Last 50 Years	1,199.26	157.95	6.79	8.34	6.17	7.90
Last 60 Years	1,241.23	279.11	11.02	16.54	7.47	6.09

Details of the construction and computation methods for each of the above series are described in *Stocks, Bonds, Bills and Inflation: The Past and the Future*. Updated figures in this table are courtesy of: *Stocks, Bonds, Bills and Inflation, 1986 Yearbook*. R. G. Ibbotson Associates, Inc.; Chicago, Illinois.

The excess returns of the small stocks far exceed the additional return that would be expected for the slight additional short-term risk. For long-term investors—those committing funds for three to six years or more—the increased risk has already been compensated for in the compound rates of return.

Although the small-stock effect has been the most studied and discussed of the apparent inefficiencies in the stock market, others do appear. Several studies have shown that low-priced stocks performed better than higher-priced issues, but when the small-stock effect was allowed for, price did not appear to be significant. Neglected stocks—those not held by many institutions and not covered by many analysts—seem to outperform the market, as do stocks of companies with positive earnings.

Based on the small-stock research and the research on the effect of neglect, the American Association of Individual Investors (AAII) developed a class of stocks that are called Shadow Stocks. These stocks meet the small-stock requirement, are not widely held by institutions and are not covered by many analysts. In isolating this group of stocks at the end of 1984, several additional criteria were added. The stocks had positive earnings for the past two years, and current information was publicly available. Initially, 440 stocks met the criteria for Shadow Stocks, and the great majority were NASDAQ issues. The number has changed over the past two years, with new companies qualifying and many stocks on the list being bought out.

While two years is a short time, the Shadow Stocks outperformed both the Standard & Poor's 500 and the R. G. Ibbotson Associates' Small-Stock Index in 1985 and 1986.

For more conservative investors, AAII will choose a subgroup of the Shadow Stocks that have lower price/earnings ratios and pay dividends. This subgroup of about 130 stocks will be monitored from 1987 onward.

One additional factor that may affect the return of a stock is the extent of management ownership. Research on this topic indicates that higher management ownership leads to higher returns, but the evidence is still insufficient. If this factor proves to be important, we would expect that higher management ownership will be more common among smaller companies and more evident in NASDAQ stocks.

Other Reasons for Considering Small Stocks

If the historical record of small stocks and Shadow Stocks does not convince most investors that this is the most fertile market from which to choose stocks, other reasons may convince them. Institutions generally cannot be in the market for smaller companies because they can't buy a substantial number of shares without owning too large a percentage of each company or temporarily inflating the price. As a result, institutions usually stick with the giant companies. The question that immediately comes to mind is: Why should individuals compete with professionals who have time, data and large-scale computers, when they don't have to?

Institutions have the advantages of manpower and information, but they have the greater disadvantage of inflexibility. Once a stock gets into the hands of institutions, it may move on institutional criteria of "looking good" rather than long-term merits. A smaller company can grow until it gets into the institutional spotlight. It then gets a great boost as institutions discover it, but that is when the time-wise individuals, having taken advantage of the institutional free ride, get off and find another "pre-institutional" stock.

In addition to the effect of institutional "me-tooism" and window dressing, the larger stocks are involved in program trading and option arbitrage strategies that can cause wide, meaningless swings in prices. The long-term individual investor is probably happier avoiding participation in such swings.

It is true that the stocks of smaller companies are not as liquid as the stocks of larger firms. That is why institutions cannot effectively invest in these companies. The lower liquidity should not have an effect on individual investors

unless they have very large portfolios. It appears that portfolios need to be more widely diversified when invested in
smaller companies than might be necessary when invested
in larger companies. This not only leads to lower portfolio
risk, but also means that fewer shares of each company are
needed, and thus buying and selling can generally be carried out within the NASDAQ bid or ask price.

What About Risk?

Many individuals worry about small com-
panies' stocks because of their greater risk. They wonder
if that makes these stocks unsuitable for those who need
a low-risk portfolio. Long-term investors (more than four
years) who are not selling off capital for current needs probably shouldn't worry about risk if they have a diversified
portfolio (at least 20 different stocks) of smaller companies.
Those living on capital or who will need their capital within
four years should certainly be risk averse. However, moving
from small-company stocks to blue chips may not be the
best way to reduce risk.

Whatever the appropriate level of risk for an individual,
numerous combinations of investments will produce portfolios of the same risk. The objective is to find the portfolio
that will produce the highest return for a given level of risk.
If the level of risk of a portfolio of blue-chip stocks seems
appropriate, it is highly likely that the investor may obtain
a higher return from a portfolio that combines T-bills and
Shadow Stocks and that has the same risk as a portfolio of
blue chips. Only the risk of the entire portfolio matters. The
individual with $1,000 in the riskiest stocks in the world and
$99,000 in T-bills has much less risk than the individual with
his portfolio entirely invested in blue-chip stocks. A portfolio of 25 percent T-bills and 75 percent small-company

stocks has about the same short-term risk as securities in the S&P's 500 but historically provides higher returns.

A Complete Investment Strategy

We can consider a fairly complete investment strategy in terms of only two kinds of investments—Shadow Stocks and money market instruments. There are, of course, other opportunities depending on an individual's tax situation and his or her ability to bear risk. Even companies smaller than the Shadow Stocks, almost venture capital in nature, may provide excellent returns for the individual investor with a portfolio large enough to diversify into 30 or more stocks or partnerships. Income-producing real estate is not really different in nature from an operating corporation, but for tax reasons, real estate ventures are usually partnerships.

For all or an appropriate part of an individual investor's portfolio, the concepts we have discerned can be brought together into an investment strategy that historically should perform well above the returns from market averages or the vast majority of mutual funds or investment advisers.

This strategy is based on smaller and less-known companies rather than NASDAQ stocks, per se. A number of small companies are on listed exchanges and some very large companies are on NASDAQ, but most of the Shadow Stocks will be found in the NASDAQ market. In outlining a Shadow Stock strategy, it becomes clear that the investor must do some work and become familiar with the concepts. Most adults can do what is necessary, but unless they want to do it themselves and have some discipline, it might be better to find a mutual fund or adviser who will do it for them.

- **Step One.** Investors must define their risk levels in terms of the percentage that should be in Shadow Stocks versus the percentage in safe, short-term investments such as insured bank accounts, T-bills, money market accounts or, for some, short-term municipal bonds. Investors must make their decisions based not only on their real financial situation, but on their psychological ability to accept the variability of risk. No investment approach will work if the investor doesn't follow it, and nothing is worth ulcers or losing sleep. As a general guide, an individual with a secure income, no need for the money for a number of years, and not a great deal of nervousness about day-to-day or year-to-year fluctuations might divide the portfolio into 80 percent Shadow Stocks and 20 percent appropriate short-term instruments.

  At the other extreme, a recently retired individual who would like to be totally safe but who needs sufficient return not just to live on but to protect the portfolio from inflation, might keep 10 percent to 20 percent in Shadow Stocks and the rest in ultra-safe income investments. Each investor must choose the appropriate portion of the investment portfolio to be in Shadow Stocks.

- **Step Two.** In choosing stocks for the portfolio, we suggest buying only 100 shares of each stock until 20 to 30 stocks are in the portfolio. Then, additional shares of previously chosen stocks can be purchased. By adding additional shares of the lower-priced stocks first, a relative balance of the dollars invested in each company can be maintained. This procedure not only provides the risk reduction of diversification, but fewer shares (in round lots of 100) of each stock will permit purchases and sales without affecting the bid or ask prices. During the selection process, investors should:

1. Concentrate on Shadow Stocks—those with total market values between $20 million to $100 million, those with fewer than 10 institutions holding shares, and those with minimal coverage by analysts. Investors should also require two previous years of positive earnings and the availability of information. If investors use a computer for screening stocks, they should choose only stocks listed on the data base they use. These screens should reduce the number of stocks to about 450.

2. Base further reduction of the potential stocks on personal preferences and more complete analysis. Some of the criteria that investors might use include:

   a. Looking for a more conservative portfolio. This could include eliminating the stocks with 25 percent of the highest price/earnings ratios and eliminating stocks that do not pay cash dividends.

   b. Reducing transaction costs by eliminating stocks priced under $7 a share and requiring minimum spreads between the bid and ask prices.

   c. Requiring three to five years of positive earnings rather than the two originally suggested. If dividend payment was a consideration, require payment for the past four years.

3. Use the direct and generalized screens above to bring the remainder of potential stocks to about 100. The selection of 20 to 30 from among them involves personal feelings about the most important criteria. Potential selection devices include:

   a. High level of management ownership of the company.

   b. Record of steady increases in earnings, dividends and sales.

   c. Conservative constraints such as debt/equity ratios, current assets and book value. These constraints,

however, may not be proper for growing companies in a service-dominated economy and may simply lead to stodgy performance.
d. An effort to diversify across other dimensions by
limiting the number of companies in any one industry or geographical area.
e. An individual with time can look beyond these
general criteria and learn more about the company,
its product, its competition and its management.

- **Step Three.** Investors should update their portfolios
by selling stocks. Stocks originally in a portfolio may
have to be replaced when they are no longer suitable.
In some instances, stocks should be sold as soon as they
fail to meet the original criteria. In other cases, they
should be held until they have exceeded the bounds
by a significant percentage or for a significant period.
I suggest the following sell rules:

1. Sell as soon as possible when: the company is bought
out; it goes into bankruptcy; it is evident it will have
a loss in the current year; it misses or reduces a dividend; or the market makes the bid/ask spreads too high.
2. Sell after a company violates the small-stock definition
($20 million to $100 million in market value) in either
direction for two years in a row. The small-stock values
can be adjusted for inflation. After two consecutive
years, it is also time to get rid of stocks with too high
an institutional interest or analyst coverage.
3. At least annually, check for other imposed criteria, such
as price/earnings levels or price.
4. Use individually chosen criteria as a sell signal on an
individually chosen time basis. In general, it is wise not
to react too quickly.

- **Step Four.** Investors should evaluate the funds committed to Shadow Stocks in terms of changes in their
own ability to accept risk. As their wealth changes, as

they move closer to retirement or as they approach a time when they wish to spend or reallocate their money, investors should adjust the percentage allocated to aggressive and safe assets.

Improving investment performance beyond the market average is not easy. I believe, however, that a little effort in the right direction and a bit of discipline can provide results that, in the long run, will beat the market. That is a result very few mutual funds or investment advisers achieve over the long haul. We can only emphasize again that individual investors should invest in that part of the market reserved for individuals. They should not invest in institutional stocks; that's best left to the institutions.

Chapter eleven

Marshall E. Blume is the Howard Butcher Professor of Finance and the Director of the Rodney L. White Center for Financial Research at the University of Pennsylvania's Wharton School. Dr. Blume has written numerous articles on financial markets, instruments and portfolio strategies. In addition, he has worked as a consultant for a large number of firms.

Irwin Friend is the Edward J. Hopkinson Emeritus Professor of Finance and Economics at the University of Pennsylvania's Wharton School and is the former Director of the Rodney L. White Center for Financial Research. Dr. Friend has lectured in numerous countries and has served as a consultant to governmental and corporate agencies throughout the United States.

Institutional Investors: A Rapidly Growing Presence in NASDAQ

by Marshall E. Blume
and
Irwin Friend

The growth of institutional investors over the past three decades is one of the most significant changes that has occurred in the structure of the U.S. capital markets. Many economists have written on this subject, especially on the increase in institutional trading on the New York Stock Exchange. In contrast, the authors of this study have compiled new data on institutional holdings of NASDAQ/OTC stocks[1] and institutional block volume in NASDAQ/NMS stocks. The findings show a dramatic rise in the

---

[1] Data do not include institutions with less than $100 million in equity holdings or foreign institutions. NASDAQ/OTC is preponderantly NASDAQ issues but also includes some other OTC and regional exchange-only issues.

presence and participation of institutions in the NASDAQ market.[2]

This chapter analyzes the trends in institutional ownership of equity for all markets together and for the NYSE, the Amex and the NASDAQ/OTC markets individually. It also analyzes the relative trends of stock ownership by different types and sizes of institutional investors. Finally, the chapter presents new data that reveal significant new trends in the types of stocks institutions own.

Study Findings

The dollar value of NASDAQ/OTC stocks in institutional investor portfolios more than tripled during the period 1980 to 1985. Our survey data show that the holdings of NASDAQ/OTC stocks in institutional portfolios rose from $20 billion at year-end 1979 to $68.6 billion in mid-1985, an increase of 243 percent. NASDAQ/OTC stocks accounted for 8.4 percent of institutional portfolios in June 1985 compared to 5.5 percent of the value in those portfolios in 1979; in the same period, NYSE stocks declined from 93.2 to 90.3 percent of institutional portfolios. Looked at another way,

---

[2] Although the volume of trading is one measure of the economic importance of institutional investors, it is not necessarily the most important from an economic perspective. The dollar value of institutional holdings may be at least as important, if not more important, in explaining the long-term effect of institutions on the prices of securities. If, as is known to be the case, institutions as a group trade their equities at a faster rate than do individuals, the frequently reported volume figures would overstate the ownership of institutions. In addition, these frequently cited volume figures usually pertain only to NYSE stocks and thus do not reflect the possible importance of institutions on other exchanges, including the over-the-counter market, consisting for the most part of NASDAQ stocks.

the percentage of the value of NASDAQ/OTC stocks held by institutions almost doubled in mid-1985, moving from 14.2 percent of the total market value of NASDAQ/OTC stocks in 1979 to 25.1 percent in mid-1985.

Investment advisers were clearly the largest segment of institutional investors in this trend, increasing their dollar value of institutional holdings by 617.1 percent, from $4.1 billion to $29.4 billion. Investment companies, principally mutual funds, were next, with a 257 percent increase from 1979 to 1985. Smaller institutional investors increased the proportion of their holdings in NASDAQ/OTC stocks even more than larger institutions did. While the largest proportion of the value of common stocks in institutional portfolios was in NYSE-listed stocks, the NASDAQ/OTC market was a rapidly growing second in importance, accounting for nearly 17 percent of the stocks held by the intermediate-sized institutions and almost 10 percent of the largest institutions' holdings.

The majority of NASDAQ/OTC stocks held by institutions with $100 million or more in equities are traded on the NASDAQ National Market System (NASDAQ/NMS)— slightly over 8 percent of the portfolios of the largest institutions and 16 percent of the portfolios of the intermediate-sized group. Amex stocks account for somewhat under 4 percent of the common stocks held by the largest institutions and 4 percent of the stocks held by the intermediate group.

About the Study

The primary data source the study uses in assessing the ownership trends of institutions is Form 13F, which any institution with over $100 million of equities under management must file quarterly with the SEC. The research reveals that a very limited number of institutions with slightly less than $100 million of equities also file these forms, although they are not legally required to do so. Thus, the institutions filing Form 13F are more accurately defined as institutions with approximately $100 million or more under management.

On Form 13F, each institution must list the number of shares of the common stock of each company in its managed accounts. The following analysis is based upon the entire universe of institutions filing Forms 13F at the end of each year from 1979 through 1984 and for the quarter ending June 1985.

Each stock was matched against the daily price files of Telstat for the same period. From this matching process, the study identifies the primary marketplace for each stock, the total number of shares outstanding, the market price of each share, the earnings per share and the dividends per share.

All common stocks covered by Telstat were used as the "universe" for this analysis. In 1985, Telstat covered 4,881 common stocks, including all NYSE and Amex securities; a large number of stocks traded in the NASDAQ market; some very small, inactive stocks traded via the "pink sheets" in a non-NASDAQ, over-the-counter environment; and a limited number of stocks with primary listing on regional exchanges.

Since Telstat does not distinguish whether the primary listing of a non-NYSE or non-Amex stock is on a regional exchange or over the counter, any non-NYSE or non-Amex stock was classified as an over-the-counter stock. For this reason, the study's estimate of the market value of over-the-counter stocks may be slightly high, although the possible failure of Telstat to include some OTC stocks with limited trading or small market value could reduce or negate this bias. External data suggest that any resulting bias is not substantial.[3]

On the basis of information provided on Form 13F, each institution was classified into one of five groups: banks, insurance companies, investment companies, investment advisers and others. Although many banks have reorganized or are currently reorganizing their investment-management function in the legal form of an investment adviser, any investment adviser owned by a bank holding company was nonetheless classified as a "bank." The "other" category represents a large number of miscellaneous activities, such as the investment activities of some very wealthy individuals or other types of non-financial organizations that for various reasons had to file Form 13F.

Ownership Trends

As of December 1979, institutions managing over $100 million of equities held $367.3 billion of common stocks. By June 1985, their holdings had increased to $817.6 billion—an increase of 122.6 percent, or 15.7 percent per year. In contrast, the total market value of all stocks outstanding grew during the same period from $1,118.5 billion to $2,053.2 billion—an increase of only 83.6 percent or 11.7 percent per year.

---

[3] According to the figures supplied by the NASD, the market value of stocks traded on the NASDAQ National Market System was $215.1 billion as of June 1985. The market value of other NASDAQ stocks was $28.0 billion, for a total of $243.1 billion. As expected, the corresponding estimate of $273.4 billion from the Telstat universe was larger than the NASD total due to the inclusion of some OTC stocks not listed on NASDAQ and some issues traded on regional exchanges. Because NASDAQ appears to account for 89 percent or more of the OTC and regional segments of the equities market, those segments are designated in this study as NASDAQ/OTC for simplicity and clarity.

INSTITUTIONAL STOCK HOLDINGS BY MARKET
1979 to 1985

Date		NYSE	NASDAQ/ OTC	Amex	Total
			Market		
A.	**Billions of Dollars**				
	12/79	342.4	20.0	4.9	367.3
	12/80	455.2	23.7	8.0	486.9
	12/81	413.7	25.8	8.1	447.6
	12/82	510.4	37.8	8.0	556.2
	12/83	625.9	55.8	12.2	693.9
	12/84	634.9	52.4	8.4	695.7
	6/85	738.5	68.6	10.5	817.6
B.	**12/79 Equals 100.0**				
	12/79	100.0	100.0	100.0	100.0
	12/80	132.9	118.5	163.3	132.6
	12/81	120.8	129.0	165.3	121.8
	12/82	149.1	189.0	163.3	151.4
	12/83	182.8	279.0	249.0	188.9
	12/84	185.4	262.0	171.4	189.4
	6/85	215.7	343.0	214.3	222.6
C.	**Totals Equal 100.0**				
	12/79	93.2	5.5	1.3	100.0
	12/80	93.5	4.9	1.6	100.0
	12/81	92.4	5.8	1.8	100.0
	12/82	91.8	6.8	1.4	100.0
	12/83	90.2	8.0	1.8	100.0
	12/84	91.3	7.5	1.2	100.0
	6/85	90.3	8.4	1.3	100.0

ALL STOCK HOLDINGS BY MARKET
1979 to 1985

Date		Market		
	NYSE	**NASDAQ/ OTC**	**Amex**	**Total**
A. Billions of Dollars				
12/79	921.8	140.4	56.2	1,118.5
6/85	1,705.4	273.4	74.4	2,053.2
B. 12/79 Equals 100.0				
12/79	100.0	100.0	100.0	100.0
6/85	185.0	194.7	132.4	183.6
C. Totals Equal 100.0				
12/79	82.41	12.55	5.02	100.0
6/85	83.06	13.32	3.62	100.0
D. Institutional Holdings to All Holdings (%)				
12/79	37.1	14.2	8.7	32.8
6/85	43.3	25.1	14.1	39.8

These institutions held 32.8 percent of all stocks outstanding as of December 1979. By 1985, these institutions' ownership share had risen to 39.8 percent of the total market, outpacing market growth by 4 percent annually.

These percentages require careful interpretation. The numbers apply only to institutional investors managing over $100 million of equities. If institutions managing less than $100 million were included, ownership percentages would be greater, but it is difficult to discern the magnitude of this increase today or the change in the relative size of this increase between 1979 and 1985.

Other factors deserve consideration. An institutional investor managing somewhat less than $100 million in equities in 1979 might be managing well over $100 million in 1985 due to the general increase in stock prices and growth through new or existing customers. This would tend to inflate the growth rate of institutional holdings reported in the table on page 197.

Changes in the importance of small institutions relative to large ones also affect the trend in growth rates of institutional holdings. If institutions managing assets less than $100 million grew at a faster rate than those with more than $100 million under management, the percentage increase in the institutional holdings reported above would be understated. If large institutions grew faster, the percentage increase would be overstated.

However, these individual factors do not have a major impact on findings regarding broad market trading patterns and, although a relatively small increase in institutional presence occurred in overall markets during the five-year period studied, the growth rate of institutional holdings by type of market differed substantially.

Institutions increased their holdings of NASDAQ/OTC stocks by 343.0 percent from 1979 through 1985. This compares with 215.7 percent for NYSE stocks and 214.3 for Amex stocks. The dramatic growth of institutional holdings of NASDAQ/OTC stocks cannot be attributed solely to growth in the market value of the total common stocks of these companies. The growth rate of the market value of NASDAQ/OTC stocks was not much greater than that for NYSE stocks.

Rather, institutions shifted a proportion of their equity investments from NYSE stocks to NASDAQ/OTC stocks. The proportion invested in NYSE stocks declined from 93.2 percent in 1979 to 90.3 percent in 1985. At the same time, the proportion invested in NASDAQ/OTC stocks increased from 5.5 percent to 8.4 percent. The proportion invested in

Amex stocks remained relatively unchanged. The percentage of institutional holdings invested in Amex stocks is considerably smaller than that of investment in Amex stocks by the overall market. In 1985, institutions invested 1.3 percent of their holdings in Amex stocks, compared with total market investment of 3.6 percent.[4]

Stock Holdings by Size and Type of Institution

These aggregate statistics hide some interesting variations in the pattern of stock holdings among different types of institutions and among different sizes of institutions. In 1979, banks managed $182.1 billion in equities—roughly three times as much as the next most important group, investment advisers. By June 1985, investment advisers saw the equities under their management increase more than fourfold to $281.2 billion, nearly matching the $301.3 billion then managed by banks. Of any group studied during this 5½ year period, banks experienced the lowest percentage growth in equities under management.

---

[4] Much of the differences between these percentages is attributable to the inclusion in the Amex figures of several large Canadian companies and some oil companies that are primarily held by investors in other countries or whose stock is held by another company for the purpose of maintaining operating control. Thus, the total market value of Amex stocks, as conventionally calculated, undoubtedly overstates the market value of stocks that are actually traded in the United States.

STOCK HOLDINGS BY MARKET

Banks
1979 to 1985

Date	Market			
	NYSE	NASDAQ/ OTC	Amex	Total
All Banks				
A. Billions of Dollars				
12/79	170.3	9.8	2.0	182.1
6/85	276.6	21.9	2.8	301.3
B. 12/79 Equals 100.0				
12/79	100.0	100.0	100.0	100.0
6/85	162.2	223.5	140.0	165.4
C. Totals Equal 100.0				
12/79	93.5	5.4	1.1	100.0
6/85	91.8	7.3	0.9	100.0
Large Banks				
A. Billions of Dollars				
12/79	96.8	4.6	1.0	102.4
6/85	191.0	12.5	1.6	205.1
B. 12/79 Equals 100.0				
12/79	100.0	100.0	100.0	100.0
6/85	197.3	271.7	160.0	200.3
C. Totals Equal 100.0				
12/79	94.5	4.5	1.0	100.0
6/85	93.1	6.1	0.8	100.0
Medium Banks				
A. Billions of Dollars				
12/79	26.9	1.4	0.4	28.7
6/85	37.8	3.2	0.6	41.6
B. 12/79 Equals 100.0				
12/79	100.0	100.0	100.0	100.0
6/85	140.5	228.6	150.0	144.9
C. Totals Equal 100.0				
12/79	93.7	4.9	1.4	100.0
6/85	90.9	7.7	1.4	100.0
Small Banks				
A. Billions of Dollars				
12/79	46.7	3.9	0.6	51.2
6/85	47.8	6.3	0.6	54.7
B. 12/79 Equals 100.0				
12/79	100.0	100.0	100.0	100.0
6/85	102.4	161.5	100.0	106.8
C. Totals Equal 100.0				
12/79	91.2	7.6	1.2	100.0
6/85	87.4	11.5	1.1	100.0

STOCK HOLDINGS BY MARKET

Insurance Companies
1979 to 1985

Date		Market		
	NYSE	**NASDAQ/ OTC**	**Amex**	**Total**
All Insurance Companies				
A. Billions of Dollars				
12/79	37.9	2.2	0.5	40.6
6/85	65.0	6.0	0.8	71.8
B. 12/79 Equals 100.0				
12/79	100.0	100.0	100.0	100.0
6/85	171.5	272.7	160.0	176.9
C. Totals Equal 100.0				
12/79	93.4	5.4	1.2	100.0
6/85	90.5	8.4	1.1	100.0
Large Insurance Companies				
A. Billions of Dollars				
12/79	14.2	0.4	0.0	14.6
6/85	39.1	3.0	0.5	42.6
B. 12/79 Equals 100.0				
12/79	100.0	100.0	N.A.	100.0
6/85	275.4	750.0	N.A.	291.8
C. Totals Equal 100.0				
12/79	97.3	2.7	0.0	100.0
6/85	91.8	7.0	1.2	100.0
Medium Insurance Companies				
A. Billions of Dollars				
12/79	9.8	0.6	0.2	10.6
6/85	9.7	1.0	0.1	10.8
B. 12/79 Equals 100.0				
12/79	100.0	100.0	100.0	100.0
6/85	99.0	166.7	50.0	101.9
C. Totals Equal 100.0				
12/79	92.4	5.7	1.9	100.0
6/85	89.8	9.3	0.9	100.0
Small Insurance Companies				
A. Billions of Dollars				
12/79	13.9	1.1	0.3	15.3
6/85	16.2	2.0	0.2	18.4
B. 12/79 Equals 100.0				
12/79	100.0	100.0	100.0	100.0
6/85	116.6	181.8	66.7	120.3
C. Totals Equal 100.0				
12/79	90.8	7.2	2.0	100.0
6/85	88.0	10.9	1.1	100.0

STOCK HOLDINGS BY MARKET

Investment Companies
1979 to 1985

Date		Market		
	NYSE	**NASDAQ/ OTC**	**Amex**	**Total**
All Investment Companies				
A. Billions of Dollars				
12/79	31.1	2.1	0.5	33.7
6/85	56.0	7.5	1.0	64.5
B. 12/79 Equals 100.0				
12/79	100.0	100.0	100.0	100.0
6/85	180.1	357.1	200.0	191.4
C. Totals Equal 100.0				
12/79	92.3	6.2	1.5	100.0
6/85	86.8	11.6	1.6	100.0
Large Investment Companies				
A. Billions of Dollars				
12/79	9.8	0.4	0.0	10.2
6/85	37.5	4.5	0.5	42.5
B. 12/79 Equals 100.0				
12/79	100.0	100.0	N.A.	100.0
6/85	382.7	1,125.0	N.A.	416.7
C. Totals Equal 100.0				
12/79	96.1	3.9	0.0	100.0
6/85	88.2	10.6	1.2	100.0
Medium Investment Companies				
A. Billions of Dollars				
12/79	10.0	0.7	0.2	10.9
6/85	7.7	0.8	0.2	8.7
B. 12/79 Equals 100.0				
12/79	100.0	100.0	100.0	100.0
6/85	77.0	114.3	100.0	79.8
C. Totals Equal 100.0				
12/79	91.8	6.4	1.8	100.0
6/85	88.5	9.2	2.3	100.0
Small Investment Companies				
A. Billions of Dollars				
12/79	11.2	0.9	0.3	12.4
6/85	10.8	2.2	0.3	13.3
B. 12/79 Equals 100.0				
12/79	100.0	100.0	100.0	100.0
6/85	96.4	244.4	100.0	107.3
C. Totals Equal 100.0				
12/79	90.3	7.3	2.4	100.0
6/85	81.2	16.5	2.3	100.0

STOCK HOLDINGS BY MARKET

Investment Advisers
1979 to 1985

Date	Market			
	NYSE	NASDAQ/ OTC	Amex	Total
All Investment Advisers				
A. Billions of Dollars				
12/79	62.9	4.1	1.5	68.5
6/85	246.7	29.4	5.0	281.2
B. 12/79 Equals 100.0				
12/79	100.0	100.0	100.0	100.0
6/85	392.2	717.1	333.3	410.5
C. Totals Equal 100.0				
12/79	91.8	6.0	2.2	100.0
6/85	87.7	10.5	1.8	100.0
Large Investment Advisers				
A. Billions of Dollars				
12/79	32.4	1.9	0.5	34.8
6/85	158.1	16.3	2.4	176.8
B. 12/79 Equals 100.0				
12/79	100.0	100.0	100.0	100.0
6/85	388.0	857.9	480.0	508.1
C. Totals Equal 100.0				
12/79	93.1	5.5	1.4	100.0
6/85	89.4	9.2	1.4	100.0
Medium Investment Advisers				
A. Billions of Dollars				
12/79	10.1	0.6	0.3	11.0
6/85	24.1	2.7	0.9	27.7
B. 12/79 Equals 100.0				
12/79	100.0	100.0	100.0	100.0
6/85	328.6	450.0	300.0	251.8
C. Totals Equal 100.0				
12/79	91.8	5.5	2.7	100.0
6/85	87.0	9.8	3.2	100.0
Small Investment Advisers				
A. Billions of Dollars				
12/79	20.5	1.7	0.7	22.9
6/85	64.4	10.4	1.7	76.5
B. 12/79 Equals 100.0				
12/79	100.0	100.0	100.0	100.0
6/85	314.1	611.8	242.9	334.1
C. Totals Equal 100.0				
12/79	89.5	7.4	3.1	100.0
6/85	84.2	13.6	2.2	100.0

STOCK HOLDINGS BY MARKET

All Other Institutions
1979 to 1985

Date	Market			
	NYSE	NASDAQ/ OTC	Amex	Total
All Others				
A. Billions of Dollars				
12/79	40.1	1.9	0.4	42.4
6/85	94.2	3.6	0.9	98.7
B. 12/79 Equals 100.0				
12/79	100.0	100.0	100.0	100.0
6/85	234.9	189.5	225.0	232.8
C. Totals Equal 100.0				
12/79	94.6	4.5	0.9	100.0
6/85	95.4	3.7	0.9	100.0
Large Others				
A. Billions of Dollars				
12/79	15.2	0.6	0.0	15.8
6/85	59.0	1.4	0.1	60.5
B. 12/79 Equals 100.0				
12/79	100.0	100.0	N.A.	100.0
6/85	388.2	233.3	N.A.	382.9
C. Totals Equal 100.0				
12/79	96.2	3.8	0.0	100.0
6/85	97.5	2.3	0.2	100.0
Medium Others				
A. Billions of Dollars				
12/79	10.4	0.3	0.0	10.7
6/85	16.1	0.7	0.5	17.3
B. 12/79 Equals 100.0				
12/79	100.0	100.0	N.A.	100.0
6/85	154.8	233.3	N.A.	161.7
C. Totals Equal 100.0				
12/79	97.2	2.8	0.0	100.0
6/85	93.1	4.0	2.9	100.0
Small Others				
A. Billions of Dollars				
12/79	14.5	1.0	0.4	15.9
6/85	19.1	1.5	0.3	20.9
B. 12/79 Equals 100.0				
12/79	100.0	100.0	100.0	100.0
6/85	131.7	150.0	75.0	131.4
C. Totals Equal 100.0				
12/79	91.2	6.3	2.5	100.0
6/85	91.4	7.2	1.4	100.0

By June 1985, investment advisers and investment companies had over 10 percent of their equities invested in NASDAQ/OTC stocks—almost double the percentage that they held in 1979. Virtually all of this increase came from a reduction in their percentage holdings of NYSE stocks. Similarly, banks and insurance companies increased their percentage holdings in NASDAQ/OTC stocks and decreased their percentage holdings in NYSE stocks, although not as dramatically as investment advisers and investment companies. Although institutions decreased their holdings of NYSE stocks as a proportion of total equity under management, the overall growth in equities under institutional management meant that the total dollars of NYSE stocks under institutional management still increased.

Within all institutional groups, the percentage of equities invested in NASDAQ/OTC stocks varied inversely with the size of the institution. Also, within all size groups, investment advisers and investment companies had greater proportions of their funds invested in NASDAQ/OTC stocks in 1985 compared to banks and insurance companies. For purposes of analysis, this study defines a small institution as one with $100 million to $1 billion under management, a medium-sized institution as one with $1 billion to $2 billion under management, and a large institution as one with more than $2 billion under management.

Characteristics of Stock Issues Held

Institutions as a group tend to tilt their portfolios more heavily toward stocks with very high market values. In 1985, institutions had placed 77.9 percent of their equity funds in stocks with market values greater than $1 billion although such large issues represented only 70.3

percent of the total market. Banks and insurance companies had an even greater concentration of equity holdings in large companies than did investment companies and investment advisers. Conversely, institutions had a smaller percentage of holdings invested in stocks with market values of less than $500 million compared to the market as a whole.

This tilt toward larger issues applies to both the NYSE and the NASDAQ/OTC markets. (The anomalous result that institutions hold a smaller percentage of the largest stocks on the Amex compared to market weights is probably due to the inclusion in the Amex of some fairly large companies that are not actively traded or widely held, at least in the U.S., as noted earlier.)

In terms of NASDAQ/OTC stocks, institutions tilt their portfolios toward issues with more than $500 million outstanding, hold almost the same overall market proportions for firms with $100 million to $500 million outstanding, and underweight firms with less than $100 million outstanding. From these results, we can infer that individuals are the dominant holders of the smallest firms in each of the three markets.

Both in the aggregate and for each individual market, institutions tilt their portfolios away from stocks with the greatest dividend yields. (This study defines dividend yield as the annual indicated dividend to the share price as given in the June 1985 data base of Telstat.) In view of the tax-free status of many clients of institutional investors, this result may be surprising. A partial explanation is that institutional investors tend to underweight utility stocks in their portfolios, and these stocks have the highest yields. For example, Simulated Environment Incorporated (SEI) reports that utilities made up 12.9 percent of the S&P 500 for June 1985, but the median fund in their universe for that date had invested only 5 percent in utilities.

DOLLAR DISTRIBUTION OF STOCK HOLDINGS BY MARKET VALUE OF ISSUES

Billions of Dollars
1985

	Categories of Market Value of Issues (Millions)					
	0-49	50-99	100-499	500-999	1,000 & Up	TOTAL
All Markets						
Banks	1.6	2.6	22.2	29.4	245.5	301.3
Insurance Cos.	0.5	0.9	7.6	7.9	55.0	71.9
Investment Cos.	0.7	1.0	7.6	9.4	45.8	64.6
Invest. Advisers	3.6	4.9	32.0	36.1	204.5	281.2
Others	0.3	0.6	4.9	7.2	85.7	98.7
All Institutions	6.8	9.9	74.2	90.1	636.6	817.6
Total Markets	54.4	57.2	266.5	232.2	1,442.9	2,053.2
NYSE						
Banks	0.2	0.8	11.4	22.8	241.5	276.6
Insurance Cos.	0.1	0.4	4.5	6.3	53.7	65.0
Investment Cos.	0.1	0.3	4.0	7.5	44.1	56.0
Invest. Advisers	0.5	1.9	17.9	28.0	198.4	246.7
Others	0.1	0.2	3.1	6.1	84.7	94.2
All Institutions	1.0	3.4	41.0	70.8	622.4	738.5
Total Market	4.1	13.4	128.6	166.1	1,393.2	1,705.3
NASDAQ/OTC						
Banks	1.2	1.6	9.6	6.1	3.5	22.0
Insurance Cos.	0.3	0.4	2.7	1.4	1.2	6.0
Investment Cos.	0.6	0.6	3.1	1.7	1.5	7.5
Invest. Advisers	2.4	2.4	12.3	7.2	5.1	29.4
Others	0.2	0.3	1.4	1.0	0.7	3.6
All Institutions	4.8	5.3	29.1	17.4	12.0	68.6
Total Market	41.3	34.5	115.8	50.6	31.2	273.4
Amex						
Banks	0.2	0.2	1.2	0.6	0.6	2.8
Insurance Cos.	0.1	0.1	0.3	0.2	0.1	0.8
Investment Cos.	0.1	0.1	0.4	0.2	0.2	1.0
Invest. Advisers	0.7	0.6	1.8	0.9	1.0	5.0
Others	0.1	0.1	0.3	0.1	0.3	0.9
All Institutions	1.1	1.2	4.1	2.0	2.1	10.5
Total Market	9.1	9.2	22.1	15.5	18.5	74.4

PERCENTAGE DISTRIBUTION OF STOCK HOLDINGS BY MARKET VALUE OF ISSUES

Totals Equal 100.0
1985

	Categories of Market Value of Issues (Millions)					
	0-49	50-99	100-499	500-999	1,000 & Up	TOTAL
All Markets						
Banks	0.5	0.9	7.4	9.7	81.5	100.0
Insurance Cos.	0.7	1.2	10.6	11.0	76.5	100.0
Investment Cos.	1.1	1.6	11.8	14.6	70.9	100.0
Invest. Advisers	1.3	1.7	11.4	12.9	72.7	100.0
Others	0.3	0.6	5.0	7.3	86.8	100.0
All Institutions	0.8	1.2	9.1	11.0	77.9	100.0
Total Markets	2.6	2.8	13.0	11.3	70.3	100.0
NYSE						
Banks	0.1	0.3	4.1	8.2	87.3	100.0
Insurance Cos.	0.2	0.6	6.9	9.7	82.6	100.0
Investment Cos.	0.2	0.5	7.1	13.4	78.8	100.0
Invest. Advisers	0.2	0.8	7.3	11.3	80.4	100.0
Others	0.1	0.2	3.3	6.5	89.9	100.0
All Institutions	0.1	0.5	5.5	9.6	84.3	100.0
Total Market	0.2	0.8	7.5	9.8	81.7	100.0
NASDAQ/OTC						
Banks	5.5	7.3	43.6	27.7	15.9	100.0
Insurance Cos.	5.0	6.7	45.0	23.3	20.0	100.0
Investment Cos.	8.0	8.0	41.3	22.7	20.0	100.0
Invest. Advisers	8.2	8.2	41.8	24.5	17.3	100.0
Others	5.6	8.3	38.9	27.8	19.4	100.0
All Institutions	7.0	7.7	42.4	25.4	17.5	100.0
Total Market	15.1	12.6	42.4	18.5	11.4	100.0
Amex						
Banks	7.1	7.1	42.9	21.4	21.5	100.0
Insurance Cos.	12.5	12.5	37.5	25.0	12.5	100.0
Investment Cos.	10.0	10.0	40.0	20.0	20.0	100.0
Invest. Advisers	14.0	12.0	36.0	18.0	20.0	100.0
Others	11.1	11.1	33.3	11.2	33.3	100.0
All Institutions	10.5	11.4	39.1	19.0	20.0	100.0
Total Market	12.2	12.4	29.7	20.8	24.9	100.0

DOLLAR DISTRIBUTION OF STOCK HOLDINGS
BY DIVIDEND YIELD

Billions of Dollars
1985

			Categories of Dividend Yield[1]					
	N.A.[2]	0	0-2%	2-4%	4-6%	6-8%	8%	TOTAL
All Markets								
Banks	0.9	12.3	35.7	121.5	71.8	47.9	11.3	301.3
Insurance Cos.	0.6	5.7	9.8	27.8	14.2	10.0	3.8	71.8
Investment Cos.	0.5	6.4	12.6	22.7	12.7	7.4	2.2	64.6
Invest. Advisers	1.4	27.4	50.3	106.7	53.9	31.5	10.0	281.2
Others	0.2	8.3	12.5	38.9	22.5	13.8	2.5	98.7
All Institutions	3.6	60.1	120.9	317.5	175.1	110.5	29.8	817.6
Total Markets	12.2	235.5	300.3	687.1	403.8	305.1	109.2	2,053.2
NYSE								
Banks	0.0	7.4	30.6	111.5	68.3	47.6	11.2	276.6
Insurance Cos.	0.0	3.6	8.3	25.7	13.7	9.9	3.8	65.0
Investment Cos.	0.0	3.2	10.5	20.7	12.1	7.3	2.2	56.0
Invest. Advisers	0.0	13.8	41.6	98.7	51.4	31.3	9.8	246.7
Others	0.0	6.7	11.5	37.6	22.2	13.8	2.5	94.2
All Institutions	0.0	34.7	102.5	294.2	167.7	110.0	29.4	738.5
Total Market	0.0	106.3	226.1	600.8	368.1	299.5	104.6	1,705.3
NASDAQ/OTC								
Banks	0.9	4.5	3.6	9.2	3.3	0.3	0.1	21.9
Insurance Cos.	0.6	1.9	1.1	1.9	0.5	0.0	0.0	6.0
Investment Cos.	0.5	2.9	1.6	1.9	0.6	0.0	0.0	7.5
Invest. Advisers	1.4	12.3	6.1	7.0	2.3	0.2	0.1	29.4
Others	0.2	1.4	0.6	1.1	0.3	0.0	0.0	3.6
All Institutions	3.6	23.0	13.1	21.1	7.0	0.5	0.2	68.5
Total Market	12.2	110.8	48.8	71.0	24.2	4.0	2.3	273.4
Amex								
Banks	0.0	0.4	1.4	0.7	0.1	0.0	0.1	2.7
Insurance Cos.	0.0	0.2	0.4	0.2	0.0	0.0	0.0	0.8
Investment Cos.	0.0	0.3	0.5	0.2	0.0	0.0	0.0	1.0
Invest. Advisers	0.0	1.3	2.6	0.9	0.1	0.0	0.1	5.0
Others	0.0	0.2	0.5	0.2	0.0	0.0	0.0	0.9
All Institutions	0.0	2.3	5.4	2.2	0.4	0.1	0.1	10.5
Total Market	0.0	18.5	25.3	15.2	11.5	1.6	2.2	74.4

---

[1]Indicated range includes upper yield but not lower yield.
[2]Not ascertained.

PERCENTAGE DISTRIBUTION OF STOCK HOLDINGS
BY DIVIDEND YIELD

Totals Equal 100.0
1985

			Categories of Dividend Yield[1]				
	N.A.[2]	0	0-2%	2-4%	4-6%	6-8%	8%	TOTAL

All Markets								
Banks	0.3	4.1	11.8	40.3	23.8	15.9	3.8	100.0
Insurance Cos.	0.8	7.9	13.6	38.7	19.8	13.9	5.3	100.0
Investment Cos.	0.8	10.0	19.5	35.1	19.7	11.5	3.4	100.0
Invest. Advisers	0.5	9.7	17.9	37.9	19.2	11.2	3.6	100.0
Others	0.2	8.4	12.7	39.4	22.8	14.0	2.5	100.0
All Institutions	0.4	7.4	14.8	38.8	21.4	13.5	3.7	100.0
Total Markets	0.6	11.5	14.6	33.4	19.7	14.9	5.3	100.0
NYSE								
Banks	0.0	2.7	11.1	40.3	24.7	17.2	4.0	100.0
Insurance Cos.	0.0	5.5	12.8	39.6	21.1	15.2	5.8	100.0
Investment Cos.	0.0	5.7	18.8	37.0	21.6	13.0	3.9	100.0
Invest. Advisers	0.0	5.6	16.9	40.0	20.8	12.7	4.0	100.0
Others	0.0	7.1	12.2	39.9	23.6	14.6	2.6	100.0
All Institutions	0.0	4.7	13.9	39.8	22.7	14.9	4.0	100.0
Total Market	0.0	6.2	13.3	35.2	21.6	17.6	6.1	100.0
NASDAQ/OTC								
Banks	4.1	20.5	16.4	42.0	15.1	1.4	0.5	100.0
Insurance Cos.	10.0	31.7	18.3	31.7	8.3	0.0	0.0	100.0
Investment Cos.	6.7	38.7	21.3	25.3	8.0	0.0	0.0	100.0
Invest. Advisers	4.8	41.8	20.8	23.8	7.8	0.7	0.3	100.0
Others	5.6	38.9	16.7	30.5	8.3	0.0	0.0	100.0
All Institutions	5.3	33.6	19.1	30.8	10.2	0.7	0.3	100.0
Total Market	4.5	40.5	17.8	26.0	8.9	1.5	0.8	100.0
Amex								
Banks	0.0	14.8	51.9	25.9	3.7	0.0	3.7	100.0
Insurance Cos.	0.0	25.0	50.0	25.0	0.0	0.0	0.0	100.0
Investment Cos.	0.0	30.0	50.0	20.0	0.0	0.0	0.0	100.0
Invest. Advisers	0.0	26.0	52.0	18.0	2.0	0.0	2.0	100.0
Others	0.0	22.2	55.6	22.2	0.0	0.0	0.0	100.0
All Institutions	0.0	21.9	51.4	20.9	3.8	1.0	1.0	100.0
Total Market	0.0	24.9	34.0	20.4	15.5	2.2	3.0	100.0

---

[1] Indicated range includes upper yield but not lower yield.
[2] Not ascertained.

In terms of earnings multiples, institutions as a group tilt their equity portfolios toward stocks with larger price/earnings ratios in comparison to market weights. Specifically, their portfolios have greater-than-market weights for stocks with price/earnings ratios of more than 10, and less-than-market weights for stocks with price/earnings ratios lower than 10. The price/earnings ratio is defined as the stock price on June 1985 relative to the immediately preceding annual earnings.

Investment advisers and investment companies hold in greater-than-market weights those stocks with price/earnings ratios of more than 20, while banks and insurance companies hold in less-than-market weights these same stocks. The three markets have minor differences in patterns of holdings by price/earnings ratio.

DOLLAR DISTRIBUTION OF STOCK HOLDINGS BY PRICE/EARNINGS RATIO

Billions of Dollars
1985

	Categories of Price/Earnings Ratios[1]						
	N.A.[2]	NEG	0-5	5-10	10-15	15-20	20+	TOTAL
All Markets								
Banks	1.1	8.5	2.5	92.2	113.9	48.2	34.9	301.3
Insurance Cos.	0.7	2.5	0.7	21.5	26.0	11.1	9.3	71.8
Investment Cos.	0.5	2.5	0.5	18.1	21.4	10.8	10.7	64.6
Invest. Advisers	1.8	10.1	4.4	76.3	93.5	49.7	45.4	281.2
Others	0.3	2.5	0.7	29.8	32.9	17.2	15.3	98.7
All Institutions	4.5	26.1	8.9	237.8	287.7	136.9	115.7	817.6
Total Markets	27.3	88.8	25.0	654.0	657.9	323.3	276.8	2,053.2
NYSE								
Banks	0.1	7.3	2.4	85.2	106.8	44.8	30.1	276.7
Insurance Cos.	0.1	2.0	0.7	20.3	24.2	10.2	7.5	65.0
Investment Cos.	0.0	2.1	0.5	16.5	19.3	9.6	8.0	56.0
Invest. Advisers	0.1	8.3	4.2	69.7	85.6	44.4	34.4	246.7
Others	0.1	2.1	0.7	28.9	31.8	16.5	14.1	94.2
All Institutions	0.4	21.8	8.5	220.6	267.7	125.5	94.1	738.5
Total Market	9.5	55.8	19.5	571.8	579.5	276.5	192.7	1,705.3
NASDAQ/OTC								
Banks	1.0	1.1	0.1	6.6	6.3	2.4	4.4	21.9
Insurance Cos.	0.6	0.4	0.0	1.1	1.6	0.6	1.7	6.0
Investment Cos.	0.5	0.4	0.0	1.4	1.9	0.8	2.5	7.5
Invest. Advisers	1.7	1.6	0.2	5.7	6.8	3.5	10.0	29.5
Others	0.3	0.3	0.0	0.7	0.9	0.3	1.1	3.6
All Institutions	4.1	3.7	0.4	15.4	17.5	7.7	19.7	68.5
Total Market	17.4	26.6	3.7	59.4	62.3	33.8	70.3	273.4
Amex								
Banks	0.0	0.1	0.0	0.4	0.8	1.0	0.5	2.8
Insurance Cos.	0.0	0.0	0.0	0.2	0.2	0.3	0.1	0.8
Investment Cos.	0.0	0.1	0.0	0.2	0.2	0.4	0.1	1.0
Invest. Advisers	0.0	0.3	0.0	0.9	1.1	1.8	0.9	5.0
Others	0.0	0.1	0.0	0.2	0.1	0.3	0.1	0.8
All Institutions	0.0	0.6	0.0	1.8	2.5	3.7	1.9	10.5
Total Market	0.4	6.4	1.8	22.8	16.2	13.1	13.7	74.4

---

[1] Indicated range includes upper ratio but not lower ratio.

[2] Not ascertained.

PERCENTAGE DISTRIBUTION OF STOCK HOLDINGS BY PRICE/EARNINGS RATIO

Totals Equal 100.0
1985

| | Categories of Price/Earnings Ratios[1] | | | | | | |
	N.A.[2]	NEG	0-5	5-10	10-15	15-20	20+	TOTAL
All Markets								
Banks	0.4	2.8	0.8	30.6	37.8	16.0	11.6	100.0
Insurance Cos.	1.0	3.5	1.0	29.9	36.2	15.5	12.9	100.0
Investment Cos.	0.8	3.9	0.8	28.0	33.2	16.7	16.6	100.0
Invest. Advisers	0.6	3.6	1.6	27.1	33.3	17.7	16.1	100.0
Others	0.3	2.5	0.7	30.2	33.4	17.4	15.5	100.0
All Institutions	0.6	3.2	1.1	29.1	35.2	16.7	14.1	100.0
Total Markets	1.3	4.3	1.2	31.9	32.0	15.8	13.5	100.0
NYSE								
Banks	0.0	2.6	0.9	30.8	38.6	16.2	10.9	100.0
Insurance Cos.	0.2	3.1	1.1	31.2	37.2	15.7	11.5	100.0
Investment Cos.	0.0	3.7	0.9	29.5	34.5	17.1	14.3	100.0
Invest. Advisers	0.0	3.4	1.7	28.3	34.7	18.0	13.9	100.0
Others	0.1	2.2	0.7	30.7	33.8	17.5	15.0	100.0
All Institutions	0.1	2.9	1.2	29.9	36.2	17.0	12.7	100.0
Total Market	0.6	3.3	1.1	33.5	34.0	16.2	11.3	100.0
NASDAQ/OTC								
Banks	4.6	5.0	0.5	30.1	28.8	10.9	20.1	100.0
Insurance Cos.	10.0	6.7	0.0	18.3	26.7	10.0	28.3	100.0
Investment Cos.	6.7	5.3	0.0	18.8	25.3	10.7	33.3	100.0
Invest. Advisers	5.8	5.4	0.7	19.3	23.0	11.9	33.9	100.0
Others	8.3	8.3	0.0	19.5	25.0	8.3	30.6	100.0
All Institutions	6.0	5.4	0.6	22.5	25.5	11.2	28.8	100.0
Total Market	6.4	9.7	1.3	21.7	22.8	12.4	25.7	100.0
Amex								
Banks	0.0	3.6	0.0	14.3	28.6	35.7	17.8	100.0
Insurance Cos.	0.0	0.0	0.0	25.0	25.0	37.5	12.5	100.0
Investment Cos.	0.0	10.0	0.0	20.0	20.0	40.0	10.0	100.0
Invest. Advisers	0.0	6.0	0.0	18.0	22.0	36.0	18.0	100.0
Others	0.0	12.5	0.0	25.0	12.5	37.5	12.5	100.0
All Institutions	0.0	5.7	0.0	17.1	23.8	35.3	18.1	100.0
Total Market	0.5	8.6	2.4	30.7	21.8	17.6	18.4	100.0

---

[1] Indicated range includes upper ratio but not lower ratio.
[2] Not ascertained.

Chapter
twelve

*E*dward J. Mathias, who joined T. Rowe Price in 1971, is a vice president and director of T. Rowe Price Associates and serves on the firm's six-member Management Committee, which establishes and implements corporate strategy and policy. He is also the president and director of the T. Rowe Price New Horizons Fund, the senior small company investment counselor to several privately managed portfolios, and the chairman of the T. Rowe Price Threshold Fund, a limited partnership investing in late-round private financings.

A Case of Increased Institutional Participation in NASDAQ: T. Rowe Price's New Horizons Fund

by Edward J. Mathias

In 1986, the T. Rowe Price New Horizons Fund held a higher percentage of assets in NASDAQ securities than ever before. When it was introduced in 1960, the New Horizons Fund traditionally bought over-the-counter stocks that would move to the American Stock Exchange and eventually be sold on the New York Stock Exchange. In recent years, the experience has been quite different, and the numbers below illustrate our increased participation in NASDAQ securities.

In 1980, the New Horizons Fund portfolio had the following composition:

NYSE securities	52%
NASDAQ securities	34%
Amex securities	14%

Over the course of the next five years, we dramatically changed the composition of our portfolio:

NASDAQ securities	64%
NYSE securities	30%
Amex securities	6%

The growth in NASDAQ securities continued into 1986, and by the end of the year, the New Horizons Fund portfolio held 69 percent of its assets in NASDAQ stocks.

The Trend to NASDAQ

New Horizons is not alone in the movement of institutions into the NASDAQ market. During the 1980s, many investment companies substantially increased their holdings of NASDAQ stocks.

One of the best measurements of this increase in activity is the change in the number of mutual funds specializing in the NASDAQ market. Lipper Analytical Services, Inc., which tracks the mutual fund industry, began following small-company growth funds as a separate group in the third quarter of 1982. At that time, the group consisted of 15 funds with just under $1.8 billion in assets. At mid-year 1986, the number of funds had more than doubled to 35 and assets totaled more than $8 billion. Twenty-five of these small-company growth funds are currently at least 60 percent invested in NASDAQ stocks.

The Growth Stock Theory of Investing

Our firm's founder, Thomas Rowe Price, pioneered the Growth Stock Theory of Investing more than 40 years ago. We base our investment approach to the NASDAQ market on this theory.

According to the Growth Stock Theory, when a company's earnings grow faster than inflation and faster than the

FUNDS OVER 60 PERCENT INVESTED IN NASDAQ

Fund	Assets ($ millions)
T. Rowe Price New Horizons	1,128
Keystone Custodian S-4	772
Evergreen	628
Fidelity OTC Portfolio	596
Pennsylvania Mutual	371
Scudder Development	281
IDS Discovery	273
Lord Abbett Development Growth	240
Over-the-Counter Securities	238
Massachusetts Financial Growth	236
Value Line Special Situations	200
American Capital Over-the-Counter	96
Delta Trend	82
Stein Roe Discovery	80
United New Concepts	60
Sigma Venture Shares	59
Babson Enterprises	48
Eaton Vance Special Equities	45
OTC 100	37
Explorer II	33
Naess & Thomas Special	32
Janus Venture	28
Hartwell Leverage	26
Nautilus	20
Westergaard	20

Sources: *OTC Review*; Lipper Analytical Services

economy in general, the stock market will eventually recognize this successful long-term record with a higher price for the stock. In addition, a company should be able to raise its dividends in line with its long-term earnings growth. However, investors should be aware of the possibility that, during periods of adverse economic and market conditions, the per-share value of an investment may not move in relation to the favorable long-term earnings trend of the individual company. Consistent with this long–term approach, investors should be prepared to maintain or add to their investments during periods of adverse market conditions.

Small, Growth Company Defined

Price Associates defines a small, growth company as one that is still in the developing stage of its life cycle, yet has demonstrated, or is expected to achieve, long-term earnings growth that reaches new highs per share during each major business cycle. Capable management and fertile operating areas are two of the most important characteristics of a growth company. Such a company should employ sound financial and accounting policies; demonstrate effective research, successful product development and marketing; provide efficient service; and possess pricing flexibility. Price Associates tries to avoid investing in companies whose operating results may be adversely affected by excessive competition, severe governmental regulation or unsatisfactory productivity.

The NASDAQ market contains the majority of growth companies that meet our criteria.

Basic Research

The U.S. economy has undergone a transition during the past several decades. Services, as opposed to manufacturing, now account for more than half of our gross national product. Personal discretionary income has risen significantly since World War II. These trends represent opportunities for imaginative companies that can offer new or improved goods or services to consumers, business and the government.

Our basic research tells us that there are new horizons for companies operating in advanced technological fields such as electronics, instrumentation, medicine, data processing and communications, and for companies making devices that result in labor savings or productivity improvement.

The industrial history of our nation shows that many small companies have successfully pioneered new products and services. Price Associates believes the American economic system will continue to provide an environment in which relatively small companies can rapidly increase their earnings.

The New Horizons Fund Approach to NASDAQ

The T. Rowe Price New Horizons Fund's approach to investing in NASDAQ stocks has not changed materially since the inception of the fund over 25 years ago, but the manner in which we execute it has changed. The driving force behind the fund remains high earnings growth. We look for companies with certain characteristics—high return on capital, reinvesting in the business, operating in a good field, good management and so forth. These are standard investment criteria.

We also look for a company that is in the early stages of corporate development. Most corporations, like people, pass through a life cycle of growth, maturity and decline. An investment in a business enterprise affords the greatest possibilities of gain and involves the least amount of risk when the company's long-term earnings trend is rising. The risk factor increases after maturity, which is when the decline normally begins.

In addition, we look for lesser-known and less glamorous growth companies—while the market, in general, pursues its preoccupation with the most glamorous and most visible companies. Furthermore, we constantly use our research resources to find stocks that are not broadly held because their valuation is likely to be more reasonable than that of the stocks everybody wants.

In light of the huge increase in the availability of information and quantitative data on small companies today, fundamental and independent research is an important commitment for T. Rowe Price Associates. We talk to the managements of companies, to their competitors and their suppliers, and we get to know the industry. We believe that through extensive research, we can pick the true growth companies.

Decision Making at New Horizons

In selecting stocks for the New Horizons Fund, we have chosen to diversify very broadly. Currently, we have over 200 stocks in our portfolio.

We have decided, through an evolutionary process, to divide the fund into five sectors: consumer products, financial, services, technology and what we call the "liquidity sector"—larger growth companies with highly liquid stocks. A veteran analyst is responsible for the buy and sell decisions in each sector. Each analyst is very knowledgeable in his or her area and works with one or two other analysts. When an analyst hits on a new investment idea for the fund, he or she visits the company, meets with its top management and circulates a candidate report on the stock to the appropriate sector head. We then discuss the idea at length before purchasing the stock.

An advisory committee handles the fund's strategic orientation. During weekly meetings, the committee asks questions such as: What is going on in each sector? How much money should we have in technology? How much money should we have in consumer stocks? Should we be adapting to any particular trends?

Thus, we have an advisory committee with portfolio perspective, sector managers with company perspective, and traders who are responsible for the execution of decisions.

Three Principles: Long-Term Investment, Diversification and Sector Balance

Three operating principles govern New Horizons' decision making.

1. **We invest for the long term.** When we look at the volatility and the nature of returns in the NASDAQ market, which the accompanying chart shows are very uneven, it reinforces our conviction that we must invest for the long term. Over the years, investors and market makers have attempted to capitalize on major swings in the market. To our knowledge, none of them have consistently succeeded.

2. **We believe in broad diversification.** Investors who pick two or three stocks and stake their fortune on them face overwhelming odds. We have found that we will have some major winners if we identify a large number of stocks within an attractive sector of the economy.

3. **We strive for sector balance.** We do not want an all-consumer fund or an all-technology fund. We do, however, gravitate to the highest growth industries. We occasionally find a few high-growth companies in deteriorating industries or problem areas, but we

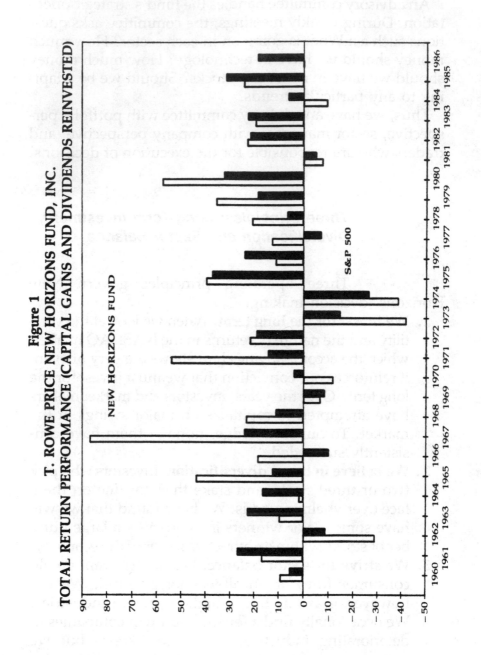

Figure 1
T. ROWE PRICE NEW HORIZONS FUND, INC.
TOTAL RETURN PERFORMANCE (CAPITAL GAINS AND DIVIDENDS REINVESTED)

usually place the bulk of our investments in the fastest growing segments. For instance, in the late '70s and early '80s we had a fairy high representation in the energy sector. Today, we have nothing there. We have to be prepared to make those kinds of shifts to the highest growth areas.

Another Key: Market Valuation

Valuation of the NASDAQ market relative to the general market is yet another key to the New Horizons Fund strategy. Figures 2 and 3, which follow, show the price/earnings ratio of the New Horizons Fund, and the New Horizons Fund P/E ratio relative to the Standard & Poor's 500 P/E ratio. The New Horizons Fund's relative P/E ratio has acted as a very good barometer of valuations in the NASDAQ/small company area and of the relative attractiveness of emerging growth stocks.

Conclusion

It is widely recognized that smaller companies and emerging growth stocks have outperformed the market over long periods. This group or sector tends to move in long valuation cycles (e.g., three to five years). Periods of poor relative performance are typically followed by lengthy periods in which stocks tend to outperform the market by a wide margin. Today, for instance, it is possible to purchase a portfolio of relatively small companies with superior fundamentals and growth prospects at approximately the same valuation afforded the S&P 500. We strongly believe that stocks of small companies will continue to provide superior returns over time.

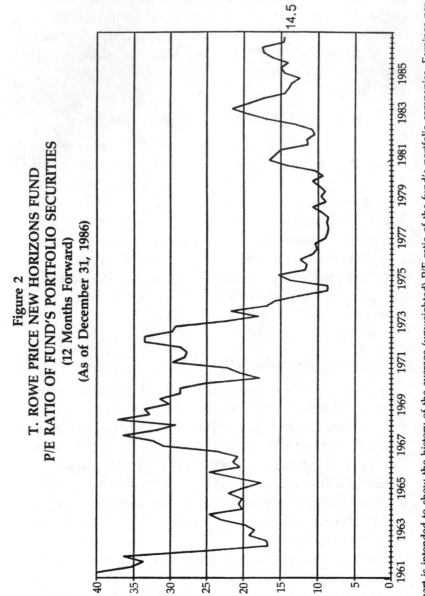

Figure 2
T. ROWE PRICE NEW HORIZONS FUND
P/E RATIO OF FUND'S PORTFOLIO SECURITIES
(12 Months Forward)
(As of December 31, 1986)

This chart is intended to show the history of the average (unweighted) P/E ratio of the fund's portfolio companies. Earnings per share are estimated by the fund's investment adviser from each quarter end.

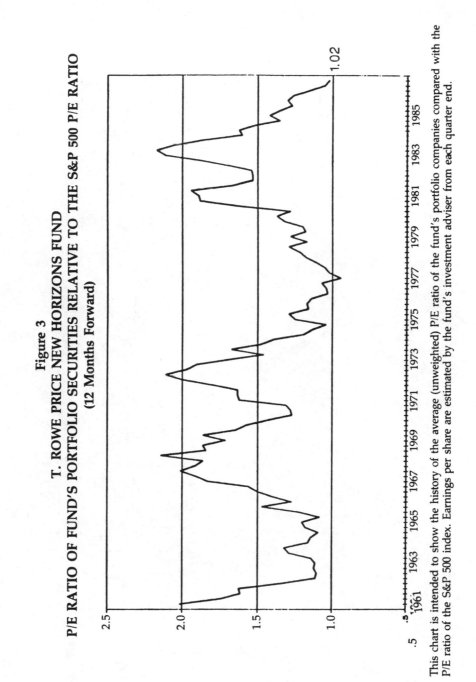

Figure 3
T. ROWE PRICE NEW HORIZONS FUND
P/E RATIO OF FUND'S PORTFOLIO SECURITIES RELATIVE TO THE S&P 500 P/E RATIO
(12 Months Forward)

This chart is intended to show the history of the average (unweighted) P/E ratio of the fund's portfolio companies compared with the P/E ratio of the S&P 500 index. Earnings per share are estimated by the fund's investment adviser from each quarter end.

Chapter
thirteen

Laszlo Birinyi, Jr., is Vice President and Manager of the Equity Market Analysis Group at Salomon Brothers Inc. A pioneer in the study of institutional and retail money flows within the stock market, Mr. Birinyi is credited with creating a trading calendar that has been widely emulated on Wall Street.

Money Flows in the NASDAQ Market

by Laszlo Birinyi, Jr.

Information is the key component to an investor's decision-making process. Investment success directly relates to the quality and timeliness of information. Recognizing this, we focus our research on situations in which market prices haven't yet fully adjusted to the information available, thus creating investment opportunities.

Investors should consider many factors when assessing a potential investment. Our approach is to evaluate supply and demand conditions for stocks in the marketplace. To provide investors with a framework to analyze supply and demand relationships in the equity market, we have developed the concept of money flows.

Money Flows: The Concept

Money flow analysis is an updated version of a very old investment technique: ticker-tape analysis. Most forms of technical analysis analyze market trends based on closing transactions, and closing prices are not necessarily valid indicators of investor demand for a stock. Money flows provide a more penetrating perspective because they capture intraday sentiment. With the aid of computer technology, we capture and analyze every trade in almost every stock. This allows us to compare actual sentiment toward a stock with its current price action. After several years of monitoring the NYSE ticker tape, we have found intraday analysis to be extremely valuable because it can detect changes in investor sentiment before that sentiment is reflected in the price.

The data are calculated quite simply. Money flows are just weighted averages of all trades in a stock: A 1,000-share trade is considered 10 times as important as a 100-share trade. Money flows are derived from the net value of all transactions done on upticks from the most recent sale versus all transactions done on downticks from the last sale. In short, money flows track investor sentiment, which we call "motivated money." For example, a trade done on an uptick is initiated when a buyer finds a situation compelling enough to buy a security at a price above the last previous transaction. Conversely, a trade done on a downtick expresses negative sentiment because the seller accepts a price that is lower than the last previous transaction.

By aggregating the net value of trades "up" and "down" over time, one can discern stock trends that portend future price movements. The importance of intraday trades in determining the sentiment toward a given stock is shown in Table 1, which illustrates trading in IBM. Table 1 shows all of the trades in IBM's stock in which there was an uptick or a downtick from 2:31 p.m. to 2:46 p.m. on January 11, 1982. At 2:31 p.m., the stock traded down to $58⅛, which represents a .2 percent loss—hardly significant in a stock of this price. However, most of the large trades were executed on downticks. In other words, the ratio of "up" volume (trades done on upticks) to "down" volume (those trades effected on downticks) was 1:19.2. During this short period,

Table 1
TIME, SALES AND NET FLOW OF IBM SECURITIES
On January 11, 1982, From 2:31 to 2:46 p.m.

Time	Price	Tick	Number of Shares	Cumulative Total Net Money
2:31 p.m.	58 1/4		800	
2:31	58 3/8	+1/8	200	11,675
2:31	58 1/4	−1/8	300	−5,800
2:32	58 3/8	+1/8	200	5,875
2:32	58 1/4	−1/8	17,800	−1,030,975
	(4 zero-tick trades)			
2:33	58 3/8	+1/8	300	−1,013,462
2:33	58 1/4	−1/8	8,100	−1,485,287
2:34	58 3/8	+1/8	500	−1,456,099
2:34	58 1/4	−1/8	16,100	−2,393,924
2:35	58 1/8	−1/8	400	−2,417,174
2:35	58 1/4	+1/8	2,000	−2,300,674
2:35	58 1/8	−1/8	1,000	−2,358,799
	(18 zero-tick trades)			
2:42	58	−1/8	17,500	−3,373,799
2:42	58 1/8	+1/8	200	−3,362,174
2:42	58	−1/8	7,800	−3,814,574
	(15 zero-tick trades)			
2:46	58 1/8	+1/8	100	−3,808,761
2:46	58	−1/8	100	−3,814,561
2:46	58 1/8	+1/8	200	−3,802,936

$3.8 million flowed out of the stock (see the Total Net Money column in Table 1) as 3,600 shares traded on upticks versus 69,200 shares on downticks—a more dramatic picture than that of a price decline of $0.13.

Divergencies: A Unique Opportunity

The IBM example illustrates what we term a "divergence." Actual investor sentiment did not support the price action. The critical factor is what investors think of the stock—are they buying it or selling it? Money flows capture this essential information. Typically, as investors buy a stock, the price should rise because money is flowing in. Conversely, as investors sell a stock, the price should fall because money is flowing out. However, in some situations near-term price action differs from investor sentiment. In these situations, price and money are divergent. We have found that a divergence persisting over time (we use two weeks) is an early-warning signal of a fundamental change in the price trend.

Stocks with persistent divergences usually recover or correct sharply. The Seagate Technology example in Figure 1 illustrates this point. When Seagate Technology experienced price weakness during late May and early June of 1985 and in 1986, investors were very willing to accumulate this stock, as evidenced by the positive slope of the total net money-line. We term this phenomenon "buying on weakness." The opposite case of price rising with money decreasing is termed "selling into strength," which denotes negative investor sentiment and results in a downward trend in price. Divergences such as the one depicted in Figure 1 usually indicate changes in price trends beyond mere trading corrections. However, a divergent situation is meant to indicate price direction and not the duration and amount of the subsequent move. In this way, money flows can be a valuable long-term investment tool.

Apple Computer is another prime example of how this tool can be useful to the investor. Throughout 1984, investors used every instance of strength in the stock price to sell their positions. Subsequently, from February 11 to August 15, 1985, Apple's stock declined by 52 percent. (See Figure 2).

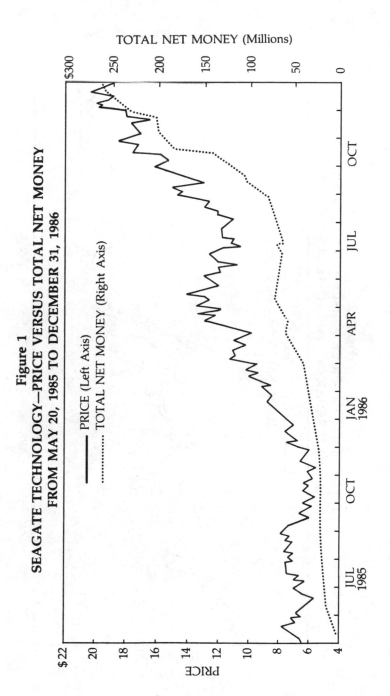

Figure 1
SEAGATE TECHNOLOGY—PRICE VERSUS TOTAL NET MONEY
FROM MAY 20, 1985 TO DECEMBER 31, 1986

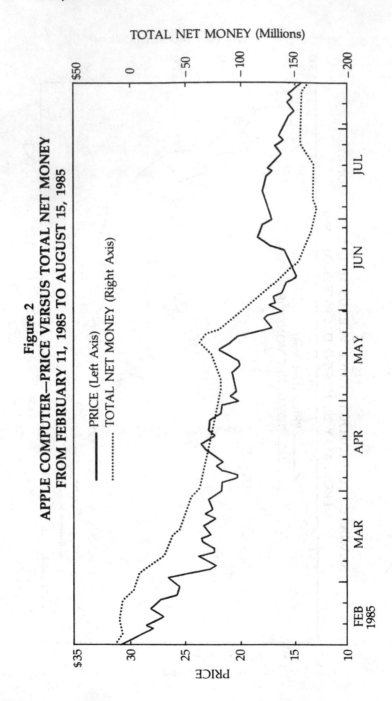

Figure 2
APPLE COMPUTER—PRICE VERSUS TOTAL NET MONEY
FROM FEBRUARY 11, 1985 TO AUGUST 15, 1985

When Apple bottomed in mid-August, investors began to buy into the price weakness. Furthermore, with each price decline, investors continued to accumulate shares, and the stock subsequently rallied by 168 percent over the period highlighted in Figure 3. Hence, money flows can enable investors to detect a major change in a price trend at a relatively early stage.

Block Versus Nonblock Money

Participants in the marketplace possess different investment perspectives and strategies. Because the marketplace was becoming increasingly institutionalized, we decided to segregate institutional attitudes from those of individuals, member firms and other participants. As a proxy for institutional sentiment, we segregated all transactions of 10,000 shares or greater and found that certain stocks and industries appear to be driven by either block or nonblock participants. For instance, consumer-oriented issues, such as food and drug stocks, tend to be nonblock driven.

However, we are most comfortable with the predictive value of money flows when block and nonblock participants are of the same opinion. The graphs of Lotus Corp. in Figure 4 illustrate this.

Capitalization: A Screening Device

Experience has also taught us that the money flow concept can be best applied to issues with large capitalizations and considerable trading volume. In fact, money flow analysis highlights divergences in only about 20 percent of cases observed. In the remaining 80 percent of the cases, either price and money are coincident, thereby simply

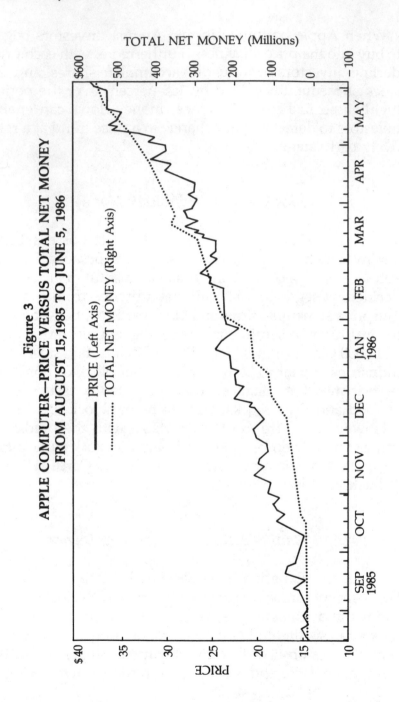

Figure 3
APPLE COMPUTER–PRICE VERSUS TOTAL NET MONEY
FROM AUGUST 15, 1985 TO JUNE 5, 1986

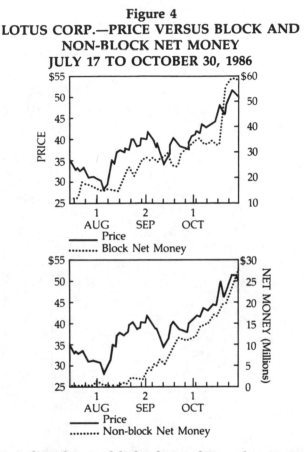

Figure 4
LOTUS CORP.—PRICE VERSUS BLOCK AND
NON-BLOCK NET MONEY
JULY 17 TO OCTOBER 30, 1986

confirming already established trends, or the capitalization and trading activity of the issue is not large enough to generate data with predictive value. While this narrows the applicable universe, we have found in past studies that a small number of stocks generally contribute a large proportion of a portfolio's return. In short, money flow divergences tend to highlight investment and not trading opportunities in the larger capitalized issues.

We currently apply this tool to New York Stock Exchange (NYSE) and NASDAQ National Market System (NASDAQ/ NMS) stocks. We first extended this concept in 1982 to the

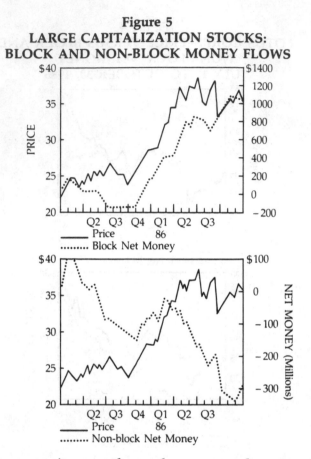

Figure 5
LARGE CAPITALIZATION STOCKS:
BLOCK AND NON-BLOCK MONEY FLOWS

NYSE because it was the only arena whose reporting mechanisms could be adapted to our computer technology. After tracking NASDAQ/NMS issues for two years, we adapted our initial methodology to these issues.

Money Flows in the Over-the-Counter Market: A New Dimension

We first created two portfolios of NASDAQ/NMS stocks—one had issues with capitalizations of at least

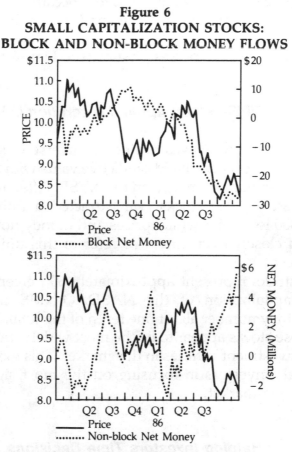

Figure 6
SMALL CAPITALIZATION STOCKS:
BLOCK AND NON-BLOCK MONEY FLOWS

$500 million, and the other had stocks with market values of less than $50 million. We did this to discover whether NASDAQ/NMS issues with large capitalizations and high trading volumes were the most appropriate for our analysis.

In examining Figures 5 and 6, it is apparent that price and money are more closely related in the larger capitalization issues. In addition, block sentiment drives the price of these larger capitalization issues more strongly than nonblock sentiment does—a trend that is not apparent on the NYSE. This could reflect the fact that institutional activity in the OTC market is a more recent and growing trend than in the

NYSE, where this activity has stabilized. Because NASDAQ/ NMS consists of smaller capitalized and more thinly traded issues, we initially experienced some difficulties applying money flow analysis to these issues (see Figure 6.)

NMS-Select: Applied Discretion Is Valuable

Our goal was to find a universe of stocks in which money flows exhibited predictive value with a similar consistency to our experience on the NYSE. After analyzing approximately 2,000 stocks, we extracted a universe of roughly 300 issues for which prices and money flows have correlated closely over time. We refer to this universe as NMS-Select.

These stocks represent approximately 60 percent of the market capitalization of the NASDAQ/NMS universe, although they number about one tenth of the total. Furthermore, these stocks appear to be the most widely traded and popular investment vehicles in this market. This tool, NMS-Select, aids investors in focusing on the most significant events in the market.

Helping Investors Time Decisions

Money flows can help investors time their decisions. For instance, by observing the Salomon Brothers NMS CAD/CAM industry group money flow (see Figure 7), the investor was warned in early 1986 that people were selling these issues. Although prices continued to rise through February, investors continued to sell into this strength. If an investor wishing to liquidate his positions in this industry had waited until prices declined, he would have experienced difficulty getting out, as the group dropped by 30 percent from mid-February to mid-March. Furthermore, each subsequent rally in the group was not supported and only resulted in trading rallies. The same concept held true for the NASDAQ/NMS stocks in the Salomon Brothers computer industry group. In early July 1985, these stocks were under accumulation, and a seller at that time probably noticed that his or her stocks were quickly snatched up because buyers accumulated stock as soon as it appeared, thus drying up the supply. Hence, the aggressive buyers— those willing to bid up the prices—disturbed the complacent ones, and forced them to be aggressive as well.

Quantifying Moves in Stocks

Once the fundamental decision has been made—for example, to buy technology stocks—money flows can help an investor identify which issues will provide the most opportunities for appreciation.

The Salomon Brothers NMS Computer Industry group experienced a sharp rally beginning in October 1985. (See Figure 8.) Subsequently, Stratus Computer (see Figure 9) and Tandem Computers (see Figure 10) also rallied in conjunction with the industry move. These issues have approximately the same value, and the price of both are in up trends. However, substantial buying in Tandem stock resulted in an extended rally of approximately 120 percent during the period highlighted. In Stratus, there was actually selling into the rally; this stock then corrected by over 25 percent in the first quarter. Hence, Stratus underwent a short-term trading rally in sympathy with the industry move. During the period that Tandem stock appreciated 120 percent, Stratus only increased about 36 percent.

The long-term investor should be wary of stocks that are

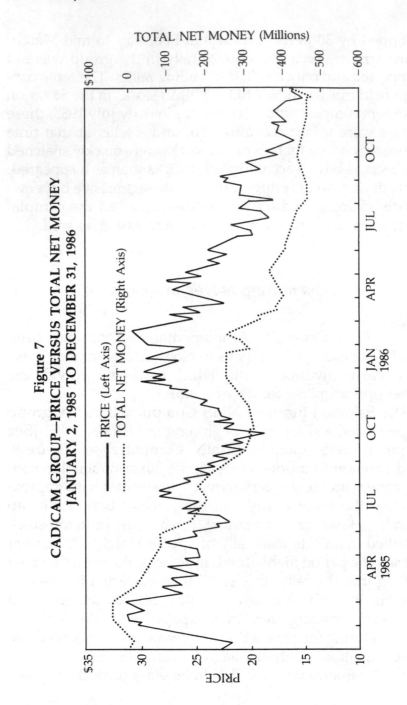

Figure 7
CAD/CAM GROUP—PRICE VERSUS TOTAL NET MONEY
JANUARY 2, 1985 TO DECEMBER 31, 1986

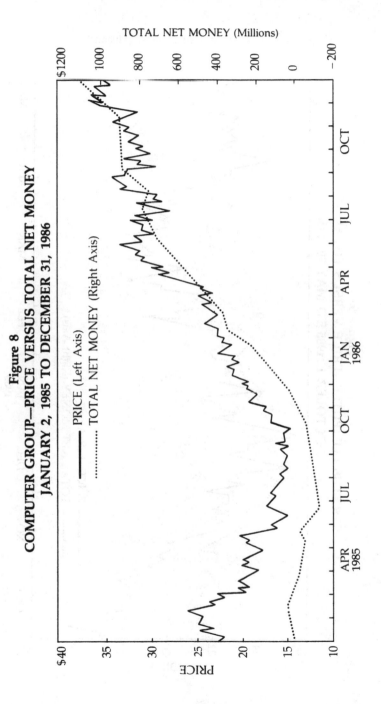

Figure 8
COMPUTER GROUP—PRICE VERSUS TOTAL NET MONEY
JANUARY 2, 1985 TO DECEMBER 31, 1986

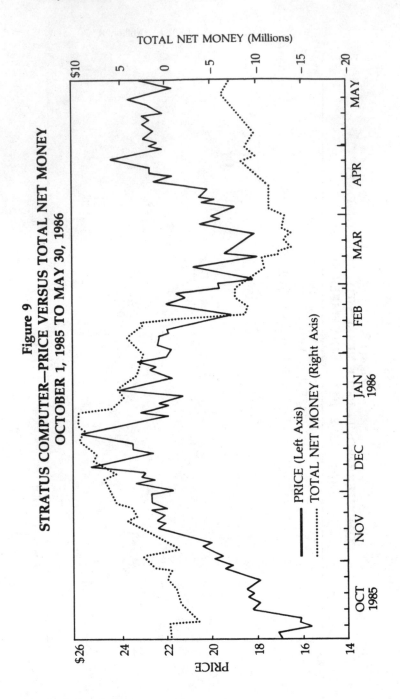

Figure 9
STRATUS COMPUTER—PRICE VERSUS TOTAL NET MONEY
OCTOBER 1, 1985 TO MAY 30, 1986

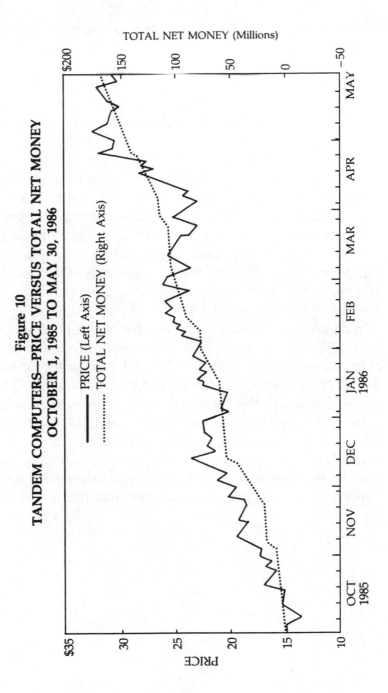

Figure 10
TANDEM COMPUTERS—PRICE VERSUS TOTAL NET MONEY
OCTOBER 1, 1985 TO MAY 30, 1986

"up on nothing," such as the Stratus example, and focus on the investment opportunities, such as the Tandem example.

Predicting the Market

We also use money flows to discern market trends. By selecting an appropriate universe of stocks, we can gauge investor sentiment toward the entire market, in addition to trends in individual issues and industry groups. For example, aggregate money flows in the 30 Dow Jones Industrial Stocks—especially the nonblock data—have been exceptional in predicting market direction. The key divergences, which had significant buying on price weakness, are highlighted in Figure 11.

In an attempt to match the success of the DJIA indicator for NASDAQ/NMS, we had to aggregate a broader sample of issues concentrated in the NMS-Select in order for money flows to be a reliable leading indicator of the NASDAQ Composite. Although the money flows in this universe are not quite as closely correlated as those in the DJIA stocks, using this as an indicator for general market direction appears valid. However (see Figure 12), this indicator has never undergone a real test of its performance in a market decline; hence, we will continue to monitor and refine the data.

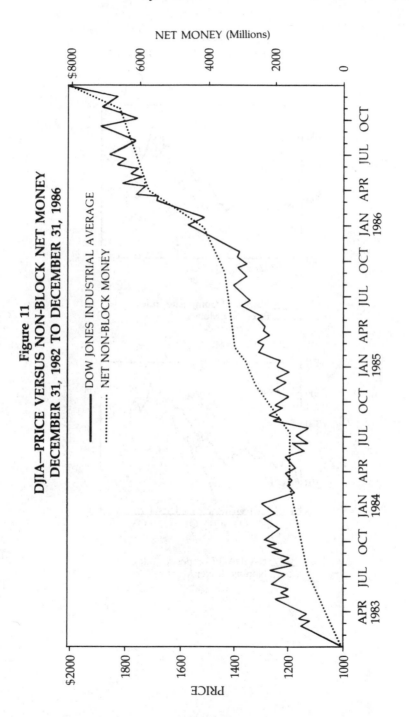

Figure 11
DJIA—PRICE VERSUS NON-BLOCK NET MONEY
DECEMBER 31, 1982 TO DECEMBER 31, 1986

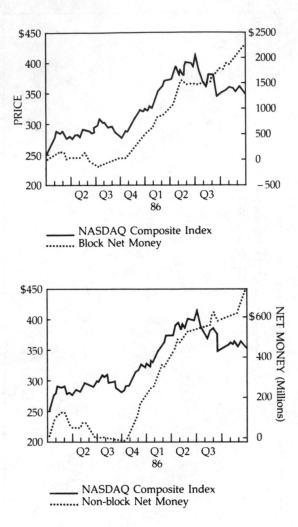

Figure 12
OTC MARKET MONEY FLOWS

Chapter
fourteen

*A*lex Hammond-Chambers is Chairman of the investment firm of Ivory & Sime plc in Edinburgh, Scotland. He joined the firm in 1964 and became a Partner in 1969 and a Director in 1975. He has had special responsibility for the management of the investment trusts that have concentrated their investment in small-and medium-sized companies in the U.S.—those typically on NASDAQ.

The European Investor in the NASDAQ Market

by Alex Hammond-Chambers

"Go West, young man and grow up with the country." With this quote from Horace Greeley begins the history of the Scottish American Investment Company, founded in 1873 to invest in, and only in, North America. Indeed the prospectus (required by a 1844 Act of Parliament) described its aim of providing "the opportunity of investing capital in the United States and British America: (1) Upon well-selected Railroad Mortgages, Government, State and Municipal Stocks; (2) Upon Mortgages over improved City and Country lots."

Scottish American was one of a number of such companies formed in Great Britain during the last half of the 19th century to take advantage of the development of America.

Great Britain was the pioneer in the world industrial revolution and because of its empire, its men of business were international in their attitudes. It was not surprising therefore that they chose to invest some of their wealth in the new developing lands which, of course, included America. Between 1870 and the First World War, foreign investments rose from about £800 million to about £3,500 million (worth about $17 billion then)—a lot of money for those days. A large proportion of these monies was invested in the United States.

The export of capital results, as one might expect, from the perception of better investment opportunities overseas. The early history of foreign investment in the United States was dominated by the British seeking suitable investment opportunities in mining, railroads and farming—the growth industries of the era.

The Forerunners of Today's Investments

The British were almost certainly the first serious investors in America. Their industrial leadership was showing the first signs of maturity during the second half of the last century; thus its industry was generating cash in excess of the opportunities for reinvestment at home and rates of interest were lower than those obtainable overseas. This was particularly true in Scotland and explains why the Scots were such prolific investors in America and why so many Scottish trusts were formed to that end. Sir Alastair Blair, former Chairman of Edinburgh American, wrote in his history of that Scottish Trust:

"The industrial revolution had brought great prosperity to the lowlands of Scotland, and the development of coal mining, iron and steel industries, shipbuilding, engineering and textiles had provided much wealth to many Scots who wanted to find safe investments in which to hold it. This might be in land, in government securities, in banks or insurance companies, but the yield obtainable on any of these was seldom above 4 percent. Equities in industrial and trading companies were largely reserved for the proprietors of these bodies, and were in any event regarded as highly speculative. So both mortgage companies and investment companies became fashionable in the seventies in all the large Scottish cities, more particularly in Dundee and Edinburgh. In deciding on investment in farm mortgages, the mortgage companies were following in the footsteps of the great American insurance offices which in the fifties, sixties and early seventies had provided over £9,000,000 of finance in this way, and reported considerable satisfaction with these investments.''

Companies were formed to invest not only in equities and bonds but also in farming mortgages, mining operations, cattle ranches, forest products and railroads. Foreign (largely British) investment played a large part in the 19th century development of America.

That the British should have invested in Canada or Australia or other parts of their empire is not particularly surprising; the administrative infra-structure existed to manage those investments; but in America that luxury had been lost in 1776 and other means were required to find, make and monitor investments. Moreover, many of these investments were made in what really was the ''Wild West.'' It was adventurous stuff. Scotsmen or Englishmen visiting from Britain made arrangements with local businessmen, accountants, attorneys, etc., to act as agents.

By 1886, the towns and cities where Edinburgh American had agents included Sioux Falls and Yankton, Dakota; Le Mars and Sioux City, Iowa; Sleepy Eye and Mankato, Minnesota; Selma, Alabama; Dallas, Austin, San Antonio and Waco, Texas; and Memphis, Tennessee. The accompanying map of the United States shows the progress Edinburgh American made during its early years as it developed its agencies and portfolio of mortgages in the U.S.

On the whole, the investments were successful, despite periods of great difficulty in the 1870s and 1890s. This history is relevant to modern-day investing because it was the fore-

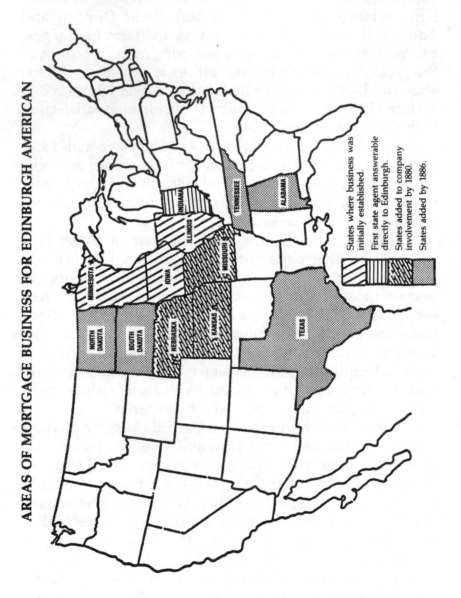

AREAS OF MORTGAGE BUSINESS FOR EDINBURGH AMERICAN

States where business was initially established.

First state agent answerable directly to Edinburgh.

States added to company involvement by 1880.

States added by 1886.

runner of today's foreign/European investment in America's growth companies—in NASDAQ companies.

Investing in the U.S. Today

The industries are now different, being computer and other technology businesses, regional banks, retailers, and new companies in new industries such as health care and aerospace. The agents are now different, being stockbrokers and investment bankers. But both the opportunities (the companies) and the agents are still spread out across America. While communication was effected by the pen, the mail, the railroad and steamship, today it is effected by the computer, the printer, the telephone and the airplane. The transactions took place in Chicago or Cleveland or California as the investor shook hands with his agent and contracts and agreements were signed; today they still take place in Chicago or Cleveland or California but via the computer. The whole process has been thoroughly modernized and is now called NASDAQ.

Why should foreigners, particularly Europeans, whose economies tend to be as mature as America's, want to invest in the United States?

Investors look overseas for opportunities if they perceive those opportunities to be more attractive than those that can be found at home. So Europeans must ask themselves a number of basic questions to determine whether to invest in America.

First and foremost, investors will always examine the prospects for sound economic growth, and overseas they will look for sounder and better economic growth than can be found at home. A cursory glance at the accompanying table illustrates what we all know: Economic growth in the United States during the last 10 to 15 years has not been significantly better than that achieved elsewhere and would

not have of itself justified serious diversion of funds into
American markets. The statistics show that not only do some
other countries have better economic records than the United
States but they also achieved these records with lower inflation, higher productivity and a higher rate of savings.

MEASURES OF ECONOMIC HEALTH

ECONOMIC STATISTICS 1970-1985

Country	Average Economic Growth	Inflation	Industrial Productivity	Average Savings Rate
	% Change			%
Japan	5	7	4½	18
Canada	3½	7½	2	14
France	3	9½	3	15
U.S.A.	2½	6½	1	7
Germany	2½	4½	3	14
U.K.	2	11½	1½	12

It would have been logical for Europeans, considering
overseas investment on the prospects for economic growth
alone, to have chosen Japan; indeed, as the next table shows,
those that did choose Japan made the right decision for the
right reason.

STOCK MARKETS' PERFORMANCE, 1975-1985

	% Change in Local Currency	% Change in Currency	Stock Market % Change In U.S. $
Japan	224	66	373
France	283	14	324
U.S.A. (NASDAQ)	319		319
Canada	198	30	257
Germany	161	52	246
U.K.	332	−29	237
U.S.A. (S & P Composite)	134		134

As we look forward from here, the prospects for sound economic growth in the United States do not appear so much better and so much sounder than in other parts of the world; we can therefore conclude that European investors are not likely to invest in the United States if only this consideration is taken into account.

Assessing National Currencies

In August 1971, President Nixon abandoned the spirit of the freedom of enterprise upon which America achieved such greatness by introducing government controls on the economic machinery of the United States and abandoned the concept of sound money by removing the gold exchangeability of the U.S. dollar. Since then currencies have fluctuated between extremes that have either seriously overvalued or undervalued their different purchasing powers. Assessment of the prospects of individual currencies now plays an important part in any investor's judgments. Clearly, chronically weak currencies can, and do, become temporarily and significantly undervalued—as the pound sterling was in November 1976, rising some 60 percent during the next five years against the American dollar.

Similarly, fundamentally strong currencies can get seriously overvalued as the yen did in 1979; it was to fall by over 30 percent during the subsequent six years. Behind these fluctuations, however, are underlying trends and when European investors review the currency world, they are likely to conclude that those fundamentals that best protect the purchasing power of money appear to be strongest in Japan, Germany, the Netherlands and Switzerland. The economics of countries such as the United States, United Kingdom, France and Italy tend to be dominated by socioeconomic politics; they are countries that tend to live beyond their means and the statistics on their savings, trade, central government budgeting and inflation illustrate this point. They all have broadly based industrial economies without necessarily achieving the best in a qualitative sense.

Currencies of these nations are therefore members of the second league. The U.S. dollar has another role to play— that of the international currency. The gargantuan American trade deficit has the effect of supplying dollars to the rest of the world. This may oil the wheels of the world economy in good times but in bad times, it merely provides a surfeit of unwanted "greenbacks." In 1985, America became for the first time a net external debtor nation, and unless things change, its external debts will dwarf Brazil and Mexico within a few years. The consequences of this will be far-reaching and unlikely to result in any long-term improvement in the value of the American dollar.

Almost certainly the dollar will once again become undervalued and the opportunist investor will have a chance to profit from the correction of that aberration. It is, however, safe to conclude that foreign investors, particularly the strong-currency European investors, will not choose U.S. markets as a haven to "play the currency" in the same way that they have chosen to invest in the German and Japanese markets during 1985 and 1986.

Assessing P/E Ratios

International investors, whether European or not, have become what I shall refer to as global money movers. Driven by the persistent pressure to perform in the very short term, they guess upon which number the roulette ball will next fall and place bets on it. If the analogy sounds a little cynical, it is meant to be, for such short-term "guesstimating" has often replaced sound fundamental assessment.

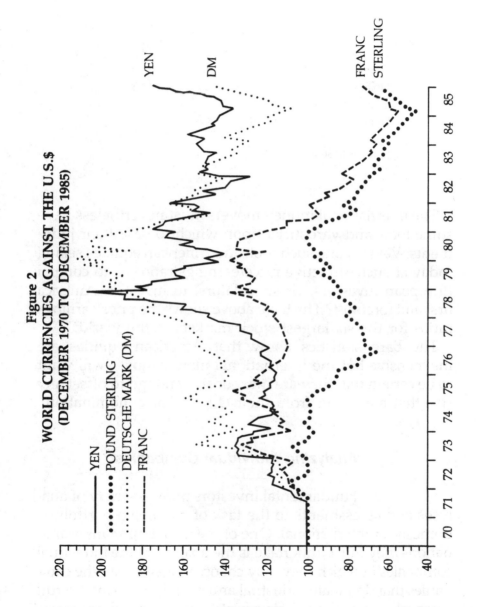

Figure 2
WORLD CURRENCIES AGAINST THE U.S.$
(DECEMBER 1970 TO DECEMBER 1985)

PRICE/EARNINGS RATIOS AS OF NOVEMBER 1986

Country	P/E Ratio
Canada	17.2
France	19.2
Germany	15.0
Japan	42.5
United Kingdom	12.8
United States	14.5

Source: MSCIP

The international money movers must nevertheless have some tools and yardsticks upon which to base their judgments: Value is one such tool. Are American equities selling today at such attractive price/earnings ratios as to compel European investors, or speculators, to invest in America first and foremost? The table above shows the price/earnings ratios for the six largest stock markets in the world.

The bare statistics show that American equities are inexpensive but the international money mover will want to be certain that they are inexpensive enough to offset any risk that may stem from their U.S. dollar denomination.

Analyzing Individual Companies

Fundamental investors bring a variety of analyses and assessments to the task of building a portfolio—domestic or international. One of the most important examinations they must undertake is the analysis of the individual companies in which they may choose to invest. Are the companies that dominate industrial and commercial America run so much better than their counterparts in other countries that fundamentalists are compelled to invest in them? The share price performances of comparable companies over long periods of time do not suggest that American companies are obviously much better in a qualitative sense nor do the superficial figures of national trade balances lend any support to this thesis. The accompanying table shows share price performance of some major companies in some important industries.

INTERNATIONAL COMPANIES' PRICE (U.S.$)
APPRECIATION 1975-1985

Retailers		Chemicals	
Ito Yokado	596%	Sumitomo Chemicals	300%
Marks & Spencer	418%	BASF	88%
Sears, Roebuck	21%	I.C.I.	66%
Horten	17%	Dupont de Nemours	61%
Banks		**Oils**	
Mitsubishi Bank	1,003%	Royal Dutch Petroleum	203%
Deutsche Bank	247%	B.P.	183%
Barclays Bank	164%	Exxon	148%
Citicorp	67%	Petrofina	51%
Autos		**Computers**	
Toyota	469%	Fujitsu	588%
Daimler-Benz	417%	Siemens	208%
Fiat	376%	I.B.M.	176%
General Motors	22%	Cit Alcatel	−50%

Americans as Entrepreneurs

For a lot of international investors, and particularly for the global money mover, American markets take their place in the cyclical scheme of things; their turn comes and goes. However, the long-term investor has an opportunity to participate in a growing part of the United States economy—that part that is so vibrant because it is run by entrepreneurs and is involved in giving birth to and exploiting the development of new technologies and their industries.

America is a country populated by those from other countries who had either the self-confidence to seek their fortune in this new country or the courage to flee the tyranny of home. This statement conveys the great strength of America, of its people and particularly from our point of view, of its economic life. It is safe to say that nowhere in the world do businessmen have the courage to start new ventures in the way and on the scale that they do in America. The very nature of young businesses means that many or most do not survive; yet many of their entrepreneurs will form new ventures and start again. This aspect of economic life in the United States is the envy of other countries because it has created much new employment at a time when bigger companies and governments have had to cut their payrolls; it has, of course, also played an important part in the leadership that the United States has achieved in so many new technologies.

As tiny companies grow and become bigger and reach a stage where they can manage their affairs as publicly quoted companies, they have a marketplace most suitably designed for their needs: NASDAQ.

It is difficult to overestimate the importance that NASDAQ plays in providing capital for young companies and liquidity for their entrepreneurs' shareholdings. The fact that it is the most modern stock market in the world, that it is the most competitive stock market in the world and that it is so widespread adds to NASDAQ's attractiveness as a marketplace for the shares of young companies. It is doubtful that any other market system could provide the necessary public sponsorship that these companies receive from their various market makers.

I do not wish to belittle or demean the role of the New York Stock Exchange by heaping praise upon NASDAQ. Large companies are quite different from small companies in nearly all of their economic characteristics. Because they are large, they are safer, more mature and have fewer growth prospects; over the long term, their profits will not perform differently from the performance of the economy as a whole.

Why Choose NASDAQ Companies?

Investing in small growth companies is not easy. They have a higher mortality rate than larger companies. Very few of them evolve smoothly from the one-man owner to a broadly based management structure involving considerable delegation. So it is that most $1 million sales companies will not attain sales of $100 million and likewise, many $100 million sales companies will not grow to $1,000 million of sales. The fact that many are called but few are chosen should in no way detract from the appeal of NASDAQ companies for investors, whether they be from the United States or Europe.

To Europeans, NASDAQ companies are particularly attractive because nowhere in their own countries, or in other countries, can they find so many diverse small growth companies.

The structure of the NASDAQ System, a computer network that joins together all the regions of America, allows regional companies with regional sponsorship to be part of a national network; it brings the shares of a modest-sized local bank to anywhere and everywhere in the United States, in a way that no centralized floor exchange can. In much the same way as Europe is composed of many countries with different economies, so the U.S. is also composed of many regions with different economies: the farm belt, the oil patch, the industrial Midwest and so on. At times, some of the micro-economies of the U.S. are growing while others are suffering. The NASDAQ network brings together the companies of different regional economies into one stock market, affording the investor the opportunity to select an area by investing in its local bank or retailer or real estate company.

Perhaps the most striking success of NASDAQ is the liquidity it affords to investors in the shares of its companies. The competitive market-making system ensures that investors can readily buy and sell shares. This is, of course, a matter of great concern for investors, particularly foreign investors, in any stock market but it assumes even greater importance when investing in small and medium-sized companies. Because their fortunes ebb and flow rather more frequently than those of the bigger companies, it is necessary for an active investor to be able to buy and sell. The fact that the number of shares traded on NASDAQ now approximates that of the New York Stock Exchange is evidence that an investor can do so.

In addition to operating the NASDAQ market, the National Association of Securities Dealers, Inc., has another important role—that of self-regulation of its members. NASD self-regulation is well organized across the United States and run by member representatives chosen for their skills in this area. The motivation of self-regulation is to ensure that ''members of the club'' conform to the rules so that the club does not lose its reputation. European investors, as well as Americans, can be assured that the highest of regulatory standards are at work in the operation of NASDAQ.

European Ownership of NASDAQ Companies Will Grow

If investing overseas is about seeking higher rewards than are obtainable at home, then a portfolio of NASDAQ companies offers such prospects; if investing overseas is about diversification, then a portfolio of NASDAQ companies offers something different from that obtainable at home—or elsewhere for that matter. Ever since those pioneering days of the last century, Europeans, led by the British, have been investors in "growth America." Today, they are investors in NASDAQ companies.

As communications continue to improve and as market makers sell their services in Europe, European ownership of NASDAQ company shares will continue to grow. It must—it makes sense.

PART IV
The Brokers
and Dealers
in NASDAQ Stocks

Chapter
fifteen

David W. Hunter is Chairman of Parker/Hunter Incorporated and has been in the securities industry for more than 30 years. An industry leader, he served as Chairman of the Board of Governors of the NASD in 1986 and Chairman of the Board of the Securities Industry Association in 1977.

Serving Individual Investors — and Grass-Roots Capitalism

by David W. Hunter

The primary function of a broker-dealer firm, to my way of thinking, is to serve the nation's nearly 50 million individual investors. Individual investors are the vital engine of our nation's economy. When they enter the market, they supply capital for job creation and economic growth. When they withhold their resources, the economy suffers.

Because they are 50 million strong, individual investors are major determinants of our country's political and economic future. We need a large percentage of Americans to understand, endorse and participate as owners in our capitalist system. Unless the capitalist system has that grass-roots support, it could gradually erode under increasing government regulation into a state-planned economy, the sure route to stagnation and lower living standards for our people.

The Individual Investor Described

I believe that anyone who has $300 or more to invest should have an investment program and that common stocks should be the mainstay of it. By investing, individuals can help the economy and capitalism. They become voters in the financial marketplace, making decisions for and against various investments. Their going to the "economic polls" is, in many ways, as important as their going to the political polls.

Intelligent, individual investors develop valuable characteristics:

- They are students, studying and learning about the performance of companies and the wide range of financial products that are available.
- They are self-confident, sure of their ability to make the right judgments over time and able to profit from their mistakes.
- They are courageous, believing that taking risks can bring rewards.
- They enjoy the challenges that investment decisions present.

Two Approaches to Investing

When investing savings, the individual basically has only two choices: lending money or acquiring ownership.

Lending money has strict limitations. The rate of return is usually fixed, or it varies within a quite narrow range. The combination of inflation and taxes may nullify or drastically diminish the profits from lending. Still, lending part of one's money—by placing it in a savings account or by buying debt instruments—makes sense: It sets aside funds that are readily available if suddenly needed.

The second approach to investing, one with greater risks and rewards than lending, is ownership. Ownership can be divided into three categories:

1. **Material goods,** such as art, antiques and precious metals. These may or may not be profitable, depending on the quality of one's taste and the vagaries of others' tastes.
2. **Real estate.** The best investment that many Americans have made in recent years has been buying their own homes. Most did not do it as an investment, but it turned out to be an excellent one.
3. **Common stock.** This category can be divided into three subsets:
   - Quiet, defensive stocks, such as utilities.
   - High-grade growth stocks. These issues have a consistent, long-term track record of price appreciation because the companies issuing them have consistent, long-term revenues and earnings growth.
   - Emerging growth stocks. These are issued by companies whose potential seems strong but has not yet been proven over time.

The NASDAQ Market for Individuals

The NASDAQ market, which offers investors all three subsets of common stocks, is pre-eminently a market for the individual investor. While institutional participation in it is substantial and growing, 70 percent of all NASDAQ securities by market value are held by individuals. They can follow the leads of the institutions, or they can invest in stocks that the institutions, given their limitations, tend to avoid. Either way, individuals, because of their predominance in the NASDAQ market, do not have to fear they will be trampled by the whims of big money.

Individual investment in the NASDAQ market can be socially useful, as well as personally rewarding. Many NASDAQ companies are small businesses. Studies show that small businesses contribute more than 60 percent of the new jobs in the U.S. economy. Those small businesses that succeed grow much faster than big, established companies. Thus, individual investment in NASDAQ companies can be a powerful force for job creation and economic growth, as well as personal profit.

How to Invest in NASDAQ: Full-Service Firms

The individual investor has three access routes to trading in the NASDAQ market:
1. A full-service broker-dealer firm.
2. A discount broker.
3. Investment companies, or mutual funds.

My firm, Parker/Hunter Incorporated, is a full-service firm. We help our clients—individuals, institutions and corporations—solve their financial problems and attain their financial objectives by providing financial advice, investments and service. In this way, our firm produces wealth for our clients, our shareholders, our employees and the communities in which we operate.

As a full-service, regional broker-dealer, my firm employs approximately 300 people, 140 of whom are investment executives committed to handling the needs of our individual clients, in 19 offices located in Pennsylvania, West Virginia, Ohio and New York City.

Like hundreds of broker-dealers, we engage in almost all aspects of the investment business, including the underwriting of corporate and municipal securities, corporate and municipal finance, venture capital, equity research, portfolio management, mutual funds, insurance, options, U.S.

government securities, market making and the handling of stock and bond transactions on most stock exchanges and in the over-the-counter market.

Most full-service broker-dealers offer their clients four primary advantages:

1. Complete investment programs that are customized to individual investors' financial needs, resources and expectations of financial risk.
2. Strong staffs of investment analysts and researchers who are familiar with NASDAQ companies, market trends and other market activities.
3. One-on-one development and management of portfolios covering a broad spectrum of investment opportunities, including stocks, mutual funds, annuities and insurance.
4. A full network of branch offices providing services to the investor at a wide range of geographical locations.

How We Work With Clients

At Parker/Hunter, we deploy our resources on behalf of an individual client much like a team of doctors would:

- In the initial meetings with a new client, an investment executive only asks questions. We determine in detail what the client is like; what his income, assets, debts and spending and saving habits are; what future financial prospects and needs he appears to have; and what his financial management objectives are. This is like a general physical examination.
- Then we explain our basic concept of creating for him a mix of lending and ownership, including another mix of ownership in quiet, defensive stocks, high-grade growth stocks and emerging growth stocks. We arrive

at an agreement in principle on the overall mix. Compare this to a course of treatment, if you will.

- In the third stage of the relationship, we recommend his specific lending and ownership investments, subject to the client's suggestions, of course. At this stage, we provide him with our own research and that of other firms. We offer the client not only our opinion but also second and third opinions.
- After the client's program of specific "medication" is set, we continually watch it and make periodic checkups. How are his various investments performing? Is the established mix still appropriate? Does it need change? Should we adjust for changes in the client's basic financial condition?

In this process, our investment executives conduct themselves like good doctors: They stick to their best professional judgment; they do not tailor their judgment to the client's whims. If a client does not like our four-step approach or our best judgment, he is free to find another broker-dealer. Our investment executives can take this position because they are supported by the full battery of Parker/Hunter's resources. They speak with informed authority.

How to Invest in NASDAQ: Discount Brokers

A second access route to the NASDAQ market is through discount brokers. Firms of this type are for individual investors who make their own stock selections and do not need the guidance of an investment executive in a full-service firm or the portfolio management services of a mutual fund.

Discount brokers do not make sales calls, provide individual advice or offer research information. Their commissions are lower than those of full-service firms because they do not offer the range of services offered by full-service firms. They are order takers and order executors.

Some discount brokers charge according to the dollar value of trades; they tend to be less expensive for individual investors dealing in lower-priced stocks. Others base their commissions on the number of shares traded; they are likely to be cheaper for investors dealing in high-priced issues. On very small transactions, a discounter may not be able to offer savings because even minimum paperwork, overhead and time costs must be adjusted to a fee schedule on which a firm can earn a profit. By comparing discounters' commission schedules, the individual investor can identify the one that best fits his or her trading pattern.

In recent years, discounters have gained roughly 20 percent of individual investors' trading activity and perhaps 35 to 40 percent of new retail accounts. Because this growth rate of new accounts may not continue, some discount firms have diversified into IRAs, Keogh plans, government securities, money market funds, mutual funds and margin accounts. Others, while still not setting up their own research departments, offer their customers free or discount-priced information produced by established research organizations. Thus, some discounters are becoming more like full-service firms, with the crucial distinction that they do not make stock recommendations or provide financial planning and portfolio management assistance to the individual investor.

How to Invest in NASDAQ: Mutual Funds[1]

As a third access route, NASDAQ investors can choose from a number of mutual funds whose portfolios

---

[1]This discussion of mutual funds is adapted from material supplied by the Investment Company Institute, the association of mutual funds, headquartered in Washington, D.C.

are composed either entirely, or to a large degree, of NASDAQ securities. Today, there are 25 mutual funds in this category with assets totaling nearly $6 billion.

The first U.S. mutual funds were organized during the 1920s. Today, mutual funds manage more than 34 million shareholder accounts valued at nearly $500 billion. They have become the nation's fourth largest financial institution—behind commercial banks, savings and loans, and insurance companies.

Some funds, known as "no-loads," distribute their shares directly to the public. No-loads advertise in magazines and newspapers, and investors can write or call for additional information. Because no sales agents are involved, these funds do not charge an upfront sales commission (or "load"), but it is up to the investor to do the investment homework.

Other funds maintain their own sales forces to help investors and do charge a commission. Some of these funds have set up retail stores in large metropolitan areas. Others can be reached through toll-free telephone numbers. Investors can write or call these funds, and a sales agent will contact them.

The money accumulated in a mutual fund is managed by professionals who decide where to invest it. These money managers base their decisions on extensive, ongoing economic research into the financial performance of individual companies and specific security issues, taking into account general economic and market trends. After analyzing the data, the managers choose investments that best match the fund's objectives. As economic conditions change, the fund may adjust the mix of its investments to adopt a more aggressive or defensive posture.

By distributing the pool of shareholder dollars across dozens of securities, the mutual fund can diversify its holdings. A diversified portfolio reduces risk if some investments turn sour and increases the chance of picking up potential winners. The average investor would find it difficult to amass a portfolio as diversified as that of a mutual fund.

While some investors prefer to pick a single fund and stick with it, others look for a "family" of funds—several different funds available under one roof. In a family, investors can transfer portions of their investment into other funds with different objectives as their own needs or financial circumstances change.

Mutual fund investors can cash in all or part of their shares at any time and receive the current value of their investment, which may be more or less than the original cost. They do not need to find a buyer; the fund is always ready to buy back, or redeem, its shares. Current per-share values are calculated daily based on the market worth of the underlying securities. These values change as the values of the underlying securities move up or down and as the fund buys new securities or sells existing ones. Investors can find the per-share calculations, which are known as "net asset values," in the financial sections of most major newspapers.

A Combination of Access Routes to NASDAQ

Many individual investors use more than one access route to the NASDAQ market. They maintain full-service accounts for those NASDAQ stocks on which they need assistance, discount brokerage accounts for trading they prefer to do on their own, and mutual fund investments for maximum diversification and the pooling of their funds with others.

The choice of access routes is as important for the individual investor as the choice of NASDAQ securities.

Selecting a full-service firm, a discounter or a mutual fund that suits individual needs is a key part of the learning, risk-taking and challenging experience that investing represents.

Investing in the NASDAQ market is an experience shared by nearly 10 million Americans of all ages. I hope that number will double, triple and quadruple, for both the personal benefits it can bring and for the assistance that it can give to the economic growth, the economic literacy and the democratic participation of people everywhere.

Chapter
sixteen

John H. Goldsmith is the Chairman and CEO of Prescott, Ball & Turben, Inc., a full-service, regional brokerage firm based in Cleveland, Ohio. Mr. Goldsmith has served with distinction on numerous securities industry committees and is currently a member of the Board of Kemper Financial Companies.

Bringing Companies Public and Aftermarket Support

by John H. Goldsmith

Before broker-dealers can trade stocks for individual and institutional investors, the companies issuing the stocks must be brought public. This is the investment banking function. The investment banker is the key figure in the flow of capital from investors to businesses that need the capital for development, expansion and growth. The investment banker's activities on behalf of companies going public make him a vital cog in U.S. progress.

The investment banker plays a particularly important role in the NASDAQ market because that is where the overwhelming majority of companies go public. In 1986, the NASDAQ market had nearly 1,000 initial public offerings (IPOs) issued by more than 700 companies.

The large, full-line investment banking firms are staffed with hundreds of people, each handling specific types of companies or specific transactions. For example, in most big investment banking houses, separate specialty groups handle finance for industry areas such as utilities, industrial companies, banking and financial services companies. Additionally, these firms might further divide industry areas by types of transactions, with one group handling equity financing and a different group handling debt financing.

At the other end of the gamut are the small, specialty boutiques that handle one industry, such as technology or banking, or one specific type of transaction, such as mergers and acquisitions. Also somewhere in the spectrum are "regional" firms, which typically handle all types of transactions for all types of companies within a defined geographical territory.

Investment Bankers and Their Customers

Investment bankers underwriting NASDAQ or other securities bring together investors and the users of capital. While it is generally accepted that investment bankers work on behalf of their corporate clients, they must also fairly represent their investor clients who are putting up the capital. In this role, investment bankers are often torn between getting the best price for their corporate clients and presenting the best investment for their investing customers. This process all starts with "selecting the right corporate client," or perhaps it would be more accurate to say "being selected as the investment banker for the right type of client."

The large investment houses that handle virtually every type of transaction primarily act for large companies with transaction sizes ranging from $10 million to $100 million or more. These houses aggressively compete for the Fortune 500 companies. Until recently, Fortune 500 companies allocated business based on long-standing relationships. Today, they look at expertise within a particular area and pricing.

The competition for the small transactions handled by regional firms and specialty boutiques is no less competitive. It is not unusual for five or six firms to fiercely compete for a $10 million to $20 million transaction. The company often makes its final decision on the basis of personalities, strengths of relationships, expertise, pricing or any combination of the above.

Once a company has chosen its investment banker, the company and its investment banker begin getting to know each other and addressing the financial needs of the company.

Should Every Company Be Public?

Whenever an emerging company needs capital, the thought of an initial public offering comes to mind. Companies often believe they can obtain capital at the lowest cost by going public. Often, quite the contrary is true. Generally, people who invest in IPOs are looking for bargains. They are looking for an opportunity to get into a new situation on the ground floor at a bargain price.

If the company is not mature and does not have a proven record of consistent earnings and growth in its earnings, it may find that the price at which its equity will be offered makes the capital very expensive. When Federal Express, Ford, Henley's Group and Coca Cola Enterprises went public for the first time, they were able to attract capital at what might be considered high prices. Why? They were mature, widely known companies with decades of earnings history.

If an emerging company can show a definite need for capital and has shown a consistent earning capability and the potential for future growth, it might be time to go public.

How to Raise the Money

The investment banker and the company must now decide how the company should raise the money it needs. To balance the company's immediate needs for capital with its more long-term objectives, a variety of factors must be considered. For instance, how would growth and the issuance of new securities affect the company's balance sheet? What is the company's ratio of debt to equity? What are current market conditions?

Although it might be advantageous for the company to improve its balance sheet by issuing equity, the market environment for an equity issue may not be advantageous. On the other hand, the company may wish to issue debt securities only to find that high interest rates cause them to be a costly financing mechanism. Other alternatives include the issuance of convertible debentures, which in essence are a compromise between debt and equity securities or preferred stock. Preferred stock is considered to be equity but has many of the attributes of debt.

Determining the size of an offering is not as simple as figuring out how much money the company needs. In many situations, the marketplace precludes the company from raising as much capital as it might otherwise like. In other instances, the market is so attractive that a company is wise to acquire more funds than it immediately needs. In either case, the banker plays a key role in advising the company about the proper balance between what the company needs and what the marketplace will bear.

Timing of the offering is a key element. An investment banker should bring the company to market with a particular type of security at a time when the market is favorably disposed to that type of security. It is not an exact science and demands a good deal of judgment.

Pricing the issue is another important element in a successful offering. Playing a critical role, the banker acts as an intermediary between the corporate client and the investing customer. Needless to say, the company wants the highest price for its common stock or the lowest interest rate for its debt. However, if the securities are priced too aggressively in favor of the corporate client, they will be unmarketable or will fare poorly in the aftermarket to the distress of the investing customer. If the investment banker errs either way, he will either have an unhappy corporate client or an unhappy investor.

For various reasons, the banker and the company may decide not to offer securities publicly, and money may be raised through a private placement. This is merely selling securities—either debt or equity or any other type of securities—privately, generally to institutional investors. This process, which does not require filing a registration with the SEC, can save the company a great deal of money in legal and printing expenses and can often significantly expedite the process of raising capital. On the other hand, only certain types of investors qualify for such offerings and the securities can only be traded by private sale because they are not registered. Private securities are generally priced in favor of the investor to reflect their lack of liquidity.

Prior to any offering, whether public or private, the investment banker conducts what is known as "due diligence." By virtue of this review, the investment banker becomes intimately familiar with every aspect of the company's business. In the process, the investment banker meets and interviews management, visits plants or retail stores, and interviews the company's directors, accounting firm and attorneys. In this way, he can uncover any areas of investor concern or special risks that may exist.

After completing the preliminary due-diligence obligations, the investment banker and the company work on the preparation of a registration statement with the company's counsel and the special underwriter's counsel, who represents the investment banker and the other underwriters. If a private placement is contemplated, a private placement memorandum is used to offer the securities instead of a prospectus and registration statement. If, however, public securities are to be issued, a registration statement is filed with the SEC. The registration statement includes a preliminary prospectus, or "red herring," that is used in the marketing effort to develop interest in the offering.

The marketing effort may also include a road show, which is a presentation organized by the investment banker and held in major cities before institutional investors and representatives of the brokerage firms that might be participating in the distribution of the issue. The speakers are generally the CEO, CFO and other top officials of the issuing company.

A registration statement is said to be "effective" when the SEC completes its review and determines the documentation is in order. The SEC does not approve the information in the registration statement and is not responsible for its accuracy. The onus for the accuracy of the information rests in the hands of the company and the investment banker with the advice of certain experts, such as public accountants and attorneys. Once the registration statement is effective, the issue is ready for market.

Underwriting and Selling the Issue

If the company and investment banker agree on a private placement, the investment banker generally handles the marketing process. He will distribute copies of the selling memorandum to institutional investors who he believes might be interested. These transactions are usually handled on a best-efforts basis, which means the banker is not underwriting the securities, he is merely committing to use his best efforts to try to place all the securities with investors. If public securities are involved, the banker generally underwrites the securities, which means he is agreeing to buy the securities from the company at an agreed-upon price and to distribute them to customers. When an investment banker underwrites the securities, he is at risk if the market moves up or down during the marketing period or if selling all of the securities proves difficult.

To spread his risk and to help market the securities, the investment banker generally puts together an underwriting syndicate composed of several brokerage firms. These firms agree to take a proportionate share of the underwriting risk and to help distribute the securities. A syndicate for a large offering may include as many as 150 brokerage firms; for a small offering it may be composed of only five to 10 firms.

While the investment banker primarily determines the character of the syndicate, the company may also exert its influence. Often a company wants its securities to be widely held, primarily by small investors in geographically diverse locations. This type of distribution would mandate either the participation of a large wire house with many offices scattered throughout the country or a large number of regional firms from various geographical areas, or most typically, a combination of the two. Other issuers prefer to see their securities held by large institutional investors, perhaps because institutions were at one time thought to hold securities longer than individuals. An institutional distribution would, of course, require a syndicate composed of specialty firms or other firms with institutional marketing capability. Generally, the investment banker and the issuer agree on a predetermined distribution between institutional and retail security sales.

When using an underwriting syndicate, the investment banker's role becomes that of managing underwriter. In this role, he is not only the intermediary between the company and the investing customers, but he is also the intermediary between the company and the other broker-dealers that are participating as underwriters in the syndicate.

As managing underwriter, he maintains primary responsibility for pricing the issue and allocates the securities among the other underwriters—a complex task. The managing underwriters must allocate securities to the syndicate, follow up with syndicate members to make sure that the securities so allocated are actually sold to investors, and constantly monitor the syndicate to ensure the securities are well placed. This latter point is critical—if the securities are in the hands of investors who sell quickly after the offering, selling pressure will be created and the price of the securities will decline.

To help ensure a solidly placed offering, the managing underwriter may often distribute more securities than are being offered as part of the issue. This creates a short position for the syndicate, which allows the managing underwriter to bid for securities in the aftermarket on behalf of the syndicate. Bidding for securities allows the manager to support the offering, thus enabling the market to stay at or above the issue price.

If the managing underwriter can build a relatively large short position and short-term investors do not create selling pressure, most issuers agree to an overallotment. Known as the "green shoe," the overallotment is a percentage of the original offering that the company agrees to sell to the underwriters to cover any short positions and to help stabilize the issue. Generally, the overallotment is up to 15 percent of the offering and covers a period of 30 days.

Once the issue is placed with the public, the syndicate is terminated and syndicate members are released from the underwriting restrictions. The issue is then free to trade in the open market. If it is a NASDAQ issue, as are many initial public offerings, some of the syndicate members usually become market makers.

The Block Transaction Alternative

While the block transaction method of distributing registered securities is rarely used for initial public offerings, it has become a popular method for large issuers to distribute new issue securities. Block transactions may involve a secondary offering, a primary offering or both. In a secondary offering, a stockholder sells stock and the proceeds go to the stockholder, not the company. In a primary offering, the company issues new stock or an initial offering of stock and the proceeds go to the company.

In a direct placement, the investment banker, who also plays the role of managing underwriter, places the securities directly with institutions. While he may have a small syndicate of one or two firms, the investment banker often handles these transactions alone. This process is similar to the private placement, except the securities are fully registered and the appropriate registration statements are filed with the SEC. Because a block placement does not involve a syndication, it is often considered a more efficient mechanism for distributing a new issue than an ordinary public offering. Consequently, the fee the managing underwriter charges for a block placement is often lower.

After the Offering

The role of the investment banker does not end when the issue is brought to market. In the case of a NASDAQ company, the investment banker generally becomes a significant market maker. Because he played the role of managing underwriter, he knows who the major holders of the stock are and who might be sellers if the price goes up or down. In general, the financial community looks at the investment banker for a NASDAQ stock as it would look to a "specialist" of an issue listed on either the New York or American stock exchange.

In addition to making markets in the securities, the investment banker must maintain a close relationship with the company to keep abreast of any future financing needs. Just because a firm handled a transaction for a company once does not mean it will handle all future transactions. If an investment banker doesn't stay abreast of new financing techniques, another firm capable of handling that type of transaction could take the client away.

In many cases, particularly with NASDAQ companies, the investment banker offers sponsorship by providing follow-up research on the company. Additionally, the banker holds management meetings with analysts or institutional investors and frequently guides the smaller companies in learning how to become a public company. Many small and some larger companies do not understand investor relations and how it influences the market price of securities. In many cases, the investment banker introduces the company to a public relations firm that specializes in investor relations. In other cases, the investment banker might recommend that the company designate a specific individual to be in charge of investor relations.

Helping a new public company deal with regulatory matters is another service the investment banker often provides. The investment banker helps the company and its counsel file all the necessary documents and may even play a small role in the preparation of an annual statement.

The necessity for continued due diligence does not end with the issuance of securities. The investment banker and the underwriters carry a great deal of the responsibility for the accuracy of the statements made in the registration statement. The investment banker who brings a small company public must be sure to the best of his ability that the way money is allocated and the way the business is managed is consistent with the prospectus.

Away From the Ordinary

A company can use four other methods to go public:

1. *A private company may purchase a public company and go public "through the back door."* The acquired public company, often no more than a shell, continues tax-loss carry-forwards from what may have been a pre-existing unsuccessful business enterprise. The acquiring company may take this step to go public in a relatively low-cost manner without issuing new securities and/or to acquire tax losses that might greatly benefit its net after-tax profits.

2. *A company may go public without a standard initial public offering by means of a spinoff.* This involves a public company's sale of a division or subsidiary to the company's shareholders through the issuance of rights to buy stock in that division or subsidiary. Often these transactions involve an underwriter or underwriting group that agrees to market any shares that are not subscribed to by the original company's shareholders. An example of this type of offering is Allied Signal Corporation's spinoff of the Henley Group, which represented one of the largest public offerings in history. Another example is the breakup of AT&T, which involved the spinoff of seven regional telephone companies.

3. *A company may opt for a leveraged buyout, which is the antithesis of an initial public offering.* A leveraged buyout is a transaction that involves a small group of investors and generally includes the management of an operating unit or an entire company. The investor group finances

the acquisition of the company or division with a small amount of equity and large borrowings (the leverage).

To finance this leverage activity, the investor group issues what are known as "junk bonds" but are more properly termed high-yield bonds. Through this method, investors have been able to take over large companies, some of them public, by tendering for the public shares at prices usually greatly above market. These tenders are financed through high-yield bonds and, upon completion of the transaction, the company is no longer public since all its shares are now held by a small, private group of investors. This is an example of taking a company private, or "going private."

4. *In the case of a hostile takeover, a company's original shareholders may be offered a package that includes stock in a publicly traded company, which is the surviving entity, and other securities, including junk bonds.* The value of this package would be the sum of the value of the bonds plus the value of the equity and typically involves a significant premium over the market value of the securities being tendered for. This transaction is also somewhat the antithesis of an initial public offering because it takes a publicly traded entity out of the marketplace and makes it part of another company, which may or may not be publicly traded.

Where Do We Go From Here?

The accompanying chart shows the number and dollar amounts of initial public offerings over the last six years. Although 1986 reflected fewer deals than the peak year of 1983, the dollar amount almost doubled, in part due to some very large transactions.

While new techniques will undoubtedly be developed, financing America's growth will always be a key role of the investment banker. As long as we have viable markets, bringing companies public will remain a popular method of raising capital.

Table 1
INITIAL PUBLIC OFFERINGS, 1981-1986

	1981	1982	1983	1984	1985	1986
Total Number of Issues	971	619	1,684	890	943	1,408
Dollar Amount	$15,312,851	$14,450,325	$37,428,993	$9,719,459	$25,157,710	$43,518,781
NASDAQ	201/$2,205,579	121/$1,768,394	364/$5,976,467	128/$1,595,731	244/$4,287,214	323/$7,048,994
NYSE	151/$8,937,061	178/$10,718,193	292/$17,200,979	81/$3,642,430	125/$11,014,168	132/$12,535,063
Amex	47/$577,672	29/$383,603	100/$1,623,499	21/$335,793	47/$1,154,929	57/$2,122,177
Initial Public Offerings	470/$3,584,139	289/$41,573,012	926/$12,732,223	659/$4,135,527	528/$8,718,461	898/$22,218,572

Chapter
seventeen

John N. Tognino is Vice President and Manager of the OTC Trading Department at Merrill Lynch, Pierce, Fenner & Smith Incorporated. He has been with Merrill for nearly 30 years and was named the 1986 "OTC Man of the Year" by *OTC Review*, the monthly magazine for over-the-counter companies.

Market-Maker Sponsorship: A Synergistic Package of Services

by John N. Tognino

More than 500 market-making firms provide a continuous stream of aftermarket support to NASDAQ securities. This support begins after securities are issued and continues year after year, while their issuers grow, mature and often become young giants. This sponsorship function of market makers is a synergistic package of four services:

1. Making competitive, efficient and liquid markets in NASDAQ securities.
2. Supporting these markets through ample capital commitments.
3. Heightening the visibility of NASDAQ stocks by quoting them on thousands of terminals in the U.S. and 36 other countries and by publicizing the stocks through careful and frequent research reports.
4. Calling worldwide attention to NASDAQ stocks through an army of securities salesmen in the 500-plus market-making firms.

All aspects of such sponsorship have expanded since the start of the NASDAQ market in February 1971. Its success has cemented the loyalty of issuers and investors. Furthermore, market-maker sponsorship of securities has gained a momentum that is making NASDAQ the role model and centerpiece of the 24-hour global dealer market.

The Expansion of NASDAQ Sponsorship

In 1970, Merrill Lynch made markets in approximately 300 over-the-counter securities. In those days, market making was done principally by a group of wholesale trading firms, without retail salesmen, without research capabilities. A telephone network hooked these firms together. The so-called "pink sheets"—printed bulletins delivered by messenger and mail, fragmentary in their information and usually out of date when they arrived—were the main communication vehicle for the market.

Then, along came the NASDAQ System on February 8, 1971. This technological innovation moved the over-the-counter market from obscurity into broad daylight, from the past into the future. Computer screens began to display reliable, up-to-the-second market-maker quotations on NASDAQ securities. The NASD established and enforced strict rules to ensure the integrity of the trading process. Overnight, the over-the-counter market began to gain credibility, liquidity and acceptance.

By 1975, we made markets in 500 NASDAQ stocks, a 67 percent increase in only four years, and market making at many other firms grew at a comparable rate. National, regional and local firms entered the NASDAQ market in force because all had confidence in it. With the reliable information available through the computer, their research could follow NASDAQ stocks; their retail salesmen could offer hard data to their clients; and their clients could follow the stocks in the newspapers. Consequently, firms could commit much more capital to NASDAQ trading and to the support of its stocks.

By 1983, our firm was trading 575 NASDAQ stocks. Then the NASDAQ National Market System took off. It introduced real-time trade reporting for selected securities, giving them all the continuous price and volume data that listed securities had on the ticker. This produced a quantum jump in the reliability, credibility and liquidity of the market. Research on NASDAQ stocks became even more sophisticated; our salesmen had still better data for their clients; and we felt confident in committing still more capital to market making.

Today, more than 500 firms have over 40,000 positions in NASDAQ stocks. Merrill makes markets in 1,300 domestic securities and 200 foreign issues. The risk capital committed to NASDAQ by Merrill and the other firms is in the hundreds of millions. The market itself has become the third largest in the world, exceeded only by the New York and Tokyo stock exchanges.

Who Recommends Stocks?

The process of sponsoring NASDAQ stocks is a serious business that may begin in a variety of ways:

- A firm may be the investment banker for a NASDAQ company, with an obligation to provide specific aftermarket support for its stock.
- A branch may be trying to sell its full range of financial services to a local company, and this could include sponsoring the company's stock.
- An outside financial adviser, a research department or traders—who are always on the lookout for additional NASDAQ stocks that could interest a firm's clients—may recommend a stock for trading.
- A NASDAQ company may ask a firm to make a market in its stock.

- Present market-making firms may ask another firm to sponsor a stock to create a larger, more competitive and more liquid market for it.

Selecting the Stock

Once we receive an initial recommendation on a stock, we follow a systematic five-step procedure:
1. The research department analyzes the company and the stock.
2. The legal and compliance department looks for anything that would impede us from making a market in the stock.
3. Our trading department closely reviews the stock's past and present price and volume activity.
4. Our sales department verifies that clients are interested in the stock.
5. We determine whether a commitment to the stock represents efficient use of the risk capital we have available for market making.

Other firms have comparable procedures. If all the indications are favorable, firms apply to the NASD to be registered as market makers in a stock. Usually within 48 hours of application, they start entering their quotes and, if it is a NASDAQ/NMS security, their transaction reports into the NASDAQ computer.

Sponsorship in Full Swing

Then sponsorship of the stock goes into full swing:
- Market makers give it additional visibility through the NASDAQ System.

- They write it up in one of their market letters or publish a full research report on it.
- They brief their registered representatives, both retail and institutional, on the stock so they can recommend it to interested clients.

This process brings a local or regional company to the attention of individual and institutional investors all across the U.S. And, today, with the rapid internationalization of the securities market, market-maker sponsorship gives an emerging growth company the opportunity to become global in scope.

Chapter eighteen

Patrick C. Ryan has been a securities trader for 26 years and is Senior Vice President, Director and Manager of Trading at Johnston, Lemon & Co. Incorporated. In 1987, he is serving as the Chairman of the NASD's District No. 10 Business Conduct Committee, and as a Director of NASD Market Services, Inc. He is 1987 Vice Chairman of the National Security Traders Association.

The Regional Market Maker: A Growing Force

by Patrick C. Ryan

Sixty percent of NASDAQ market-making firms are headquartered in cities other than New York. From 1982 to 1986, the number of NASDAQ market makers grew from less than 400 to more than 525. Yet, no new national firms were established in those years. The entire increase can be attributed to regional and local firms, showing clearly that they can compete with national firms, and be profitable, as NASDAQ market makers.

Regional, Local Firms Increase Market Share

Johnston, Lemon, which is a medium-sized regional firm, has increased its NASDAQ market share in recent years. Many other regional and local firms—such as Piper, Jaffray in Minneapolis and Bateman Eichler in Los Angeles—have increased their share as well. We have been able to do this for three principal reasons.

1. **We attract and retain top-notch professionals.** I believe that regional and local firms attract the same quality of talent as the big national firms.

In addition to myself, we have four people on our trading desk; the oldest is 29. All have college degrees, and three have graduate degrees. The fourth was an NCAA championship golfer who started as a securities salesman but quickly switched to trading because it required the same precision, judgment, risk taking and competition that made him so good on the links.

One of our traders specializes in taxable, fixed-income securities but he also handles NASDAQ trading when we need him. Formerly with a local bank, where he traded bonds as well as equity issues, he thrives on the electric atmosphere—and more attractive compensation—of a securities firm.

I recently hired another trader who took a pay cut to come to us. He is running our computer and monitoring trading patterns, while training to become an equity trader. Although he has traded currencies in New York and London, he says the prospect of being an equity trader thrills him more than anything else he's ever done.

A locally based, medium-sized regional firm offers traders and would-be traders full scope for their brains, boldness and prudence, in a non-assembly-line workplace, set in an unpressurized living environment. It combines the best of the professional and personal worlds. That's why we attract top-flight people.

2. **We try harder.** A regional broker-dealer is always in the position of Avis, compared to the giants of the securities industry, the Hertzes. We not only have to try harder, but we also have to do better to compete. For instance, we often are required to supply a much more in-depth analysis of a stock and a company than the widely followed research of a national firm. We also

often must supply a quote superior to that of the national firms to attract order flow.

What particularly keeps the regional market maker on its toes is the firm's retail clientele. In our trading operations, the retail client and our account executives come first.

Our clients and account executives are never disadvantaged by a principal transaction in a security in which we make a market. To ensure this, we follow two basic principles in our market making:

- We obtain best execution for the clients' accounts. This means that our clients never pay more or receive less than they would have paid or received had we acted as agent with another market maker in the security. In reality, we strive for a trade in which the firm's client pays less or receives more.
- We offer our account executives a fair and competitive sales credit (or commission). We never ask an account executive to execute a trade on a principal basis in a security in which we make a market and receive less than the normal agency commission.

3. **We can compete because of NASDAQ.** Before NASDAQ, when the "pink sheets" and the telephone were the only means of communication in the OTC market, regional firms had to fight for recognition. They had little visibility, and the order flow went to the big-name firms.

Once NASDAQ began operation, the regionals could display their prices on the screen, nationwide, alongside the prices of the giants. This allowed individuals and institutions to find out who we were, to start paying attention to us and to start dealing with us. Almost overnight, the financial community became aware of the viable and strong market-making community which the regionals constitute—and we were off to the races.

The Markets We Make

Today, Johnston, Lemon makes markets in some 70 NASDAQ securities, and most of them are NASDAQ/NMS securities. They include many local banks, technology firms and service companies. However, because we are visible on NASDAQ, we also trade securities from all over the country—from Clearwater, Florida, Ann Arbor, Michigan, Clovis, New Mexico, and Seattle, Washington, to name just a few.

I won't trade a stock unless I can make an institutional-quality market in it. I can't run the risk of offering second-class merchandise—stock that is not competitively priced. Nor can I trade in small size and have to tell clients I can't handle a 10,000- to 20,000-share buy or sell. If I don't make institutional quality markets, people are going to stop calling me. And I can be profitable in a stock only if I can capture a significant portion of the order flow in it.

Tomorrow—To the Top

The NASD gave our visibility another boost in 1984 when it introduced the Small Order Execution System (SOES). Through SOES, people see even more of our market-maker identifier, JOLE, on the screen. After completing several SOES trades—up to the SOES 1,000-share limit—and obtaining good execution, they start calling us for the 10,000-share orders.

Competition for order flow among market makers has always existed but today there is the very real threat of competition from yet another source, the stock exchanges.

Stock exchanges historically have traded only those securities "listed" on their exchanges. But today, due largely to the dynamic growth of the NASDAQ market, many exchanges are preparing to move outside their walls and trade the most active NASDAQ securities. Exchange quotations usually include the size of both the bid and ask. (Size is the amount of shares to be purchased or sold.) Regional market makers are, as always, prepared to compete and if size display becomes commonplace, it will, in my opinion, be a major plus for the regional firms who can then "advertise" on a firm basis the true depth of their markets and go right to the top of the market, not only in this country but in the world.

NASDAQ SECURITIES AND MARKET MAKERS
1977-1986

Year	No. of Securities	Active Market Makers	Market-Making Positions	Average Market Makers Per Security
1986	5,189	526	41,312	8.0
1985	4,784	500	40,093	8.4
1984	4,723	459	38,739	8.2
1983	4,467	441	32,923	7.4
1982	3,664	407	27,734	7.6
1981	3,687	420	26,935	7.4
1980	3,050	394	22,360	7.3
1979	2,670	364	21,768	8.2
1978	2,582	355	19,898	7.7
1977	2,575	353	19,479	7.6

MARKET-VALUE DISTRIBUTION
ACCORDING TO NUMBER OF MARKET MAKERS

Market Makers	NASDAQ/NMS		Total NASDAQ	
	Issues	Average Market Value ($000s)	Issues	Average Market Value ($000s)
Less than 3	72	39,477	313	27,198
3-5	777	63,330	1,764	34,560
6-10	1,010	85,175	1,878	50,851
11-15	497	133,508	801	91,720
16-20	207	261,953	283	200,423
21-25	70	352,428	81	314,426
26 or more	62	643,311	69	605,164

NASDAQ MARKET MAKERS
(As of December 31, 1986)

States by Number of Market Makers		States in Alphabetical Order	
State	**Market Makers**	**State**	**Market Makers**
New York	206	Alabama	5
California	37	Arizona	4
Colorado	30	Arkansas	2
New Jersey	26	California	37
Minnesota	19	Colorado	30
Illinois	16	Connecticut	6
Pennsylvania	16	District of Columbia	4
Florida	15	Florida	15
Texas	14	Georgia	5
Massachusetts	13	Illinois	16
Missouri	13	Indiana	4
Utah	13	Iowa	1
Michigan	12	Kansas	3
Ohio	11	Kentucky	1
Washington	9	Louisiana	2
Virginia	8	Maryland	5
Connecticut	6	Massachusetts	13
Alabama	5	Michigan	12
Georgia	5	Minnesota	19
Maryland	5	Missouri	13
Oregon	5	Montana	1
Tennessee	5	Nebraska	1
Arizona	4	Nevada	1
District of Columbia	4	New Jersey	26
Indiana	4	New Mexico	1
Wisconsin	4	New York	206
Kansas	3	North Carolina	3
North Carolina	3	Ohio	11
Oklahoma	3	Oklahoma	3
Arkansas	2	Oregon	5
Louisiana	2	Pennsylvania	16
Rhode Island	2	Rhode Island	2
Iowa	1	Tennessee	5
Kentucky	1	Texas	14
Montana	1	Utah	13
Nebraska	1	Virginia	8
Nevada	1	Washington	9
New Mexico	1	Wisconsin	4
TOTAL	**526**	**TOTAL**	**526**

Chapter nineteen

*P*eter J. DaPuzzo has been involved in OTC trading for nearly 30 years. As the Senior Executive Vice President of Shearson Lehman Brothers, Inc., he heads one of the largest over-the-counter trading departments on Wall Street. He is also responsible for all retail equity trading for the firm, including listed securities, options, convertibles and international equities.

The Drama of Market Making in a National Full-Line Firm

by Peter J. DaPuzzo

In 1986, Shearson Lehman Brothers renamed its over-the-counter operation the National Market System Department to identify ourselves with the top tier of the over-the-counter market and to recognize the growth of this technologically advanced segment of the NASDAQ market.

Our NMS Department makes a market in more than 2,800 stocks and expects to reach 3,500 securities by 1990. This large roster of issues comes from our investment banking activities, our research and requests from our sales force.

We usually make a minimum of 5,000-share markets in everything we trade with our retail and institutional clients. In 200 to 300 of the stocks we trade, we are constantly trying to buy and sell blocks of 200,000 to 300,000 shares.

On the retail side, we allow our markets to be held out on AES, an automatic execution system through which we will buy or sell a maximum of 2,000 shares. Clients can enter an order anywhere—New York, Paris or Hong Kong—to buy or sell any security in which we make a market, and their orders are executed instantaneously.

We commit more than $120 million in capital. While this represents less than 5 percent of the $2+billion in capital that Shearson Lehman Brothers has at its disposal, we contribute a much larger percentage of the firm's revenue stream. We create about 15 percent of retail revenue stream, the second largest contribution in a firm with over 200 products and 5,600 financial consultants. We generated over $302 million in OTC revenue in 1986. Our target is to create $500 million in principal revenue and $150 million in agency commissions by 1990, with a capital commitment that would approach $200 million.

In 1986, we estimate that we executed about 11 percent of the 28.7 billion shares traded on NASDAQ, or 3.2 billion shares.

Managing an Over-the-Counter Department

The secret of effective management in a large over-the-counter trading department is maintaining close contact with employees, fostering a friendly atmosphere and keeping all employees involved in the growth of the department. It involves centralized and decentralized management.

Centralized management at Shearson Lehman Brothers' NMS Department is the responsibility of the NMS Planning Group, which includes nine senior staff members who meet weekly to discuss department policies and procedures. Each person represents a different specialty or area of the department. This management team helps me stay in touch with the many members of our staff in New York and around the world. Even with all the time I spend on the trading desk, they are my eyes and ears.

Decentralized management is practiced by our trading groups, where a senior market maker oversees the activities of one or two junior market makers and two or three assistants. Each trading group has one profit-and-loss statement, which fosters a team effort in the trading of 100 to 150 securities. Each group also serves as a training ground for younger members of the department, who after two to three years of serving as junior market makers may become senior market makers and later team leaders themselves.

Relationships, Relationships, Relationships

Successful trading is a product of the people who trade. It's a people business. My most valuable assets walk out the door—sometimes run—at 5 p.m. or so every day. And the people who generate tickets—our 5,600 retail and institutional financial consultants—also have to be treated as valuable friends and clients. At Shearson Lehman Brothers, we consider ourselves partners with our sales force; our profitability and credibility are tied to their profitability and credibility.

That's why I emphasize to my senior market makers, juniors and assistants that cementing relationships with the sales force is crucial to their success and to the department's success. In essence, my staff has to do what any successful sales force does daily. It has to prospect for new accounts, maintain and improve existing accounts, and periodically visit all accounts, even in-house accounts.

Marketing managers and liaisons visit branches, host regional road shows and participate in divisional conferences. Institutional sales traders and market makers host lunches, dinners and conferences for other traders, salesmen and accounts throughout the country. We entertain, we educate and otherwise keep ourselves visible. I try to talk to all of our accounts, our salesmen and branch managers at least once a quarter or more often. I talk to the press and have been quoted frequently and featured in major periodicals, television programs and radio shows. It's all a part of keeping our name in front of our clients, the sales force and the investing public.

Having strong relationships with the firm's investment banking, research and executive services (144) departments has also been a factor behind our firm's success in over-the-counter trading. We work with our investment bankers before we bring a deal public. As member of the firm's Equity Marketing Committee, for example, I provide feedback on potential retail and institutional demand for a security before we bring it public or bring out a secondary offering. I also help our investment bankers attract corporate clients by meeting the management of potential client companies. Management representatives tour our trading floor and see first-hand the size and scope of our operation. My top trading manager or I personally trade all initial public offerings on the first one or two days, as this period is crucial for the success of the new issue. After the initial offering, the NMS Department maintains contact with the investment banking and syndicate department to provide early after-market support for our corporate clients.

We also work closely with our research department. Shearson has five research departments and more than 80 analysts headquartered in New York, Atlanta, San Francisco, Seattle, London and Tokyo. Maintaining close contact with these analysts and their ideas requires a special effort. We keep in touch by utilizing our divisional traders and liaisons, by attending all research meetings and presentations, and by reading and distributing to our market makers all research on the securities we trade.

Often our market makers and analysts go to dinner to get to know each other and their crafts in a quiet and relaxed atmosphere. In 1986, when the Statue of Liberty was rechristened, we rented a yacht and invited our research department on a mid-day cruise to watch "Operation Sail" in New York Harbor. In turn, we ask analysts to call and otherwise keep us abreast of developments in their industries and the companies they follow. We view our relationship with research and investment banking much the same as our relationship with our retail and institutional sales force. We are partners, and we continually want to improve and expand the partnership.

Shearson's NMS Department coordinates its marketing activities through its National Sales and Marketing Group. Together, we generate brochures, advertisements and marketing campaigns to promote our over-the-counter trading strength. For instance, when we renamed our trading operation, the National Sales and Marketing Group developed a full page ad that ran in *The New York Times* and *The Wall Street Journal*. The advertisement offered readers the opportunity to write or call for a brochure about the NASDAQ National Market System. Ten thousand calls and letters came in the first day, giving our sales force 10,000 new prospects.

Of course, we have to be careful when talking to other departments. We don't share secrets, trade on rumors, or front-run recommendations. If there is a question of legality, we turn to our attorneys or outside counsel.

How Are Stocks Selected for Market Making?

When selecting issues to add to our list of 2,800 securities, we adhere to a number of guidelines. First, we want to know if our firm will be a factor in the stock. Will a research analyst be following this stock? Do our investment bankers have a relationship with the company? Does a salesperson in the field have a contact in management at the company, or is regional interest strong in the stock? If an issue meets most of these criteria, we are ready to consider it for market making.

The next test an issue must pass is quality. Stocks in which we will make a market should be selling over $3 per share and have merit as a potential investment for our clients. We look to see if other quality market makers are trading the issue.

Some market makers will trade a stock that has a high beta, which means the stock is volatile. A volatile stock may swing 4 or 5 percent of its price every day—for a $50 stock, that could mean 2½ points. We call high-beta stocks "animals," meaning they are hard to control and demand a lot of market-maker attention. If a market maker trades 30 to 50 issues, one high-beta stock may lead to trading losses. Stocks that are quiet, dull and don't trade very much could create more profit in the long run.

If our corporate finance department is bringing a company public, we must make a market in the stock. This is one of the largest sources of new issues for our market makers because our firm has a constant flow of new issues or secondaries.

The other factor we consider when deciding whether to trade an issue is the "blue sky" status of the stock. Blue-sky laws are state laws that require issuers of stock to register their offerings and provide financial data. The state will then determine if the stock can be sold in that state on a solicited basis (a salesperson asks a client for the order) or an unsolicited basis (the client asks the salesperson to buy the stock). If a security is not "blue-skied" in many states, we would not be interested in making a market in the stock.

When Shearson Lehman Brothers (SAXP) becomes a market maker, we stay in the stock for at least three months. Generally, however, when we go into a stock we remain a market maker for a long time.

The Trading Process: Training Traders

Our firm trains traders through the team approach, which allows junior and assistant market makers, as well as clerks, to work under the supervision of a senior market maker. It also allows our clerks, assistants and juniors to teach a thing or two to our senior market makers. Many of these younger people have M.B.A.s or other degrees, while most traders who began in the late '50s and early '60s came straight out of high school. Old-time traders often trade stocks with little more knowledge of the company than its name and stock symbol; they trade by "feel" of the stock or its group. They have innate trading ability and street smarts. Our younger clerks, assistants and junior market makers may have been trained in economics or security analysis. They also may be adept with computers.

Therefore, beyond keeping books and records for a senior market maker and possibly trading a small list of stocks, younger assistants watch and analyze news and economic developments that may affect the stocks their group trades. They read analyst reports and keep our senior market makers abreast of changes in opinion.

Before new staff members even sit at a desk, they have to work in the back office for several weeks or months. They spend time on the agency desk to get a feeling of what it's like to buy and sell securities from others when they don't make a market. Next, a new employee moves to the belt system to get familiar with how orders come in, how they go out and how we process them. Then, when the clerk sits with a senior market maker, he or she listens, watches, and asks questions for weeks and months.

I can generally tell within the first few weeks whether a clerk or assistant has the ability to be a trader. If an assistant works hard, thinks fast and is quick with numbers, he or she may make it but not without a steep learning curve. After several months, he or she will join a senior trader as an assistant. If things work well and the assistant trader keeps up on changes on his or her machine, remembers phone messages and quotes, processes orders quickly, and watches the news and research on the market maker's list of stocks, it may be time to move up. Typically, an assistant trader is on the job no less than two years before assuming responsibilities such as making position bids and committing capital.

Another key to effective trading is the ability to "see" both sides of a transaction: to think and act like both a buyer and a seller. It has a lot to do with psychology, being able to talk a buyer or seller into making a trade at one price while he or she wants a different one. It involves convincing the buyer or seller that this trade should be done now, at this price and with this trader.

Psychology is very important. In fact, on resumes of young traders, I look to see if they have taken any psychology courses or had any business dealings with people across a counter. Convincing a person who wants something but can't make up his mind is the key to selling and trading. A good salesperson, and a good trader, will help a buyer make that decision to buy.

When I entered the business, I was a runner, taking messages from building to building. I posted for senior traders. At 19, I began filling in for senior traders when they were on vacation. When I was 20, I was so eager to be a market maker, I was jumping out of my skin. I wasn't old enough to get registered, however; you had to be 21. My strengths were in the areas discussed: quick with numbers, aware of the movement in stocks, and a flair for creating urgency and excitement in a trade. I suppose that's why my department's training is structured the way it is—it worked for me.

For continuing education, traders must read everything that is available on the stocks they trade, the market and the industry. Industry periodicals, such as *Investment Dealers' Digest* and *OTC Review*, are required reading. Daily newspapers, such as *The Wall Street Journal*, *Investor's Daily* and

The New York Times, keep a trader in touch with company and industry developments.

For a successful market maker, the day doesn't close with the market at 4 p.m. Market makers should be active in trade associations, such as the Security Traders Association of New York and the National Security Traders Association. They should volunteer to be on NASD subcommittees and Securities Industry Association committees. This lets traders have a voice in development of the industry. It also gives the firm representation in the industry and provides another source of continuing education for senior and junior market makers.

Before the Market Opens

The market may open at 9:30, but a sharp market maker's day starts at about 7 a.m. At this time, a market maker reads the morning newspapers. He or she studies the previous day's trading activity in the stock listings. Did the firm participate in much of the volume in the over-the-counter market? And more important, did the market maker participate in the volume in the stocks he or she trades? If not, the market maker checks on the Autex, a computerized advertisement system to find who traded the big blocks. With that information, the buyer or the seller from yesterday can be located today: There might be more to buy or sell.

The market maker also looks for any discernible trends in the market. For instance, were insurance, savings and loan or technology stocks strong as a group the day before and, if so, will that trend continue today? Were earnings released for any of the stocks he or she trades? Were they better than expected, worse than expected, or in line with analysts' estimates, and how will the stock react today?

A market maker should next look at yesterday's profit-and-loss statement before trading begins. Does the position tally for today coincide with what the market maker thought he or she had the previous night? Is the market maker long or short and, if so, how long or short in each stock? Does he want to be as long or short as he is? If not, positions must be adjusted during the trading day.

Much of the trading process involves technology. A great deal of automation has been introduced in the over-the-counter market during the last several years. The NASD Small Order Execution System (SOES) allows broker-dealers to trade up to 1,000 shares at the best bid or lowest offer automatically, without human intervention. Most major firms also use AES, an automatic execution system that executes internal orders of up to 2,000 shares from retail salespeople.

By providing an automatic market in stocks to broker-dealers, institutional and retail clients, traders can find themselves with sizable positions they may or may not want to own. I tell my traders they should make up their minds minute to minute—and certainly hourly—about which stocks they wish to be short or long in. The morning is the most important time to check positions, but market makers must stay aware of their automatic trading systems and positions throughout the day.

Meetings, Meetings, Meetings

At about 8 a.m., the research and trading meetings begin. In a conference room at headquarters, block traders, institutional salespeople, research analysts, market technicians and investment strategists report on the previous day's trading activity. They also discuss today's buying and selling interest, market and economic developments, and specific recommendations. This discussion is broadcast throughout the firm, in New York and at 360 regional and international branches. Any piece of news—a new recommendation, a favorable or negative economic report, or an institutional buying program that includes over-the-counter stocks—can affect a market maker's list of stocks and may affect the looks of the profit-and-loss statement at the end of the trading day.

The over-the-counter traders meet at 8:45 with regional trading offices connected to New York on a conference call. We exchange ideas for today, discuss yesterday's activity and update market makers on departmental news. This is another forum for continuing education, and market makers learn from the mistakes and successes of the day before.

At about 9 a.m., market makers move to their trading turrets. They examine every order left from the previous day, regardless of how far away in potential transaction price it might seem to be at the time, and call salesmen and other firms to renew orders. Yesterday's tough trade may get easier when the market opens and the stock moves into range.

At 9:15, the morning product call begins. Our national sales manager, along with sales managers from most other product areas in the firm, relays to our retail sales force what occurred in the markets yesterday, what is expected today and what special offerings are available this morning.

"We can offer 50,000 ABCD at 9¾ net, with a ½ point sales credit," the sales manager may tell our 5,600 salespeople. That means that a market maker is offering to sell to the sales force, at the opening and during the morning, 50,000 shares of ABCD at a price that is better than the best offer quoted on the screen. Clients and salespeople would typically have to buy a stock at the offer, plus a mark-up (much like a commission). With morning specials, our sales force earns larger sales credits, equivalent to the ½ point the firm offers, while the client pays the offered price of 9¾.

The Trading Process Begins

At about 9:25, the noise level begins to increase in the room. Telephones begin to ring, with early indications of where stocks may be headed and who's doing the buying or selling today. At 9:30, the room explodes with energy. The 120-button banks of telephone wires connecting Shearson Lehman's market makers with market makers and retail traders at other firms and institutional clients around the country light up, almost in unison.

Assistants picking up telephones begin relaying bids and offers to market makers. Retail and institutional salespeople begin to phone in large orders to retail and institutional liaisons, while smaller, routine orders are entered over the automatic execution system. The overhead intercom begins to sound off with questions and trading commentary. "George, pick up Troster" (asking a market maker to pick up his or her counterpart at another firm); "59½ bid, 1,000 EFGH, bought stock away" (meaning another broker-dealer wants to purchase 1,000 EFGH at 59½ and has already bought some away from our firm); "no automatics, LMNO" (meaning no automatic executions will be accepted on LMNO because the stock may be opening much higher or lower today).

The silent salesmen, as automatic trading systems like the Small Order Execution System and Instinet are known, are also at work as trading begins. Indications of interest and offers to buy and sell stocks blip on the screens in front of market makers. Their eyes are glued to SOES for automatic executions, the NASDAQ terminal for current markets and volume in their stocks, the Dow Jones Newswire for news and headlines and five other screens of trading and market information that can be called up in quadrants on a screen. The telephone keeps ringing.

Calls are going out as fast as they come in. A block of 750,000 shares of BCDE is available; the market is $15 bid-$15¼ offer. The market maker and I determine that we could probably buy the block at $14½, a discount to the market because of the large size of the block.

Should We Get Involved?

We next determine whether the firm should get involved in the trade. Is the stock attractive at this price? A call goes to the firm's technical analyst: "Does the technical price chart look right, with support for the stock near the current bid?" A call is made to the analyst who follows the stock: "Would the analyst recommend the stock at this time? Could any news on the near-term horizon affect the stock?" Before the firm commits its capital at risk by buying BCDE, we want to limit our risk by assessing the timeliness of the offering. The technician and the analyst like BCDE, and we move to the next step.

Shearson Lehman starts to "shop" the BCDE block. Time is of the essence because a large block of BCDE for sale could pressure the stock price lower if the Street sees it is not quickly snapped up by buyers. Institutional sales traders call their trading counterparts at institutions. Would they like to buy BCDE? A computerized listing can be called up showing institutions currently holding BCDE, or any given security, as of the past 30 days. This allows us to "know where the bodies lie" in a stock. A call goes out to the company to see if it would like to repurchase the block. Retail liaisons on the over-the-counter desk call retail salespeople whose clients hold BCDE; once again we have technology that can tell us at the press of a button "where the bodies lie."

Our national sales managers initiate a call on the internal radio network connecting New York with the 360 branches, featuring the research analyst who covers BCDE going over the sales points on the stock and discussing the probable terms of the offering. Occasionally, another market maker involved in the stock calls to indicate he or she has some interest in BCDE. And the silent salesman is put into play, as the firm advertises to institutions on the Instinet, Autex or Bridge system that 750,000 BCDE are about to trade. (These systems connect market makers with institutions around the country.)

The market maker, working with institutional and retail liaisons, begins to build a book of indications for BCDE. An institution is interested in buying 100,000 BCDE but only at $14⅜, or ⅝ below the bid. Retail liaisons have indications for 450,000 BCDE from 150 salespeople at $14½. A bid for 150,000 BCDE appears on Instinet at $14⅜.

The book has been built to 700,000 shares of BCDE. The size of the block is 750,000 shares. Although the firm will be left with a 50,000-share position in BCDE after the trade, the market maker can justify the risk of 50,000 shares in a large 750,000 share trade. The market maker calls the seller, bidding $14⅜ for the BCDE shares. "Sold," says the seller.

Institutional and retail liaisons move fast to contact those salespeople and accounts who gave indications on BCDE. Retail interest could build now that we have bought the block at $14⅜, below the $14½ price mentioned while soliciting indications. Therefore, the remaining 50,000 may also be easily sold.

Other Buying Decisions

The BCDE trade could be one of a dozen or more large special offerings in which our firm is involved on any given day. Smaller trades of 100 to 100,000 shares make up the remainder of the 9,000 tickets that are written in the department on an average day.

Buying decisions could involve an existing purchase order that we have received from an institution or retail sales-person. Market makers often take positions to facilitate sell orders, even if there are no buyers of the stock. In these cases, the market maker puts capital at risk by buying the block of stock from the seller and holding it in inventory until a buyer or buyers for the stock can be located. We routinely put capital at risk for blocks worth $500,000 or less. For larger blocks, the firm will put its capital at risk if the seller is a valuable account with which we do regular business. Even if the firm loses money on a trade, we know that over a year, the order flow generated by an account will more than offset any one loss on a trade. These decisions are based upon the quality and importance of the client.

A market maker will almost always buy several thousand shares of stock from a retail seller even though there may not be an immediate outside bidder to whom he or she can sell the stock. This is because the NMS/OTC department operates as a service center for retail and institutional salespeople and clients. The stock may have been recommended by our research department. It may be a corporate client that our investment bankers brought public. Even though money may be lost on the trade, we have to service our sales force and clients efficiently.

What Traders Learn From the Screen

A NASDAQ terminal allows market makers to view all bids and offers for a stock, as well as to input their markets in a stock. The trader can often tell who the major players are in any stock, by seeing who consistently has the highest bid and lowest offer on the screen. For each stock they trade, market makers should know which firm was the underwriter (brought the company public or managed secondary offerings of securities) and which firms have research coverage. Knowing this, a market maker will know which firms can possibly have an "axe" (a major buying or selling interest), even if that firm doesn't show up on NASDAQ as the high bid or low seller. A NASDAQ screen shows a market maker's up-to-the-minute trading data for all NASDAQ National Market System securities, including last-sale prices, high and low prices for the day, and current volume.

Instinet is another on-screen service that a market maker watches during the day. It links market makers with more than 100 major financial institutions and 300 broker-dealers throughout the United States and Europe. Anonymous negotiations take place between sellers and buyers. Only after a transaction is complete will a market maker learn the identity of the buyer or seller, and both the buyer and seller pay a fee to Instinet for using the system. This permits institutional investors to deal with other firms and market makers without prejudice. The only concern is making the trade at the best price for all parties.

Autex is somewhat like Instinet. On the Autex Trading Information System, market makers see the flow of block trading in their stocks. They advertise (list) executions of blocks. This real-time computer network links more than 800 broker-dealers and institutional investors. Market makers can often locate the other side of a trade by advertising their interests in blocks. Institutions see buyers and sellers without exposing their interests.

Autex also offers market makers historical files of indicated and executed trades. They see the number of shares and blocks having been traded. In essence, Autex is an advertisement of interest: Traders can decide to buy or sell before any transaction takes place.

Bridge Data, another on-screen service, provides on-line software that can call up, for example, stock price charts for recent days, months or years. These charts can show price and volume trends in a security over a given time period. With this information, market makers make technical timing decisions. They may buy or sell based on the chart, which can reveal technical support and breakout points. Employed in conjunction with fundamental data that can be called up on the screen—such as earnings results, estimates and dividends—Bridge can facilitate the decision to buy or sell a stock.

Finally, another on-screen system traders use is the Quotron System. Quotron has Market Minder, a screen that allows a trader to monitor the trading activity of stocks he or she chooses. Traders can call up any stock by symbol to see its latest trade. They can view recent and past news stories that appear on the Dow Jones Newswire. The stocks that are on Market Minder flash when a trade has occurred, changing the price, and an asterisk appears when a news story affecting the stock has been reported on the Dow Jones Newswire. Quotron also features a service from Computer Directions Advisers, which lists all institutional holders of a stock (institutions are required to file this information 30 days after purchase). Market makers can also see on Quotron current news headlines and a great deal of statistical data, such as 52-week high and low prices.

At Shearson Lehman, we have eliminated the need for traders to turn from screen to screen during the trading day. All of these services—NASDAQ, Instinet, Bridge Data and Quotron—are available on one screen. Market makers can view four of these services at one time because the screen is divided into quadrants. One keyboard can control all four screens and, in fact, it can allow access to four additional screens if necessary.

Trading on the Telephone

Even with all the technological developments and on-screen trading tools, the telephone still plays an invaluable role in negotiating transactions. There is nothing like a one-on-one conversation with a retail or institutional salesperson to convince him or her that a stock is a timely trade. While institutions can deal with us through the Autex or Instinet systems, our sales-traders and salespeople can generate many times more volume than our "silent salesmen" by talking with accounts over the telephone.

Shearson Lehman's institutional sales traders in the OTC area have private lines connected with more than 300 institutional accounts throughout the country. Our market makers each have private telephone wires to well over 100 broker-dealers throughout the country. Automatic systems can handle smaller trades, but it is necessary to negotiate larger transactions over the telephone.

Negotiating means not just doing trades on the bid and ask. More than 70 percent of large transactions are done away from the inside market because of the size of these blocks and the capital risk our firm takes in buying such a large position. We negotiate these trades primarily over the telephone, although we can also negotiate via computer.

A typical conversation between a market maker and a retail trader or institutional client could go like this:

Retail (or institutional) trader: "I see you are 10 bid on ABCD. I also see that another firm is 10 bid away from you. (Two market makers are willing to buy ABCD at 10.) But I have a good relationship with you. I'll offer you 10,000 shares at 10; can you use them?"

Market maker: "Thanks for the preference (for calling me). Let me buy a couple of thousand shares now and call you back on the rest right away. I need to call my buyer." (Of course, if he has a big order in hand, the market maker would just say "Buy it, thanks.")

The market maker calls his potential buyer, who could be an institutional account, a retail salesman or another brokerage firm. The company itself may be the buyer. If the market maker connects with a buyer who agrees to purchase the stock, the deal is completed.

Market maker: "I buy that 10,000 shares at 10. Thank you."

A transaction has been completed. If the stock is part of the NASDAQ National Market System, the market maker then reports the price and size of the transaction on his NASDAQ screen within 90 seconds of the actual transaction.

Evaluating the Competition

Every market maker is in competition with other market makers. All are trying at different times to locate the same sellers and buyers, and one may outbid other market makers to get the order.

Market makers tend to evaluate their competition by past experience. Reputations take years to build. As a breed, market makers are professional. They can handle themselves under pressure. You come to know who the seasoned professionals are in any one stock or in general.

A market maker earns respect by being competitive and consistent. Being competitive means that a market maker will buy and sell at the best prices, even if the trade does not fit, or will come back with a counter-proposal that makes sense. As a result of having a good reputation, a market maker will often receive preference calls even if he or she is not high bid or low offer. Being consistent simply means that in good markets and bad, a market maker sticks by his or her word with clients. For example, if the firm is an investment banker or has research coverage for a stock and the market maker agrees to take all clients' orders in that stock, consistently sticking to that promise is essential to remaining credible and professional.

A market maker will never—ever—hurt a caller by running ahead of an order. If an account wants to buy 100,000 shares of ABCD, the market maker may say he cannot accommodate the trade. Why? Because he or she may be short the stock, may have another buy order, or may have a long position that he or she wants to maintain and not sell to the account. If the market maker then goes into the market as a buyer of ABCD, this is known as running ahead of the order; it hinders the customer in completing a transaction by beating him into the Street to buy the stock.

A good market maker practices consistency and competitiveness, but the best market makers practice creativity. A creative trader knows all the places to turn to transact a buy or sell order. For example, an account may call a market maker with an order to buy 100,000 shares of a stock that may not have traded much in the past several weeks. The first step is not necessarily to go high bid on NASDAQ; the creative market maker will advertise interest in the stock on Instinet and Autex. He or she would then look to create sellers. A call could go to an investment banker, who together with the market maker could call management and other insiders at the firm: Would they like to sell some of their holdings?

The creative market maker might have to convince the parties that selling their 144 holdings would be positive, as the institutional buyer's order would be filled, rather than leaving the buyer disgruntled and potentially losing interest in a stock that could not be purchased in sufficient size. The market maker may call other holders and suggest they sell the stock, offering another similar stock as a substitute.

In the case of a large sell order with no substantial buying interest at the current bid, a creative market maker might assure the seller that an order will be executed, although the price cannot be guaranteed. The market maker might begin to sell a portion of the order, allowing the stock to find the level at which it can trade (the price at which buying interest begins to appear). A creative trader would then become a patient seller of the stock; instead of dumping the position at the new low bid, he or she would negotiate the sale of the stock at a somewhat higher price. The trader would have to know the trading activity of the stock before attempting this, however, because there is the risk of "breaking" the stock to lower prices, which would bring out more sellers.

Another part of evaluating the competition is knowing the strengths and weaknesses of competing organizations as well as individuals. Integrated houses, such as Shearson Lehman, have the advantage of investment banking relationships, research coverage, large retail sales networks and institutional clients. Investment banking houses have strong relationships with their corporate clients; their buyers and sellers will primarily consist of institutional accounts. Regional firms, such as William Blair in Chicago and Robinson Humphrey in Atlanta, have localized investment banking and research efforts; they typically have hands-on relationships with their corporate clients. Wholesalers, such as Troster Singer and Herzog Heine, Geduld, have a high profile in, and close contact with, the broker-dealer community.

Making Markets: A Long-Term Commitment

When we decide to make a market in a stock, it's a long-term decision. We scrutinize stocks carefully and therefore expect to trade them for a long time. If a stock becomes inactive or highly volatile, we may change market makers, as each has a different style. For instance, some are better with active stocks, while others trade inactive stocks well. We discontinue making a market only when a company is taken over, goes out of business or otherwise disappears from the NASDAQ market.

The Future of Market Making

I believe the NASDAQ market and negotiated trading over electronic networks will be the dominant forms of trading in the future. Talented, intuitive and creative market makers will always be necessary because computers will never replace the human mind and feeling in this industry.

As I said at the outset, our firm now makes markets in 2,800 securities, and by 1990, we expect to make markets in 3,500. We have room in New York for 12 more market makers on the trading desk, and we have room for another 12 in our regional locations. In London and Tokyo, another 25 market makers could be employed before 1990.

With "Big Bang" in London creating a principal market-making capability, the concept of a global marketplace has moved a step closer to reality. London's Stock Exchange Automated Quotations system already connects with the NASDAQ System, and it is only a matter of time before more international markets are connected electronically. This will create the need for expanding our market-making capabilities in the U.S. and abroad. We have already begun to distribute research from our U.K. subsidiary, L. Messel & Co., and we make markets in more than 500 international securities.

As I said before, my department in 1986 committed about $100 million in capital to over-the-counter trading and generated about $300 million in sales credits and agency commissions. By 1990, capital commitment should increase to about $200 million, while sales credits and agency commissions should top $500 million.

As a firm, Shearson Lehman is committed to increasing the size of our sales force by 50 to 100 percent. Given the growth in our distribution channels, as well as the increase in U.S. and international investment banking and research, I may well have to exceed my budgeted additions to staff. I may also—hopefully—exceed my revenue projections for this period.

PART V
NASDAQ as a National Economic Institution

PART V

Chapter
twenty

James H. Lorie is the Eli B. and Harriet B. Williams Professor of Business Administration at the Graduate School of Business at the University of Chicago. Dr. Lorie has written extensively on marketing, consumer spending and business finance and served as a consultant to many governmental and private agencies.

Economic Efficiency
and NASDAQ

by James H. Lorie

We are now deluged with news of movements in stock prices. Newspapers, radios, television sets, and even recorded phone messages tell us almost continuously what is happening to "the market." It would be understandable if the nearly 50 million people who own stocks in this country became so preoccupied with short-term fluctuations in their wealth that they lost sight of the purpose of organized markets. Their primary purpose is to reduce the cost of transacting. Reducing this cost is obviously important to investors; less obvious, perhaps, is its importance to the economy as a whole. This general importance stems from the fact that a reduction in the cost of buying and selling securities makes them more liquid and hence more valuable and thereby reduces the cost of capital for the corporations (or governments) which issue them. And this reduction in the cost of capital makes it possible to build more plants, roads and other durable facilities and to buy more equipment, or to do these things more cheaply. Everyone benefits.

A second important function of organized markets is to determine the prices of securities. These prices determine the cost of capital for issuers of securities and channel investors' funds to various enterprises in accordance with their risk and promise of gain.

347

By any international standard of comparison, our principal securities markets are very efficient in performing their functions of reducing transaction costs. Thus, they decrease our cost of capital below that which would exist with the relatively inefficient markets of many countries and appear to achieve an economic allocation of resources. The cost of capital in the United States is almost certainly significantly higher than in Japan, but this American disadvantage is attributable to our tax on capital gains.

There are many organized markets for securities in the United States. The two largest stock markets are the New York Stock Exchange (NYSE) and NASDAQ. The NYSE is much larger and older; NASDAQ is more technologically advanced and rapidly growing. They are organized in different ways and operate according to different principles.

The central problem of any market is to bring buyers and sellers together so that a seller has a chance to deal with the buyer making the highest bid, and a buyer has a chance to deal with the seller making the lowest offer. The NYSE solves this problem by having all bids and offers come together at specialist posts. "Specialists" are persons or firms who are given franchises, which in practice have amounted to monopolies, to match orders to buy and sell specified stocks. Brokers with orders from customers converge at the posts of specialists and either deal with each other or with the specialist, who can act as a dealer and buy or sell for his own account or act as a broker on behalf of a customer. In exchange for a monopoly, specialists take on affirmative and negative obligations designed to protect the public investor. Perhaps the most important of these obligations is to provide instant liquidity by buying or selling for their own account when there is an imbalance in the flow of public orders to buy and sell. Other obligations are to preserve an "orderly" market, maintain reasonable spreads between bids and offers and execute public orders ahead of their own.

The NASDAQ System solves the problem of bringing buyers and sellers together in a totally different way. Instead of relying on monopolists with obligations designed to protect the public, NASDAQ relies on competition. The competition is between dealers, called market makers, who buy for and sell from their own inventories.

In discussing the way in which NASDAQ contributes to economic efficiency, it will be useful to compare the different ways in which it and the NYSE solve the basic problem of organized markets—bringing buyers and sellers together. Before doing that, however, a benchmark for both modes of organization can be provided by describing an ideal market.

An Ideal Market for Stocks

Unconstrained by reality, it is easy to describe an ideal market. It would deal with the component problems of organizing a market as follows:

Information. Investors would be quickly, cheaply, completely and accurately informed about all the factors pertinent to making an investment decision. This information would deal with facts about the issuers of securities as well as facts about the market. Among the former would be data on earnings, dividends, orders, shipments, product development and the myriad other details that affect a company's future prosperity; among the latter would be data on prices, bids and offers, and trading volume. The optimum frequency and substance of the flow of information may vary for different securities and the ideal market will accommodate such differences.

Equity. Notions of equity are necessarily subjective, but there is a strong consensus as to what constitutes equity in a financial transaction: The consummation of a transaction should depend exclusively on its terms rather than on the characteristics of the persons doing the transacting. As a matter of law, we do not discriminate with respect to color, creed, sex or age. Perfect equity in financial transactions requires that we go further and renounce discrimination based on factors such as location, the size of the transaction, the historical business or personal relationships which often do not have an economic significance. The only things that should matter are the price at which the investor is willing to transact and the time at which he makes his commitment.

For convenience, this principle is called "price-time priority." A higher bidder gets stock before someone making a lower bid, and a lower offeror makes the sale before a higher offeror. If two bidders or offerors are willing to transact at the same price, the one who made the commitment first takes precedence, whether the bid/offer is that of "Aunt Jane," a large institution or a professional dealer.

Efficiency. "Efficiency" is used in two senses. In the first, the word refers to the cost and speed of the various tasks necessary to the completion of a transaction. These include communicating between the investor and the broker, communicating between the broker and brokers representing other investors, making the deal, notifying the clearing corporation and the transfer agent, notifying the investors who completed the transaction, possibly delivering the stock, etc. An ideal market would perform these tasks quickly, at minimal cost and without error.

In its second sense, "efficiency" refers to the speed with which prices in the market adjust to changed perceptions of value (i.e., pricing efficiency). In an ideal market, prices adjust instantaneously. Any impairment of the adjustment process would be unfair to either buyers or sellers. If prices did not rise in response to perceptions of increased value, sellers would be disadvantaged; if prices did not fall in response to perceptions of decreased value, buyers would be harmed. Ideally, the price adjustment mechanism should favor neither buyer nor seller.

Integrity. Everyone is for integrity. Integrity of financial markets means a number of things. Investors must have absolute confidence that contracts will be honored. Buyers must know that they will receive the stock for which they have contracted, and sellers must know that they will receive their money. Investors must feel that there is a level playing field. They must feel that they are not at a disadvantage with respect to other players in the information that is available or the priority given their orders. Investors must be protected against fraud and manipulation by a strong surveillance system and vigorous enforcement of laws and regulations.

The elements of a system that is very close to ideal have been conceived, designed and tested on a small scale. In the mid 1970s, Peake, Mendelson and Williams, on the one hand, and Merrill Lynch on the other, made public proposals which, in theory, seemed radical but very promising.[1] Their market would be organized around a system of computers and telephone lines, which would solve most of the problems discussed above. Orders could be entered by any qualified broker-dealer (without limit as to number), either for its own account or for the account of public customers. These orders would be stored in a central computer where automatic execution would take place whenever bids and

---

[1] J. W. Peake, M. Mendelson, and J. Williams, "The National Book System," April 30, 1976, and Merrill Lynch, Pierce, Fenner and Smith Incorporated, "Proposal for a National Market System," October 16, 1975.

offers matched. Execution would be in accordance with price-time priority. Obviously, all orders to buy or sell would interact, thus ensuring that sellers would hit the highest bid and that buyers would cross with the lowest offer. All information on bids, offers and transaction prices would be available to everyone, unlike the system on the NYSE where information on bids and offers "away from the market" is restricted to specialists.

Efficiency, in the first sense, would be achieved because almost all communication would be instantaneous and electronic. The only remaining voice communication would be between the investor and the broker when the public order was placed; other communication, between broker-dealers and with the clearing corporation and the transfer agent would be automatic. Efficiency, in the second sense, would be achieved because there would be no impediments to the instantaneous adjustment of prices to market forces as reflected by the flow of orders. Surveillance would be effective and relatively cheap because there would be an almost permanent record in the computer of the parties responsible for all bids, offers and transactions. Because of price-time priority, complete disclosure of bids, offers, and prices, and the easy possibility of effective surveillance, investors would have almost all the elements necessary for high confidence in the integrity of the system. The missing element is information about the issuers of securities, and this is not an integral part of the trading mechanism, although it is important for the market.

The conceptions of an automated market discussed here have been tested on a small scale at the Cincinnati Stock Exchange and on a system called Instinet. Although neither market has achieved a very large trading volume, nothing in their experiences suggests that there are technological obstacles in the way of developing an automated system for the scale of trading on the NYSE or NASDAQ.

Both the NYSE and NASDAQ have been evolving in ways that bring them closer to the ideal system, but, for reasons discussed later, NASDAQ is more likely to reach that goal.

Some Comments on NASDAQ and the NYSE

NASDAQ and the NYSE rely on the same information systems to inform investors. All firms listed on NASDAQ or on the NYSE are required to make annual reports, quarterly reports and other more detailed reports to the Securities and Exchange Commission. The definitions and procedures underlying the data in these reports are prescribed by the SEC. Further, both the NASDAQ National Market System (NASDAQ/NMS) and the NYSE continuously provide during trading hours the same information on transaction prices with approximately the same speed. The two markets differ with respect to information on bids and offers. NASDAQ displays on desktop terminals throughout the world the bids and offers of registered market makers in each stock, together with an indication of the number of shares that must be bought or sold in response to a public order. The NYSE discloses only the specialists' bids and offers through the same terminals.

The surveillance systems of the two markets differ. The NASDAQ System has the more precise audit trail, permitting the reconstruction of all transactions, but the NYSE is also sensitive to fraud and manipulation.

The competing market makers of the NASDAQ System have more capital for market making than the specialists, but the NYSE has adapted to the need to trade large blocks of stock by arranging for them to be traded through upstairs traders who work away from the exchange. As a result, there is probably not much difference in the liquidity of the two systems. A recent comparative study shows that the distribution of trades by size of trade is similar for the two markets.[2] There have been other comparative studies of the two markets.[3] They differ in details and in some conclusions because of differences in concept and econometric techniques, but it is reasonable to conclude that in today's environment there are not important differences in the efficiency with which the two markets perform their basic economic function. If that were not true, we would observe the hundreds of firms on the NASDAQ National Market System that qualify for listing on the NYSE moving to that exchange. Or, we would see a reverse movement.[4]

In the market environment of the future—probably the near future—the trading mechanism of NASDAQ is likely to prove decisively superior. The important change that is taking place is the globalization of securities trading.

Recently, United States firms were allowed to join the Tokyo Stock Exchange and several did. And the number of United States companies listing on the Tokyo Stock Exchange is increasing.

---

[2] Laszlo Birinyi, Jr., and Julie M. Morrison, *The Over-the-Counter Market, Analysis, Groups, and Flows,* Salomon Brothers Inc., July 1985.

[3] See, for example, H. K. Baker and J. Spitzfaden, "The Impact of Exchange Listing on the Cost of Equity Capital," *Financial Review,* September 1982, pp. 128-138; K. Cooper, J. C. Groth, and W. E. Avera, unpublished working paper, 1983; David A. Dubofsky and John C. Groth, "Exchange Listing and Stock Liquidity," *The Journal of Financial Research,* Winter 1984, pp. 291-302; F. K. Reilly and W. Wong, "The Effect of a Stock Exchange Listing on Trading Volume, Market Liquidity, and Stock Price Volatility," unpublished paper, 1982; W. W. Reints and P. A. Vandenberg, "The Impact of Changes in Trading Location on a Security's Systematic Risk," *Journal of Financial and Quantitative Analysis,* December 1975, pp. 881-890.

[4] A reverse movement, i.e., from the NYSE to NASDAQ, is seriously impeded by the contract that firms sign with the NYSE when they list. This contract prohibits delisting unless approved by owners of a super-majority of the shares entitled to vote.

On October 27, 1986, The Stock Exchange of London had its "Big Bang." The rules changed in London to require competitive commissions and to permit individual firms to act as both brokers and market makers. The result was an influx of financial firms into the London market and a decision by many firms to act as both brokers and market makers.

Now there are three great international financial centers: New York, London and Tokyo. One or more of these markets is open through 20 hours of every business day. The volume of international capital flows is enormous and increasing. The United States in the past 10 years has, to a significant degree, gotten over its long-standing provincialism and is increasingly turning to foreign securities. The trend toward international diversification is based on sound reasons and is going to increase.

Issuers of securities are acting more and more on the realization that there is a global market for securities. Firms in the United States and in other developed countries are raising capital in the national markets that seem most favorable and are denominating securities in the currencies best suited to their individual circumstances.

In this global market, the kind of trading mechanism used by NASDAQ is likely to be superior to the mechanism of the NYSE. The NASDAQ mechanism has the ability to evolve easily until it is like the ideal system described earlier. That system differs from NASDAQ in important respects, but none of the differences is hard to overcome. The most important difference is that NASDAQ does not have a consolidated book. That is, the bids and offers of the individual market makers are listed separately rather than being consolidated. As a consequence, orders must be manually transmitted to individual market makers. In the event that an order, because of its size, requires the participation of more than one market maker, more than one order must be transmitted. In an era of many large blocks and volatile markets, the need to communicate with more than one market maker to consummate an order is a significant shortcoming. A consolidated book in which all bids and offers at the same price are consolidated eliminates this problem.

If NASDAQ consolidates its book, the System must decide how to choose the market maker to whom to direct an order among the several having a common bid or offer. As discussed above, the equitable way is to allocate the order to market makers in accordance with the times at which they made their commitments—the price-time priority principle. There is no technological obstacle to doing this.

At present, the NASD's Small Order Execution System is limited to orders of not more than 1,000 shares for companies on NASDAQ/NMS and 500 shares or less for other NASDAQ stocks. There is no technological or economic reason for this upper limit. Dealers' bids and offers must be good for orders up to these limits. This requirement prevents the entry of improved bids or offers on behalf of public customers. If that limit were removed and the other changes discussed above were made, the NASDAQ System would be the ideal system.

The superiority of such a system for purely domestic trading is substantial in comparison to either NASDAQ or the NYSE. For global trading, the superiority is overwhelming. It is easy to see the efficiency and general attractiveness of a global system which simultaneously informs all broker-dealers of the information in the consolidated book and permits the automatic execution of orders from any broker-dealer, wherever he may be on the face of the planet.

The NASDAQ System can easily evolve into such a global trading system. The evolution of the trading mechanism of the NYSE into such a system is probably impossible as long as all orders must be channeled to the specialist for his participation. Thus, although there is probably no significant difference in the efficiency of NASDAQ and the NYSE for domestic trading, the NASDAQ System can evolve into an ideal global trading system while the NYSE system cannot.

Chapter
twenty-one

John C. Groth is Professor of Finance in the College of Business Administration at Texas A&M University. Dr. Groth serves as a consultant and expert witness in the areas of corporate finance, investments and management education. His research has focused primarily on the efficiency and functioning of the securities markets and the resultant implications with respect to corporate finance and investments.

David A. Dubofsky is an Assistant Professor in the College of Business Administration at Texas A&M University. Dr. Dubofsky's articles on corporate finance and investments have appeared in such publications as the *Southern Economic Journal, Journal of Financial Research* and the *Financial Review*.

The Liquidity Factor

by John C. Groth
and
David A. Dubofsky

Liquidity, one of several factors that affect the value of an asset, varies by asset and characteristics of the market(s) for the asset. This chapter focuses on the liquidity of equity securities.

Liquidity is critical to some investors, less important to others. Most institutional clients and some individual investors regard the liquidity of assets as very important because they place a premium on being able to buy or sell a number of shares in a short time without a significant price concession. For individual investors with modest investments held for extended periods, liquidity is not usually an issue.

Liquidity is of interest to both providers and users of capital because asset prices (and therefore rates of return demanded by market participants) are sensitive to liquidity. In addition, the price of liquidity translates through to a higher cost of capital for firms that issue securities.

This chapter begins by reviewing a few concepts related to liquidity; the focus then shifts to the liquidity of stocks and particularly the relative liquidity of the NASDAQ market versus the exchanges. It also discusses economic studies on the liquidity of common stocks and some reasons for the observed differences in liquidity in these markets.

The Concept of Liquidity

Liquidity, sometimes called marketability, reflects two dimensions of a desired transaction: First, whether the asset can be either bought or sold at or near the prevailing market price, or the "realization factor;" and second, the time needed to effect the trade at or near the prevailing market price, characteristically called the "speed of transaction."

There is generally a tradeoff between price realization and transaction time. For example, suppose you decide on a stormy Thursday afternoon in March to try to sell an antique piano. Absent the chance meeting with an antique piano buff, you could probably not get rid of it on that day except at some ridiculously low price. Patience over several months would likely net a much better price. However, you would have to hold the piano and sacrifice immediacy of sale.

When an individual purchases something that might later be resold, liquidity becomes important and it will affect the price paid for the item. It may be difficult, for example, to find ready buyers for some assets such as antiques, houses, collectibles and shares of stock in a closely held corporation. These investments are relatively illiquid. On the other hand, assets such as 100 shares of General Motors Corporation and 90-day U.S Treasury bills can be quickly sold at a price that is at or between the bid and offer prices posted just prior to the initiation of the sale. The degree of confidence with which one can quickly buy or sell an asset close to the current market price is a factor contributing to its value.

To the extent that market participants want both dimensions of liquidity, prices will reflect those market characteristics that affect the asset and transaction elements of liquidity. For example, suppose a woman wishes to sell a house. A careful study of previous sales of houses of similar size, location, age and condition leads her to believe that the value of the house is $85,000. In a highly liquid market, she could sell her house quickly—perhaps in a week or less—for $85,000. As market liquidity declines, she would have to accept less than $85,000, or wait in hopes of realizing $85,000.

Conversely, the market for large, actively traded shares of a stock listed on NASDAQ or on the New York Stock Exchange (NYSE) is highly liquid. You can make a phone call to your broker, get a price quote summarizing the information that millions of investors have concerning the value, at the margin, of the stock of interest. Then you could sell or buy shares, within seconds, at or close to the quoted market price. Obviously, the market environment is different than the markets for the house and antique piano.

On NASDAQ, competing dealers or market makers continuously quote two-sided bid and offer markets for securities. On the NYSE, a single dealer (specialist) maintains a book of limit orders and bids and offers for his own account when the book bid and offer are too far apart. When there are many shares outstanding and many shareholders, the chances are greater that public orders will intersect from the buy and sell sides as market orders are executed against limit orders on the book. The existence of dealers ensures a buy and sell price even in the absence at the desired trading times of matches between buyers and sellers. Thus, dealers in the stock market contribute significantly to the liquidity of equity securities.

However, liquidity differs considerably for the shares of large companies, such as the General Motors, IBMs, MCIs and Exxons of the world, and for the shares of small companies with relatively few public shares. Shares that are less actively traded and those of firms with fewer shareholders and with fewer outstanding shares may not enjoy high levels of liquidity.

In some instances, interest in a company is so limited and shares are so infrequently traded that no dealer is attracted to making a market in the stock. On the NYSE, all common stocks have an assigned specialist but frequently preferred stocks do not. These would be called "post 30" stocks, reflecting the location of trading on the floor. In the over-the-counter (OTC) market, such inactive securities are quoted in the "pink sheets."[1] NASDAQ lists only stocks that have at least two market makers quoting a two-sided market.

Market Differences That Affect Liquidity

The exchanges and the NASDAQ market differ in a number of ways. Some of the differences appear to affect the setting of prices and the filling of buy and sell orders. The differences affect both the returns to providers of capital and the capital costs for firms.

1. **Competition.** The NASDAQ market consists of competing dealers. Each market maker quotes a price at which he or she is willing to buy (the bid) and a price at which he or she is willing to sell (the asked) a company's stock. In 1986, NASDAQ had over 525 dealers, with the average security having more than eight market makers. As Table 1 reveals, a very high percentage of stocks had four or more market makers.

---

[1] "Pink sheets" are daily quote sheets disseminated each day by the National Quotations Bureau. They are received by traders by 10 a.m. each day, and they contain quotes as of 2 p.m. the prior day.

Table 1
DISTRIBUTION OF NASDAQ SECURITIES
BY NUMBER OF MARKET MAKERS
(As of December 31, 1986)

Number of Market Makers	NASDAQ/NMS	Non-NASDAQ/NMS	Total NASDAQ
3 or Less	278	575	853
4 to 5	571	653	1,224
6 to 10	1,010	868	1,878
11 to 15	497	304	801
16 to 20	207	76	283
21 to 25	70	11	81
26 or more	62	7	69
Total	**2,695**	**2,494**	**5,189**
Percent of Total Having 4 or More Market Makers	89.7%	76.9%	83.6%

On the other hand, each stock traded on the NYSE and the Amex is assigned to a specialist who is charged with "maintaining fair and orderly markets." A specialist often acts as a "broker's broker," executing orders for a commission, or as a dealer, trading for his or her own account.

It would appear that specialists have an inherent conflict of interest. They are required to maintain an orderly market for their assigned stocks yet they wish to earn profits for their activities by trading for their own accounts. At times, market stabilization activities could lead to actions that result in zero profits or even losses. In these instances, it would seem that the market-making activities versus the specialists' personal risk and wealth circumstances could be at variance.

The specialist was once regarded as a monopolist in providing "liquidity services" for investors. While today's specialists still possess monopolistic information by knowing limit orders ("the book"), they compete with floor traders, investors' limit orders, regional exchanges and also NASD dealers who make markets in listed stocks away from the floor of the exchange in the "third market."

To be sure, NASDAQ market makers also have their economic interests close at heart. But in the case of securities traded through NASDAQ, market makers continually face competition as well as the threat of immediate additional competition from other market makers. As depicted in Table 1, the competition among multiple market makers vying for business enforces a competitive discipline on the market.

This competitive-dealer mechanism versus the single-specialist, market-making mechanism is a primary difference between the NASDAQ market and the exchanges. Because of the unrestricted entry into NASDAQ market making, firms with sufficient capital and the willingness to bear risk can become market makers without much difficulty.

Relatively free entry is an important issue. If economic profits become "excessive," added competition will arise and the price of liquidity (in part reflected by the bid/ask spread) will be driven down to competitive or zero economic profit levels. On the other hand, restricted entry could keep prices of liquidity services unduly high on the organized exchanges. As noted earlier, there is some competition for the specialist, but a glance at any day's volume figures on different markets will show that much of the competition is at the fringe of the market. Floor traders at the exchanges allow for trades between the specialists' bid/ask quotes, but this is tantamount to one dealer maintaining his bid/ask quotes and only occasionally transacting at a price between those quotes.

Others have assessed the specialists' returns and concluded that specialists earn high profits from brokering and dealing activities. Sobel calls the $720,000 earned by one specialist "monopoly returns."[2] But perspective demands consideration of the amount of capital the specialist has invested in providing a service as well as attendant risk exposure.

2. **Distribution of Risk.** Liquidity offered by market makers is likely to be sensitive to the capital available and the willingness to expose that capital to risk. In this case as well, the system of multiple market makers is potentially superior to the specialist system for two reasons. First, the total amount of aggregate capital available to several NASDAQ dealers for making a market in a given stock exceeds the amount available to a single exchange specialist. The second advantage of the multiple market-maker system might be termed a risk-willingness "portfolio effect." The risk associated with a given amount of capital is spread or diversified over several market makers. Each market maker bears only a portion of that risk. If only one individual market maker is willing to bear a level of risk slightly greater than his or her proportional share, that capital along with the capital from the remaining market makers would yield increased liquidity.

---

[2] Robert Sobel, *Inside Wall Street*, W.W. Norton and Company, New York, 1977, p. 51.

3. **Depth of Market.** Another aspect of markets that affects liquidity is the readiness to effect a trade for minimum transaction volume. Thus, the minimum number of shares that must be available at the quoted prices is relevant to liquidity. Each specialist's bid/ask quote holds for at least 100 shares. Similarly, each market maker must be willing to trade a minimum of 100 shares. Thus, if several dealers all quote the same or nearly the same bid/ask prices, then jointly they are effectively "good" for several hundred shares at posted prices.

4. **Access to Information.** Some suggest that NASDAQ dealers perform an information function because many communicate with and follow closely the managements and the performance of firms in whose stock they make markets. A recent study finds evidence that the impact of informational processes on stock prices in the competing market-maker system is comparable to that of exchanges.[3]

Just as multiple market makers compete for business, its seems logical that they would compete for information. To be sure, the specialist is constantly trying to glean information from the environment that might affect security prices, and both specialists and market makers likely contribute to the efficiency of the market for information. However, multiple market makers, each motivated by economic interests, may more effectively unearth information and capture it in share price.

---

[3] Donna J. Shores, *Differential Information and Security Returns Surrounding Earnings Announcements on the Over-the-Counter Market*, Ph.D. Thesis, Stanford University, August 1986.

That is, multiple market makers may cause information to be more accurately reflected in share price.

5. **Inventory Adjustment.** Last is the issue of inventory adjustment. It appears that there is a difference between internal and external adjustment of inventory. Assume that a specialist and a NASDAQ market maker desire to adjust their inventory positions in a stock. Each could be motivated by a variety of reasons. Factors related to the particular stock could prompt the specialist or market maker to want to alter inventory, or factors not at all related to the stock could cause an inventory change. For example, a change with respect to investments other than the stock in question might lead to an inventory change.

Whatever the motivation, the methods of adjustment seem different for the specialist than for a NASDAQ market maker. It would seem that the specialist must make inventory adjustments against the market, that is, by adjusting prices against the external market. Those price adjustments have their origin in the personal circumstance of the specialist rather than in economic factors related to the firm's stock.

In the case of multiple market makers, the worst case inventory adjustment is the same as with the specialist. But the presence of several market makers allows for something better than the worst case. Suppose one or more market makers desires to alter his or her inventory in a particular stock. There exists the prospect of making such adjustments internally, against other market makers who desire to alter their inventory in a counter way. Thus, there exists the chance of internal, cross market-maker inventory adjustment. The result is that it may not be necessary to in effect charge the external market for the cost of market-maker inventory adjustments.

Measuring Liquidity

There is no single, unambiguous, theoretically (or otherwise) correct measure of liquidity. One that has often been used is the bid/ask spread. It is widely used as a measure of "immediacy."[4] In other words, an investor who wants to buy (or sell) shares can do so at the ask (or bid) price quoted by the specialist or NASDAQ market maker. In the NASDAQ market, the investor would preferably trade at the highest bid or lowest asked price. These are called "inside" quotes and may be those of two or more different dealers.

The development of NASDAQ has reduced the costs of determining inside quotes to near zero. The bid/asked spread is also called the "price" that market makers charge for liquidity services.

In establishing a true cost of trading on either exchanges or NASDAQ, any brokerage commissions might also be added, since they too are effectively part of the price concession one makes in quickly selling an asset.

However, spread is only one dimension of liquidity. The bid/ask spread fails as a liquidity measure because it does not account for the number of shares that can be traded at the quoted price. In addition, it does not reflect the price change that is necessary for a large block of shares to trade. Last, it fails to capture the fact that trades can and do take place within the quoted spread.

Liquidity measures should account for both trading volume and concurrent price changes. A liquid market for a stock can absorb large volume with little price change. An

---

[4] Harold Demsetz, "The Costs of Transacting," *Quarterly Journal of Economics*, January 1968, Vol. 82, pp. 33-53.

illiquid market for a stock will experience low trading volume and price jumps when dealers experience an increase in the order rate.

The Amivest Liquidity Ratio is one measure of liquidity. Like most generally accepted measures of liquidity, it measures the dollar volume of trading per percent of price change. The liquidity of a stock is measured as follows:

$$\frac{\text{Total dollar volume of a stock traded during the previous 4 weeks}}{\text{The sum of the absolute value of daily price changes during the previous 4 weeks}}$$

Symbolically, the liquidity of stock i on day t, L_{it}, is:

$$L_{it} \frac{\displaystyle\sum_{t=-1}^{-20} P_{it} V_{it}}{\displaystyle\sum_{t=-1}^{20} \left| \% \, \Delta P_{it} \right|},$$

where,

P_{it} = the price of stock i on day t

V_{it} = the volume of stock i on day t

$\left| \% \, \Delta P_{it} \right|$ = the absolute value of the percentage change in the price of stock i on day t

A high value of L_{it} means that many shares are traded with little change in price—a property possessed by a liquid stock. The four-week (20-trading day) period was chosen because it is the time period used by most practitioners.

Other variants of the Amivest Liquidity Ratio have been proposed. For example, some suggest that a better liquidity measure would utilize intra-day high and low prices. After all, a stock could experience wide fluctuations in price on one day, yet close unchanged in price from the previous day.

The list of possible liquidity measures could be extended; there is some debate about what is "best." However, the three studies that will be reviewed here employed the Amivest Liquidity Ratio. This ratio reflects the conventional approach to measuring liquidity, is easily computed and understood, and captures the elements of liquidity that are important for investors: price fluctuations and volume. It is a good measure of liquidity in that it reflects the practical ability to effect trades at prices close to posted prices.

Trading Location and Liquidity

Since the method by which markets are made differs on an exchange and NASDAQ, an interesting and important question is whether trading location affects liquidity. A series of academic papers have used the Amivest Liquidity Ratio to examine this question.

A paper published in the February 1985 *Journal of Economics and Business* entitled "Liquidity, Exchange Listing, and Common Stock Performance," by Kerry Cooper, John C. Groth and William E. Avera compares the liquidity of similar-sized firms that trade in different markets. Size is measured in terms of equity capitalization, which is defined as the number of shares outstanding multiplied by share price. There are intuitive reasons why stocks with a high market value (price times shares outstanding) would possess greater liquidity. It is also true that many of the largest stocks (those with greatest market value) trade on the New York Stock Exchange. The concern was that relative size not cloud observations regarding liquidity. The approach was to examine liquidity in the different markets with samples arrayed and matched according to size.

Using the Master File of Media General Financial Services Data Bank as the data source, the authors sort all NYSE, Amex and 1,015 NASDAQ/OTC common stocks by their market capitalization. Next, they place the stocks into one of 10 market capitalization deciles, arbitrarily demarcated so that a reasonable sample size of stocks from each trading location would fall into each decile.

Using the Amivest Liquidity Ratios as of April 30, 1981, as supplied by Media General, Cooper, et al., compute the summary statistics presented in Table 2.

Observations. First, the results support the preconceived notion that greater market value would tend to accompany greater liquidity. However, size does not always lead to higher liquidity. As evidenced by the liquidity ratio range, at least one firm on the NYSE, Amex and OTC had very low liquidity. Liquidity ratios of zero exist in the Amex and OTC markets because some stocks had zero volume in the 20-day period.

Of greater interest is the comparison of average liquidity ratios for similar-sized companies that trade on the NYSE, Amex and OTC. The average liquidity ratios for OTC-traded stocks exceeded those of Amex-listed stocks in every decile. In addition, in comparing the NYSE with the Amex, liquidity for the NYSE exceeded that of the Amex except for the third decile.

With the exception of the very smallest companies (decile 1) and the very largest companies (decile 10), the average liquidity ratio of OTC-traded stocks also exceeded those of NYSE-listed stocks. In deciles 2 through 9, the liquidity of OTC stocks exceeded the liquidity of both NYSE- and Amex-listed stocks.

The researchers conclude that "the over-the-counter market appears to offer liquidity that is very competitive with that offered by the New York and American Stock Exchanges."

Table 2

LIQUIDITY RATIO OF COMMON STOCKS SORTED BY AGGREGATE MARKET VALUE

Decile	NYSE			Amex			OTC		
	Number of Stocks	Average Liquidity Ratio*	Liquidity Ratio Range	Number of Stocks	Average Liquidity Ratio*	Liquidity Ratio Range	Number of Stocks	Average Liquidity Ratio*	Liquidity Ratio Range
1	10	7.900	(1-38)	206	3.369	(0-34)	157	7.420	(0-58)
2	44	15.545	(1-65)	154	12.636	(0-60)	163	30.135	(1-417)
3	58	26.069	(2-151)	101	35.148	(2-1099)	115	49.009	(4-328)
4	51	41.510	(12-164)	65	36.508	(5-135)	85	57.671	(4-280)
5	59	57.407	(8-212)	47	46.149	(5-325)	68	120.029	(9-1923)
6	50	58.580	(10-207)	28	54.429	(8-257)	52	116.885	(5-328)
7	103	94.524	(17-275)	51	82.392	(5-290)	63	142.555	(1-589)
8	73	124.685	(27-430)	23	81.435	(14-186)	47	158.191	(29-517)
9	228	223.364	(34-1491)	57	135.948	(0-510)	118	293.873	(16-936)
10	839	1699.181	(34-35579)	69	530.623	(1-5557)	96	668.885	(9-3579)

*Read: Thousands of dollars required to effect a 1% change in market price.

In a subsequent study, David A. Dubofsky and John C. Groth used a different approach to examine trading location and liquidity. The results are summarized in "Exchange Listing and Liquidity," published in the Winter 1984 *Journal of Financial Research*.

As background, it should be acknowledged that several previous studies have concluded that trading location has no consistent impact, one way or the other, on stockholders' returns or firms' cost of capital. In spite of these findings, some corporations change their trading locations, citing higher stock returns and lower capital costs as one consideration prompting a switch. Other reasons often mentioned include the greater prestige of an exchange such as the NYSE and the added liquidity that exchanges offer.

To test the belief that an exchange listing improves liquidity, Dubofsky and Groth examined liquidity changes for three groups: for 112 stocks switching from OTC to Amex; for 128 switching from OTC to NYSE; and for 104 switching from Amex to NYSE. These represent virtually all of the switches that occurred during 1975 through 1981. Whereas the first study compared the liquidity of stocks of similar size, this one focused on changes in liquidity of stocks that actually made the switch.

Using the Media General Daily Price History Tapes for price and volume data, Dubofsky and Groth performed for each switching stock a time-series analysis of liquidity ratios after each calendar switch date, which they call the "event day."

Figures 1 through 3 summarize the results. In each group, different calendar days for the individual stocks are all grouped and examined relative to the switch day. Thus, although the switches occurred on different calendar days, for each switch liquidity is examined for the same number of pre- and post-days around the event day.

Figure 1
LIQUIDITY OF STOCKS SWITCHING FROM OTC TO NYSE
N = 128

Observations. The findings depicted in Figure 1 indicate a sharp and apparently permanent decline in average liquidity for securities switching from the OTC to the NYSE.[5]

---

[5] These daily liquidity ratios are averaged in event time. For example, day 46 is the switch date, and the liquidity ratio of a stock on day 46 utilizes price and volume data over the previous 20 days relative to its switch date. Each stock has its own given switch date in calendar time, and there is a liquidity ratio for each on day 46—its switch date. To get the average liquidity ratio for all switches on day 46 for the 128 (or 112 or 104) observations, day-46 liquidity ratios were averaged. The same was done on each of 108 days.

Liquidity declined 24 percent from the switch day (day 46) to day 66, and declined an additional 13 percent thereafter. These results should not be extended beyond the range of the sample or be interpreted to mean that all securities moving from the OTC to the NYSE will suffer a decline in liquidity.

Figure 2 illustrates average liquidity of the 112 stocks that switched from the OTC to the Amex. These stocks were in general less liquid than those switching to the NYSE from the OTC (note that the values on the vertical axis of the graphs differ in Figures 1, 2 and 3). Average liquidity increases as the switch date nears, from 50.0 on day 1 to 57.7 on day 46. Once a stock is listed on the Amex, however, average liquidity declines by 26 percent. The pre-listing improvement might be attributable to the increased publicity and market attention on the stock, or a "using up" of latent liquidity, which is followed by a decline after listing.

Finally, Figure 3 summarizes the findings for stocks switching from the Amex to the NYSE. These stocks realize an increase in liquidity just after the switch date, followed by a gradual decline to near pre-switch levels.

Dubofsky and Groth used another liquidity measure developed by Martin[6] and drew conclusions identical to those above: Securities moving from the NASDAQ market to either of the organized exchanges decline markedly in liquidity.

Historically, bank stocks have tended to trade OTC. That observation led to a third study by Donald R. Fraser and

---

[6] Peter Martin, *Analysis of the Impact of Competitive Rates on the Liquidity of NYSE Stocks*, Economic Staff Paper 75-3, Securities and Exchange Commission, July 1975.

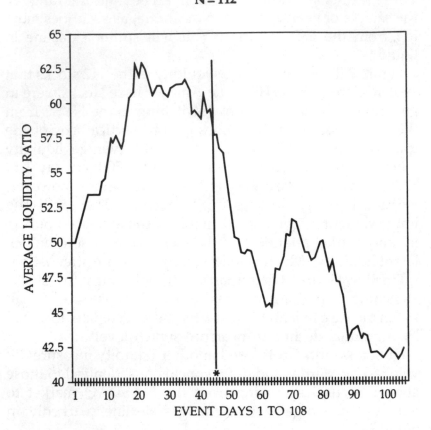

Figure 2

LIQUIDITY OF STOCKS SWITCHING FROM OTC TO AMEX

N = 112

EVENT DAYS 1 TO 108

John C. Groth, which examined the liquidity of bank stocks. "Listing and the Liquidity of Bank Stocks," published in the autumn 1985 issue of the *Journal of Bank Research*, presents their findings. The authors regress liquidity ratios on a set of explanatory variables, one of which is trading location (exchange listed vs. OTC; the variable was a "dummy variable" that took on a value of 1 if the bank stock was listed). This approach takes account of differences in

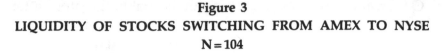

Figure 3

LIQUIDITY OF STOCKS SWITCHING FROM AMEX TO NYSE

N = 104

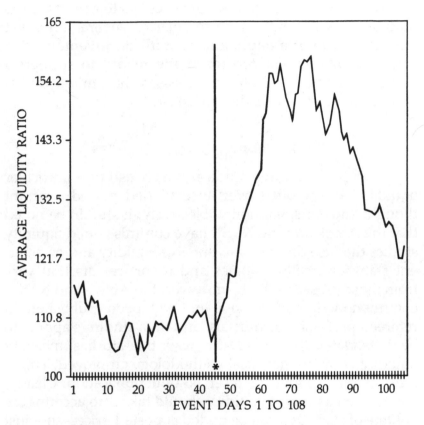

characteristics of the firms traded on the exchanges and OTC, such as differences in size.

The regression yielded a coefficient of −148.8 for the trading location variable, a value statistically different from zero at the 5 percent level of confidence. This means that all else being equal, $148,000 more in dollar volume of trades would be required to move the price of bank stocks 1 percent if the stock traded OTC rather than on an exchange. In other words, the results indicate that the liquidity of an

OTC-traded bank stock was considerably greater, after removing the effects of different company characteristics, than bank stocks listed on an organized exchange.

Fraser and Groth attributed their results to aspects of the trading mechanism: "The presence of several...market makers may offer a depth and breadth of 'inventory' and greater capital committed (or at the ready) to support a buy/sell willingness that far surpasses the limited capital and/or commitment of the specialist."

Conclusions

The three studies, which use one particular liquidity ratio applied over an extended period, warrant thought and consideration. Objectively, it should be noted that the Amex and the NYSE have commissioned liquidity studies that use different measures of liquidity and/or different statistical methodologies and report results that vary from those presented here. However, the Amex- and NYSE-commissioned studies have not yet been published in refereed professional journals, and their findings appear to be invalidated by either the way the studies measure liquidity or by the statistical methodology employed. Therefore, comment should be reserved until publication. Clearly, any new measures of liquidity should take into account the volume of stock that can be traded at posted prices—not just spreads and the behavior of spreads.

We view the use of a conventional liquidity measure such as the Amivest Liquidity Ratio to be important. It measures the dollar volume of trades per percentage of price change. Because it captures both volume and concurrent price change, it is an appealing practical measure. For findings to be valid, tests of liquidity should control for the size of the company and reflect trading over a reasonable period of time.

All three of the papers discussed here cover approximately the same period. The Cooper, Groth and Avera study and the Fraser and Groth study use liquidity ratios measured during the 20-day period ending April 30, 1981. However, the Dubofsky and Groth study covers switches in trading location over an extended seven-year period ending in 1981. Although relative liquidity could differ for other periods, the nature of the OTC dealer market vis-a-vis the exchange specialist system appears to create different degrees of liquidity for similar stocks when size and time factors are adequately considered.

Chapter
twenty-two

H. Kent Baker is Professor of Finance at the Kogod College of Business Administration, The American University in Washington, D.C. Dr. Baker, a Chartered Financial Analyst, has written more than 100 articles appearing in such publications as the *Harvard Business Review, Journal of Finance, Journal of Accountancy* and *Financial Management.*

The Cost of Capital to NASDAQ and Exchange-Listed Companies

by H. Kent Baker

       Each year many companies are approached by the American Stock Exchange (Amex) or the New York Stock Exchange (NYSE) for listing. Although a few decide to list on an exchange, most join or remain on the NASDAQ System even though they meet the financial requirements of the NYSE and Amex. In fact, there is a clear trend for firms to remain with the NASDAQ System rather than to list on the Amex or the NYSE. For example, from January 1980 through December 1986, the number of companies on NASDAQ grew from 2,543 to 4,417, a gain of almost 74 percent, while Amex listings decreased over 15 percent from 931 to 791 and NYSE listings increased slightly from 1,570 to 1,573.

The intense competition for listings among these market-places underscores the difference in views about them. Some people believe that exchange listing benefits the company and its stockholders while others do not. Prior to the advent of NASDAQ, it was commonly held that listing improved marketability, provided more efficient pricing, reduced transaction costs to investors, reduced flotation costs of future equity financing, or lowered the cost of capital to the company.[1] Numerous economic studies attempted to confirm these beliefs.

While clear confirmation of these beliefs was difficult even prior to NASDAQ, the development of NASDAQ, by increasing the efficiency of the OTC market, has altered the equation sharply and there is no longer undisputed evidence to support a decision to list. In fact, the presumption in favor of listing has clearly changed, and a majority of companies now reject listing after careful analysis of the relative merits of NASDAQ and the exchanges as markets.

Past studies shed some light on both the motivation for and the economic impact of exchange listing. For example, Baker and Petit[2] surveyed 613 financial managers to ascertain their motives for listing and to determine why qualified companies elected not to list. The sample represented 242 NYSE and 171 Amex companies that listed from 1975 to 1980 and 200 over-the-counter (OTC) stocks that met the minimum requirements for Amex listing. The findings show that the twc most frequently cited reasons for listing were visibility and prestige. Although some of the motives given had economic implications, such as improving future financing alternatives and marketability, the major reasons for listing were not economic in nature. The financial managers of OTC companies decided not to seek exchange

---

[1] F. J. Fabozzi, *Financial Management*, "Does Listing on the Amex Increase the Value of Equity?," Spring 1982, pp. 43-50.

T. Grammatikos and G. Papioannou, *Journal of Financial Research*, "Market Reaction to NYSE Listings: Tests of the Marketability Gains Hypothesis," Fall 1986, pp. 215-227.

[2] H. K. Baker and G. Petit, *Akron Journal of Business and Economics*, "Management's View of Stock Exchange Listing," Winter 1982, pp. 12-17.

listing for one of two reasons. They preferred market makers to specialists, or they saw no advantage to listing.

However, listing studies must be continually updated because of the rapid and continuing relative improvement in the NASDAQ System. Each year brings changes that tend to make study findings less valid with age.

This chapter examines one potential motive for exchange listing: Does exchange listing reduce a company's cost of equity capital? For convenience, this issue is labeled the "reduced cost of capital hypothesis." It is of interest not only to the academic community but also to representatives of different marketplaces and to corporate managements.

The impact of exchange listing on the cost of capital is perennially debated by representatives of the exchanges and the OTC market. In prospecting for new listings, the Amex and the NYSE maintain that listing is advantageous in terms of lowering the required rate of return on a company's common stock. On the other hand, the NASD asserts that listing does not significantly affect the company's cost of capital.

The issue of whether or not listing lowers the cost of capital is also relevant to corporate managers. The term "cost of capital" means the rate that the company must pay for its funds or the minimum required rate that a company must earn on new investments to maintain the market value of its common stock. The cost of equity capital is a positive function of the market's perception of the risk associated with the company's common stock. Since the company's overall cost of capital consists of the costs of both debt and equity, reducing the cost of equity capital would also affect the firm's overall cost of capital. In theory, management attempts to find some optimal balance of debt and equity that simultaneously maximizes the firm's total market value and stock price while minimizing its average cost of capital.

Thus, if listing in a particular market reduces a company's cost of equity capital, a firm would receive something of value by listing on that market.

Managers also want to lower their cost of capital because it affects corporate decision making. For example, corporate managers use the company's cost of capital for making capital budgeting decisions and capital structure decisions. The cost of capital provides a hurdle rate for determining the acceptability of projects when discounted cash-flow techniques are used. The cost of capital also measures the effectiveness of the firm's capital structure. That is, the company is able to approach its optimal capital structure by lowering its cost of capital.

This chapter is divided into three major parts. The first part gives the theoretical underpinning for any impact of exchange listing on the cost of equity capital. The second part reviews the relevant research evidence. The third part provides the main conclusions based on the research and suggests avenues of future investigation.

Underlying Theory

In it simplest form, the theoretical underpinning for the reduced-cost-of-capital hypothesis centers around the concept of the risk/return tradeoff. The risk/return tradeoff states that investors expect to be compensated for taking higher levels of risk by receiving higher returns. If listing reduces the market's perception of risk associated with the company's common stock, then it should also reduce the investors' required return and consequently the firm's cost of equity capital. Thus, the cost of equity capital would be reduced if investors require a lower rate of return on the newly listed company's common stock than they did prior to listing.

It is sometimes argued that systematic risk, as measured by beta, can be expected to decline when a security qualifies for listing. In theory, a forecast of a diminished post-listing beta could be based upon an assumption that trading liquidity will increase or that there will be a decline in the perceived inherent risk of the security due to its new status.[3] This second assumption for a lower post-listing beta may in turn be partly based upon information factors surrounding the announcement. Chapter 21 discusses the relationship between liquidity and exchange listing. Therefore, attention here is focused on the relationship between perceived risk and information. In that regard, two controversies exist: One centers around whether or not a listing action contains information content and the other centers around whether or not exchange listing increases information availability.

According to the information-content view, the listing action has information content that affects the risk and return of the securities. Ying, Lewellen, Schlarbaum and Lease[4] (hereafter referred to as YLSL) contend that eligible candidates for listing are companies that are experiencing significant growth in assets and earnings, and thus are making the transition to established business entities with records of profitable operations. Therefore, market participants may view the listing application as a signal expressing managerial confidence in the company's business prospects. The allegedly positive information content of the listing action may result in less perceived risk and may thereby lower the firm's cost of equity capital.

---

[3] L. K. W. Ying, W. G. Lewellen, G. G. Schlarbaum and R. C. Lease, *Journal of Financial and Quantitative Analysis*, "Stock Exchange Listing and Securities Returns," September 1977, pp. 415-432.

[4] Ibid.

Opponents of this information-content view contend that while a change in trading location may be the result of change in a company's character, i.e., a developmental step in its growth process, this change should already be reflected in the company's stock price. Any shift in stock returns, risk or cost of capital should occur over time and should not be a consequence of listing unless listing reflects new information. If listing does convey new information, then in an efficient market, prices of individual securities should adjust very rapidly to a new equilibrium. A securities market is said to be efficient if the price instantaneously and fully reflects all relevant available information.

The issue of whether listing has information content may be determined by examining stock price behavior surrounding the listing action. If listing has information content, it is reasonable to hypothesize the possible existence of abnormal positive investment returns surrounding the listing action. Capital-market theory is pessimistic about the possible existence in the market of locales of persistent opportunities for the realization of "superior" investment results, i.e., abnormal risk-adjusted returns.

According to the information-availability view, exchange listing increases information availability, which reduces perceived risk concerning the company's current and future affairs.[5] It is argued that this reduction of perceived risk makes listed securities relatively more attractive to investors, and it thus lowers the cost of capital to firms. Proponents of this view contend that unlisted firms may suffer from an information deficiency relative to listed firms. There

---

[5] D. S. Dhaliwal, *Journal of Business Research*, "Exchange-Listing Effects on a Firm's Cost of Equity Capital," Spring 1983, pp. 139-151. Dhaliwal presents several arguments that an increase in financial information should reduce the dispersion of security prices and reduce the cost of equity capital.

is considerable debate, however, on how to measure this information deficiency. The lower riskiness of listed shares may also lead to lower flotation costs, which would reduce the cost of raising external equity.

The argument that increased availability of financial information is likely to reduce the cost of equity capital has been advanced by several authors.[6] For example, Dhaliwal[7] states that:

> ...exchange-listing is likely to reduce the cost of equity capital to the firm because the investment community is likely to gather and disseminate more financial information on a firm once it becomes listed. This increased availability of information reduces the uncertainty about the present and future affairs of the company, and the company is therefore perceived to be less risky. Consequently, investors are willing to accept a lower rate of return on their investment, which means that the cost of equity capital to the firm is reduced.

Opponents of the information-availability view, such as Phillips and Zecher,[8] argue that having more information available or distributed more broadly does not guarantee that investors will lower their perception of a firm's risk, causing a change in the cost of capital. Opponents also contend that

---

[6] W. W. Alberts and S. H. Archer, *Journal of Financial and Quantitative Analysis*, "Some Evidence on the Effect of Company Sizes on the Cost of Equity Capital," March 1973, pp. 229-245.

F.D.S. Choi, *Accounting and Business Research*, "Financial Disclosure in Relation to a Firm's Costs," Autumn 1973, pp. 159-175.

Dhaliwal, pp. 139-151.

[7] Dhaliwal, p. 140.

[8] S. M. Phillips and J. R. Zecher, *Capital Market Working Paper*, "Exchange Listing and the Cost of Equity Capital," Securities and Exchange Commission, Washington, D.C., March 1982.

if this lack of information is a source of risk, such risk can be diversified away. Thus, investors should not expect to be compensated for the risk that results from the lack of information about firms and the securities they issue.

According to the capital-asset pricing theory, investors are rewarded only for accepting systematic risk, as measured by beta. In a reasonably efficient capital market, the decision to list would not change the level of systematic risk. If both listed and unlisted markets are reasonably efficient, then each market would offer an equal opportunity for issuers to minimize their cost of equity capital. Thus, trading location would not affect a company's systematic risk level and consequently would not affect its cost of equity capital.

More recent research, however, by Arbel[9] and Barry and Brown[10] suggests that, even in an efficient market, investors should expect a higher return on shares of firms for which relatively little information is available. If risk is measured by traditional methods such as beta, without adjusting for the relative information of the securities, then securities for which there is relatively less information would appear to earn excess returns.[11] Yet, the returns would actually not be excessive if information factors were included in the measurement of risk.

---

[9] A. Arbel, *Journal of Portfolio Management*, "Generic Stocks: An Old Product in a New Package," Winter 1985, pp. 4-13.

[10] C. B. Barry and S. J. Brown, *Journal of Portfolio Management*, "Limited Information as a Source of Risk," Winter 1986, pp. 66-72.

[11] The quantity of information (information deficiency) related to a particular security is difficult to measure. Barry and Brown (pp. 66-72) suggest several measures such as the period of listing, extent of analyst agreement or disagreement about the prospects of a security, firm size and the number of citations of news items regarding a security in key financial publications.

Observers also note that several developments resulting in the upgrading of the OTC market now make any information gap between marketplaces less likely to exist. These developments include the SEC amendment of 1964, which expanded the periodic information disclosure requirement to OTC firms, the introduction of NASDAQ and the ensuing tighter internal regulation of OTC dealers, the interlinkage of the various markets, the increased number and activity of institutional investors, and the growth in newspaper coverage of the NASDAQ market.[12]

For example, 73 newspapers carried information about NASDAQ securities in 1980, but the number had increased to 165 by 1986. Other factors contributing to the narrowing of any information gap between listed and unlisted stocks include increased computerization and electronic communication[13] and the development of the NASDAQ National Market System (NASDAQ/NMS). As noted earlier, the findings of past studies must be evaluated in the context of the rapidly changing NASDAQ environment.

Research Evidence

The broad question of whether stock exchange listing represents something of value has been debated and studied for many years. The following discussion investigates the findings of empirical research on whether exchange listing reduces the cost of the firm's equity capital.

---

[12] Grammatikas, pp. 215-227.

[13] J. F. Weston and T. E. Copeland, *Managerial Finance, 8th ed.*, The Dryden Press, Hinsdale, Illinois, 1986, p. 38.

Early empirical studies on listing that predated NASDAQ focus on the relationship between listing and price behavior, whereas later studies directly examine the relationship between listing and the cost of equity capital.[14]

Using the earlier approach, Ule[15] examined stocks that moved from the OTC market to the NYSE from 1934 to 1937. He observed price increases before listing and concluded that market participants bid up equity prices, thus yielding abnormal returns to the shareholders of those companies. The price increases were attributed to the anticipated benefits expected to result from listing.

In four studies conducted during the 1960s, Merjos[16] investigated the price behavior of newly listed stocks on four dates: three months before listing, the day of listing, the day after listing, and one month after listing. The performance of these stocks was compared to the Dow Jones averages. Merjos found that newly listed securities increased in price, relative to the overall market, before listing and decreased after listing. In three of the samples, the market outperformed the samples after listing, which resulted in a loss of much of the pre-listing gain. The pre-listing price performance was attributed to the expected benefits of market participants from listing, such as improved prestige.

---

[14] Fabozzi, pp. 43-50, and Phillips and Zecher provide a detailed review of the early literature on the impact of stock exchange listing.

[15] G. M. Ule, *Journal of Business*, "Price Movements of Newly Listed Common Stocks," October 1937, pp. 346-369.

[16] A. Merjos, *Barron's*, "Going on the Big Board: Stocks Act Better Before Listing Than Right Afterward," January 29, 1962, pp. 5, 14-15; *Barron's*, "Stricken Securities," March 4, 1963, pp. 9-10; *Barron's*, "Like Money in the Bank: Big Board Listing, the Record Suggests, is a Valuable Asset," July 8, 1963, pp. 9, 13; *Barron's*, "Going on the Big Board," May 1, 1967, pp. 9-10, 15.

Problems with these early studies included the failure to use tests of statistical significance to identify or measure price changes and the failure to account for other concurrent influences on stock price performance. Several later studies attempted to overcome these shortcomings by more carefully examining price behavior of stocks newly listed on a major exchange.

For example, Van Horne[17] studied stock price behavior before and after listing after adjusting for market and industry effects. His sample consisted of 80 new listings on the NYSE between 1960 and 1967 and 60 on the Amex between 1962 and 1967. Van Horne found the usual price pattern of newly listed stocks—prelisting prices increased through the listing date and decreased after listing. After adjusting for transaction costs and certain biases in the use of industry averages, he concluded that listing was not "a thing of value." He also noted that investors could not profit from a strategy of buying a stock when an imminent listing is announced and selling upon listing.

Furst[18] and Goulet[19] reached similar conclusions. Furst examined 198 issues that changed trading location from the OTC market to the NYSE between 1960 and 1965. Using multiple-regression analysis, he found that dividends, growth rate in dividends, earnings instability, leverage and company size were significant in explaining price changes before and after listing, but trading location did not have a significant impact on market price. Goulet reported that the pre-listing price behavior for a sample of 113 issues newly

---

[17] J. Van Horne, *Journal of Finance*, "New Listings and Their Price Behavior," September 1970, pp. 783-794.

[18] R. Furst, *Journal of Business*, "Does Listing Increase the Market Price of Common Stocks?", April 1970, pp. 174-180.

[19] W. M. Goulet, *Financial Management*, "Price Changes, Managerial Actions and Insider Trading at the Time of Listing," Spring 1974, pp. 30-36.

listed on the Amex between January 1968 and September 1970 was similar to that found in previous studies. His investigation of post-listing price changes suggests that the price declines in the post-listing period may be due to the fact that firms frequently sell additional shares shortly after listing.

The later studies also failed to adjust for the differential risk characteristics of the securities involved. YLSL[20] attempted to correct this problem by testing whether the systematic-risk characteristics of the securities considered were the same after listing (or application for listing) as before. They examined the price behavior of a sample of 248 firms whose common shares were listed for the first time on either the NYSE or Amex from 1966 to 1968. The period covered was 24 months before and 24 months after the listing date.

The YLSL study produced two important findings. First, the difference in the means of the pre- and post-listing betas was both small and not statistically significant. Second, positive abnormal returns were associated with the pre-listing period and a modest surrendering of some of these gains occurred in the post-listing period. The pre-listing price behavior was attributed to the continued emergence of progressively more favorable news items during that period about the firms involved. YLSL concluded that "listing did indeed 'have value' for the companies examined."[21] However, it should be noted that these studies were pre-NASDAQ.

In a study of listings shortly after the start-up of NASDAQ, Fabozzi investigated the price behavior of newly listed companies on the Amex to see if listing reduces the cost of

---

[20] YLSL, pp. 415-432.

[21] Fabozzi, pp. 43-50, questions the validity of the YLSL, p. 430, findings because of the long pre-listing period and the benchmark-performance model they employed.

equity before flotation costs. An analysis of the residuals generated from the market model was used to assess the market's reaction to the news of listing for a sample of 83 firms that shifted trading location from the OTC market to the Amex between 1972 and 1975. He found that listing did not change systematic risk and that the market reacted favorably to the news of listing. However, the price behavior after the week of listing largely offset the initial gain. Fabozzi concluded that "...the present study does not support the hypothesis that listing on the Amex reduces the cost of equity before flotation costs."[22]

Other studies investigated the relationship between listing and systematic risk (beta), which is a proxy for the cost of equity capital. For example, in a pre-NASDAQ study, Reints and Vandenberg[23] tested the hypothesis that changes in trading location do not affect a company's systematic risk. For the 32 companies in their sample that moved to the NYSE between May 1 and August 31, 1968, they found no significant change in the systematic risk of the stock after listing. Fabozzi and Hershkoff[24] extended the work of Reints and Vandenberg by examining companies that shifted trading locations from the OTC market to the Amex between 1972 and 1975. Their results agreed with the findings of Fabozzi, Reints and Vandenberg, and YLSL. A change in trading location did not affect the stock's systematic risk and hence the firm's cost of equity capital.

---

[22] Fabozzi, p. 49.

[23] W. W. Reints and P. A. Vandenberg, *Journal of Financial and Quantitative Analysis*, "The Impact of Changes in Trading Location on a Security's Systematic Risk," December 1975, pp. 881-890.

[24] F. J. Fabozzi and R. A. Hershkoff, *Review of Business and Economic Research*, "The Effects of the Decision to List on a Stock's Systematic Risk," Spring 1979, pp. 77-82.

Dhaliwal took an approach completely different from that of previous studies that examined price performance before and after listing. He hypothesized that exchange listing is likely to reduce the cost of equity capital to the company because of the increased availability of financial information. Matched pairs (based on asset size and industry) of 35 exchange-listed and OTC companies were used to test for the existence of a statistically significant difference between the average number of news items appearing in *The Wall Street Journal* during 1972 for the two groups of stocks. The results indicated that the average number of news items for the exchange-listed companies was significantly larger than that for similar OTC companies.[25]

Dhaliwal also tested for a statistically significant difference between the exchange-listed and OTC companies with respect to their costs of capital, alternatively measured by the systematic risk and the total risks associated with companies' rates of return.[26] Based on a cross-sectional

---

[25] E. B. Grant, *Journal of Accounting Research,* "Market Implications of Differential Amounts of Interim Information," Spring 1980, pp. 255-268. Grant shows that more information is released to the public through *The Wall Street Journal* on NYSE companies than on OTC companies. However, he ignores the fact that NYSE firms will normally be larger than firms traded in the OTC market. Dhaliwal overcomes this problem by matching listed and OTC companies based on asset size.

[26] Beta may be a less-than-satisfactory surrogate for the cost of equity capital. For example, W. W. Alberts and S. H. Archer in the *Journal of Financial and Quantitative Analysis,* "Some Evidence on the Effect of Company Sizes on the Cost of Equity Capital," March 1973, pp. 220-245, argue that where the major conditions of the capital-asset pricing model are violated, the strongest substitute for beta is the total risk (standard deviation) of the rate of return. R. Roll, *Journal of Financial Economics,* "A Critique of Asset Pricing Theory's Tests," October 1977, pp. 129-176; and H. Levy, *American Economic Review,* "Equilibrium in an Imperfect Market: A Constraint on the Number of Securities in the Portfolio," September 1978, pp. 643-658, provide additional support for the use of the standard deviation as a reasonable surrogate for the cost of equity capital.

analysis of 29 of the original 35 matched pairs used to test for information availability, Dhaliwal concluded that the exchange-listed company's cost of equity is less than that of the comparable OTC company.[27]

Phillips and Zecher performed the Dhaliwal statistical tests using more recent data and extended the analysis by examining the market-adjusted portfolio returns surrounding the event of exchange listing. An examination of two risk measures, beta and standard deviation of returns, for 26 pairs of OTC and listed companies matched by asset size, industry and trading volume for 1978 and 11 pairs for 1972 revealed no clear tendency for either the OTC or listed stocks to have consistently higher risk.

A second set of tests was performed for a random sample of companies that listed on the Amex and the NYSE during 1977 and 1978. The findings show no differences in risk associated with listing on the Amex or the NYSE. Phillips and Zecher concluded: "In sum, listing does not affect risk or the cost of capital for companies of similar asset size, industry group and trading volume. Further, the decision to list does not appear to have any predictable effect on risk or the cost of capital for the listing company."[28]

Baker and Spitzfaden[29] examined whether any advantage accrued to the issuer of listed vis-à-vis NASDAQ securities regarding the cost of equity capital. Their study attempted to correct several conceptual and methodological flaws that may have biased the findings of previous research, especially those in Dhaliwal's study. For example, their study distin-

---

[27] Dhaliwal, p. 146.

[28] Phillips and Zecher, p. 20.

[29] H. K. Baker and J. Spitzfaden, *The Financial Review*, "The Impact of Exchange Listing on the Cost of Equity Capital," September 1982, pp. 128-141.

guished between the potential impact of listing on the NYSE from listing on the Amex and sampled securities traded on NASDAQ rather than OTC-traded securities in general.

Baker and Spitzfaden addressed the impact of exchange listing on the cost of equity capital from three perspectives. First, they matched 15 NASDAQ-Amex and 14 NASDAQ-NYSE firms to determine media visibility, as measured by news items in *The Wall Street Journal* over the 1978 through 1980 period. The companies were matched on asset size, industry, and debt ratio. The results showed that the number of news items reported for Amex stocks was significantly greater than for their NASDAQ counterparts but that there was no statistically significant difference between the NASDAQ and NYSE members of matched pairs.

Second, they used a cross-sectional analysis to determine whether the cost of equity capital, using beta and standard deviation of returns as surrogates, was lower for exchange-listed firms than for comparable NASDAQ companies. They found no significant differences in the cost of equity capital between members of matched pairs.

Finally, they used a time-series analysis of the pre- and post-listing performances of 15 former NASDAQ companies that listed on the Amex and 23 former NASDAQ companies that listed on the NYSE to determine whether exchange listing lowered the cost of a firm's equity capital. Again, their findings showed no significant differences in either of the two risk measures.

Thus, Baker and Spitzfaden concluded: "Although some differential amounts of news coverage appear to exist between comparable listed and NASDAQ stocks, these differences did not appear significant enough to reduce the perceived riskiness of listed stocks, to lower investors' rate of return, or to reduce the cost of equity capital."[30]

---

[30] Ibid., pp. 135-136

Baker and Petit took a different approach to investigating issues surrounding listing. Instead of examining market data, they surveyed a sample of financial executives of newly listed NYSE and Amex companies during 1975 to 1980 and OTC firms that met the minimum requirements for listing on the Amex. The findings showed that the respondents did not perceive listing as having substantial price effects. Furthermore, the managers on average disagreed with statements such as "investors are willing to accept a lower rate of return on listed securities than they otherwise would require if the same securities were unlisted" and "listing reduces the cost of equity capital." Baker and Petit concluded that "the managers surveyed did not feel that listing led to either stock price enhancement or to reduced equity costs."[31]

Conclusions and Future Research

Because year by year the markets are improving, continuing research is needed to provide current evidence about the reduced-cost-of-capital hypothesis. However, taken as a whole, the research to date generally has not supported the reduced-cost-of-capital hypothesis. With the exception of the Dhaliwal study, which was contradicted by two subsequent studies, the findings have shown that listing status has not altered the risk attributes and hence the cost of equity capital of the companies studied. The implication of this finding is that the NASDAQ System offers a marketplace equal to the major exchanges for issuers to minimize their costs of equity capital. Corporate managers cannot anticipate reduced equity costs from listing.

---

[31] Baker and Petit, p. 17.

Finally, the evidence on whether listing improves the availability of financial information has been both limited and mixed. Studies by Dhaliwal and Baker and Spitzfaden, which use the number of news items reported in *The Wall Street Journal* as a proxy for information availability, have provided a starting point for investigation. Further research is needed that would use other measures of information availability and that would take into consideration the view that information availability may be a function of factors other than listing.

Chapter
twenty-three

*H*ans R. Stoll is the Anne Marie and Thomas B. Walker, Jr., Professor of Finance at Vanderbilt University's Owen Graduate School of Management in Nashville, Tennessee. Dr. Stoll has taught management and finance courses for more than 20 years and has written extensively about domestic and international markets. He has also worked as a consultant to governmental and private agencies.

The Economics of Market Making

by Hans R. Stoll

A market maker facilitates trading. The particular services provided by a market maker depend on the market structure in which he operates and range from purely clerical services to active involvement as a principal.[1] In auction markets, such as some of the European markets, a market maker may simply facilitate trading by others, rarely taking positions for his own account. In NASDAQ and other U.S. markets, market makers play a much more central role by trading as principals and by making two-sided markets.

In this chapter, the term "dealer" is used instead of the more general term "market maker" when trading as a principal is to be emphasized. It is important to recognize that a market maker does not set the fundamental price of a security; price is determined by much more powerful forces. Instead, he sets a price for the services he provides. In NASDAQ and other U.S. dealer markets, dealers stand

---

[1] For a description of alternative roles of market makers, see Hans R. Stoll, *Market Making and the Changing Structure of the Securities Industry*, "Alternative Views of Market Making," In Amihud, Ho, and Schwartz (eds.), Lexington Books, 1985a.

405

ready at any time to buy at the bid price or sell at the ask price. They are therefore said to provide the service of immediacy.[2] The economics of market making, therefore, deals with the demand for and the supply of this service, not with the demand for and supply of securities.

Partly by coincidence and partly by cause, the transformation of the over-the-counter stock market from a sleepy, paper-oriented market in the late 1960s to a modern, computerized system coincided with the growth of academic research on the economics of market makers.[3] Stigler, in 1964, reacting to the SEC's *Special Study of the Securities Markets,*[4] and Demsetz, in 1968, provided the first look at the economics of the market maker.

Stimulated by Smidt's work in the SEC's *Institutional Investor Study,*[5] Tinic, in 1972,[6] developed a model of the New York Stock Exchange specialist and carried out empirical tests of the effect of competition on the bid/ask spread. Stoll,

---

[2] H. Demsetz, *Quarterly Journal of Economics*, "The Cost of Transacting," February 1968.

[3] G. J. Stigler, *Journal of Business*, "Public Regulation of the Securities Markets," April 1964.

[4] U.S. Securities and Exchange Commission (SEC), *Report of the Special Study of Securities Markets*, 88th Congress, 1st Session, U.S. Government Printing Office, Washington, D.C., 1963, Chap. 5.

[5] U.S. Securities and Exchange Commission (SEC), *Institutional Investor Study Report*, 92nd Congress, 1st Session, U.S. Government Printing Office, Washington, D.C., 1971.

S. Smidt, *Financial Analysts Journal*, "Which Road to an Efficient Stock Market? Implications of the SEC Institutional Investor Study," September-October 1971, Vol. 27.

[6] S. Tinic, *Quarterly Journal of Economics*, "The Economics of Liquidity Services," February 1972, Vol. 86, pp. 79-93.

in 1978,[7] provided an explicit theoretical framework for the dealer based on the inventory risk facing the dealer and a variety of other factors.

Empirical tests of the factors affecting bid/ask spreads both on exchange markets and the over-the-counter market—volume, risk, stock[8] price, competition—appeared in the mid-1970s.[9] More recently, theoretical models have been developed[10] of the spread as a means to protect the dealer against adverse information possessed by other traders.

---

[7] Hans R. Stoll, *Journal of Finance*, "The Supply of Dealer Services in Securities Markets," September 1978a.

[8] The term "stock" is generally used because most analyses have been made using common-stock data. In nearly all instances, the statements are also true for securities generally. The term "security" is used in certain instances because the narrower term "stock" might be misleading.

[9] Seha Tinic and R. West, *Journal of Financial and Quantitative Analysis*, "Competition and the Pricing of Dealer Services in the Over-the-Counter Market," June 1972, Vol. 7, pp. 1701-1728.

Ben Branch and W. Freed, *Journal of Finance*, "Bid/Asked Spreads on the AMEX and the Big Board," 1977, Vol. 32.

Hans R. Stoll, *Journal of Finance*, "The Pricing of Securities Dealer Services: An Empirical Study of NASDAQ Stocks," September 1978b.

J. Hamilton, *Journal of Financial and Quantitative Analysis*, "Competition, Scale Economics and Transaction Cost in the Stock Market," December 1976, Vol. 11, pp. 779-802.

[10] T. C. Copeland and D. Galai, *Journal of Finance*, "Information Effects on the Bid/Ask Spread," December 1983, Vol. 38, pp. 1457-1469.

Lawrence R. Glosten and Paul R. Milgrom, *Journal of Financial Economics*, "Bid, Ask and Transaction Prices in a Specialist Market with Heterogeneously Informed Traders," 1985, Vol. 14.

More complete reviews of the burgeoning literature on market making are contained in K. Cohen, S. Maier, R. Schwartz and D. Whitcomb, *Journal of Financial and Quantitative Analysis*, "Market Makers and the Market Spread: A Review of Recent Literature," November 1979, Vol. 14; and Stoll, 1985a.

Suffice it to say that academic study of market making is nearly as hot a topic as NASDAQ itself.

Demand for and Supply of Dealer Services

The demand for dealer services arises from imbalances between public buyers and public sellers in a particular security. Suppose that fundamental information justifies a price of P* for a security. An imbalance arises if buyers at that price exceed sellers at that price, as shown in Figure 1 (the amount, A-B). Such imbalances are almost inevitable since one cannot expect public sellers to match public buyers during any particular interval of time. In the

Figure 1

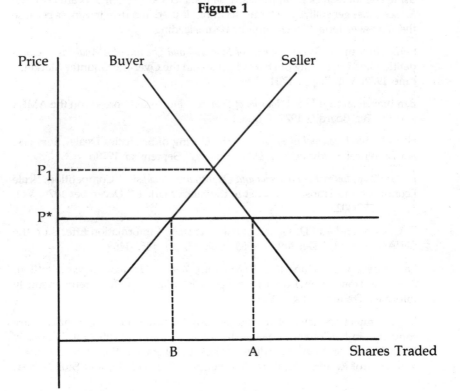

absence of intervention by a dealer, certain buyers would not trade and other buyers would trade only at a high price, P_1, in excess of the true price, P^*. A dealer would be willing to intervene by selling shares below P_1 and above P^*, thereby limiting unjustified deviations of transaction prices from the true underlying prices.

In every type of market, including most call-auction markets that have no dealers, a mechanism exists for responding to the type of imbalances pictured in Figure 1. Sometimes other investors or floor traders are able to respond to imbalances (for example, scalpers in futures markets). Sometimes trading is carried out periodically so that many orders may be batched and imbalances publicized before transactions occur. Call-auction markets operate in this manner. But call-auction markets have the disadvantage that investors are not able to trade at all times. That is, the service of immediacy is not provided. Furthermore, a call-auction market does not eliminate the need for participation by market professionals. In most call-auction markets, professional traders intervene on one side or the other to prevent the transaction price from deviating too much from the true underlying price.

Organized dealer markets, such as NASDAQ, are distinguished by the fact that professional traders—dealers—are prepared continuously to quote a two-sided market. They do not respond to an imbalance after the fact, as might be the case in call-auction markets. They limit imbalances before they have the opportunity to arise. Market-making services are supplied in response to economic rewards—the profit realized from buying at the bid price and selling at the ask price.

In competitive markets, the bid/ask spread reflects the cost of providing dealer services—for dealers will not stay in business unless they are compensated for their costs, and new dealers will enter if profits are too great. Fluctuations of transaction prices around the true price, as in Figure 1, are limited by the bid/ask spread established by dealers. The higher the cost of providing dealer services, the larger the bid/ask spread and the wider the possible fluctuations of the transaction price around the true price.

A desirable characteristic of a market is, therefore, to provide dealer services at a cost that is as low as possible. This cost depends on the economics of the individual dealer and the degree of competition among dealers.

The Economics of the Individual Dealer

Three types of costs facing an individual dealer may be distinguished: order-processing costs, risk-bearing costs and adverse-information costs. The profits earned from buying at the bid price and selling at the ask price must cover these costs if a dealer is to stay in business.

1. **Order-Processing Costs.** Order-processing costs include fixed- and variable-cost components. Some costs are fixed over a particular planning horizon, such as a month or year. These include the cost of space, the cost of communications equipment, most labor costs and the cost of the dealer's time. Certain other costs are fixed with respect to a particular transaction and do not depend on the size of the transaction. These might include a fixed minimum cost for communications and a fixed minimum cost for clearing. Certain costs may vary with the size of a transaction. For example, larger transactions incur larger clearing costs and may require more attention from the dealer. However, because of the fixed-cost component, economies of scale are said to exist in trading. In other words, the per-dollar cost of handling a transaction is lower for larger transactions than it is for smaller transactions because the fixed costs of a large transaction can be spread over more dollars.

2. **Risk-Bearing Costs.** By buying at the bid price or selling at the ask price, the dealer takes on an inventory position (either "long" or "short") that imposes inventory risk. The risk arises from unpredictable changes in the stock price after the dealer takes on inventory. The larger the variance of the rate of return of the stock and the larger the transaction size, the larger the risk. Risk has a greater effect on the dealer the lower the capitalization of the dealer and the more risk averse the dealer.

   Stoll and Ho[11] show how the dealer spread is influenced by inventory risk. They also show that the dealer changes his bid and ask prices after taking on inventory to create incentives for public traders to even out his inventory position. For example, after a dealer buys stock, he lowers his bid price to discourage further sales to his own inventory, and he lowers the ask price to encourage purchases of the inventory from him. Thus, while the spread between the bid and the ask prices need not change, the parallel shifting of the bid and the ask prices encourages public transactions that even out the dealer's inventory position.

3. **Adverse-Information Costs.** Because the dealer quotes prices at which he will trade a stated amount, he can be victimized by traders who possess superior information. Thus, a trader with information that justifies a price below the dealer's bid price will sell to the dealer at the bid price, and the dealer will tend to lose to this information trader.

---

[11] Hans R. Stoll, *Journal of Finance*, "The Supply of Dealer Services in Securities Markets," September 1978a; Thomas Ho and Hans R. Stoll, *Journal of Financial Economics*, "Optimal Dealer Pricing Under Transactions and Return Uncertainty," March 1981, Vol. 9.

Papers by Copeland and Galai[12] and Glosten and Milgrom[13] show that the spread must be widened to offset the adverse effects of information trading. In principle, the spread is established so the dealer's losses to information traders are offset by the dealer's gains from traders without information.

The Quoted Bid/Ask Spread

The quoted bid/ask spread that appears in the newspapers or is available from computer quotation services reflects two underlying economic forces. First, the quoted spread of any dealer must, at a minimum, cover the dealer's "reservation spread." Second, the quoted bid/ask spread may exceed the "reservation spread" to the extent allowed by demand conditions and the competitive environment.

"The Reservation Spread." The reservation spread is the spread at which the dealer just covers the marginal costs of carrying out the next transaction. That spread reflects the marginal order-processing, risk-bearing and adverse-information costs described previously. From time to time, the reservation bid or ask price can be quite favorable to public investors.

For example, suppose a dealer has a long position in a particular stock. In this circumstance, the dealer may be willing to sell at a low price simply to dispose of his inventory. Alternatively, a dealer with a heavy fixed investment

---

[12] T. C. Copeland and D. Galai, *Journal of Finance*, "Information Effects on the Bid-Ask Spread," December 1983, Vol. 38, pp. 1457-1469.

[13] Lawrence R. Glosten and Paul R. Milgrom, *Journal of Financial Economics*, "Bid, Ask and Transaction Prices in a Specialist Market with Heterogeneously Informed Traders," March 1985, Vol. 14.

in personnel and computer equipment may be willing to execute a transaction at a bid or ask price that fails to make a contribution to these fixed costs. However, as in any business, market-demand conditions must allow the dealer to price sufficiently above the reservation spread so as to make a contribution to overhead that over the long term covers the fixed costs of being in the dealer business.

The Role of Competition. Competition determines the extent to which dealers can quote bid and ask prices that exceed their reservation prices. In a market without competition, in which a dealer has a monopoly, quoted bid and ask prices can be set in excess of the reservation spread to yield a monopoly profit that exceeds the fixed costs of being in business. In other words, in a market without competition, the dealer has the opportunity to consistently set the bid price below the reservation bid price and to set the ask price above the reservation ask price. NASDAQ's requirement that each NASDAQ security have at least two market makers limits the monopoly pricing power of any dealer. Table 1 shows that most NASDAQ securities have more than two dealers; 90 percent of the NASDAQ/NMS securities have four or more market makers; 75 percent of the non-NASDAQ/NMS securities have four or more dealers.

Competition among dealers is important for two reasons. First, in a market without competition, the quality of the market in a stock depends on the characteristics of the dealer making a market in that stock. If that dealer has excessive risk aversion or inadequate capital, the market in that stock tends to be poor. In a market with competition, investors have the opportunity to seek out dealers that are less risk averse and better capitalized. Second, in a market without competition, even well-capitalized dealers that are willing to take risks tend to charge excessive bid/ask spreads because of their monopoly positions.

Table 1

DISTRIBUTION OF NASDAQ SECURITIES
BY NUMBER OF MARKET MAKERS
(As of December 31, 1986)

Number of Market Makers	Number of Securities	
	NASDAQ/NMS	Non-NASDAQ/NMS
3 or less	278	575
4 to 5	571	653
6 to 10	1,010	868
11 to 15	497	304
16 to 20	207	76
21 to 25	70	11
26 or more	62	7
Totals	2,695	2,494

Aside from competition from other dealers, competition can arise from limit orders placed by investors. On the New York Stock Exchange, where specialists have monopoly franchises in their stocks, individual investors who find the spread too large have the opportunity to place limit orders inside the spread. This competition from limit orders has the effect of narrowing the spread on the New York Stock Exchange relative to the spread that would exist in the absence of limit orders.[14]

The Inside Quote. When there are several dealers in a stock, bid and ask prices can vary across dealers. The "inside

---

[14] The economics of the specialists and the role of the limit-order book in narrowing the spread are discussed in Hans R. Stoll's *Monograph Series in Finance and Economics*, "The New York Stock Exchange Specialist System," 1985b, p. 1985-2.

bid/ask quote'' is the highest bid price of any dealer and the lowest ask price of any dealer. Competition and the tendency of order flow to go to the best dealer keeps the bid and ask prices of different dealers from deviating from each other very much. However, inventory differences and other factors may cause different dealers to quote different prices. As a result, the inside quote generally involves two different dealers.

Determinants of the Quoted Bid/Ask Spread

A casual examination of inside quotes in NASDAQ stocks or in stocks in other markets indicates that spreads differ substantially across stocks. The economics of market making should explain these variations of spreads across different stocks—for if it could not, one would be compelled to argue that spreads are due to haphazard factors.

That spreads vary across stocks is shown in Table 2. For example, consider NASDAQ/NMS stocks, which are subject to real-time, transaction-price reporting. Ten percent of the financial stocks have proportional spreads of less than .0064, and 90 percent have proportional spreads less than .0345. The variation in spreads is greater for industrial stocks and for non-NASDAQ/NMS stocks.

Economists have attempted to explain the cross-sectional variation in spreads as a function of observable variables that represent the theoretical constructs discussed previously. While it is not always possible to find observable variables that adequately represent all the theoretical factors, a number of variables consistently seem to be related to differences in spreads. Some of these include:

1. Spreads tend to be smaller the greater the volume of trading in a stock. This is, in part, because a stock with high volume shortens the dealer's holding period, and

Table 2

DECILE VALUES OF THE PROPORTIONAL SPREAD*
BY TYPE OF COMMON STOCK

Decile	NASDAQ/NMS Stocks		Non-NASDAQ/NMS Stocks	
	Financial	Industrial	Financial	Industrial
Lowest	.0039	.0046	.0053	.0078
1	.0064	.0121	.0174	.0294
2	.0082	.0158	.0272	.0388
3	.0098	.0197	.0333	.0486
4	.0117	.0246	.0408	.0579
5	.0138	.0284	.0503	.0712
6	.0176	.0343	.0611	.0848
7	.0219	.0400	.0775	.1003
8	.0281	.0472	.0964	.1278
9	.0345	.0613	.1481	.1857
Highest	.2302	.2296	.4615	.6667
Observations	166	748	406	1231

* Data are from October 1984; the spread for each stock is the average proportional closing "inside quote" in October, and deciles are determined from this number.

therefore, lowers his inventory risk. Also, high-volume stocks may enable a dealer to achieve certain economies of scale in order processing.

2. More volatile stocks tend to have wider spreads. For a given holding period, a stock with larger variance in rate of return imposes greater risk on a dealer than a stock with low variance in rate of return.

3. High-priced stocks tend to have smaller proportional spreads than low-priced stocks. The price of the stock per se should have little effect on the proportional bid/ask spread. The fact that it does is ascribed to the

possibility that the price of the stock may proxy for certain other factors, such as the risk of the stock or the size of the issuing company. In addition, dollar transaction sizes in low-priced stocks tend to be small and require a larger proportional spread to cover the fixed costs of the trade.

4. The more dealers in a stock, the lower the spread. The greater the number of dealers, the greater the competition, which tends to limit any deviations of the spread from the reservation spread of any dealer. In addition, stocks with a large number of dealers tend to be high-activity stocks in which the risks to the dealer are small.

The importance of these four factors on the spread is reflected in the following cross-sectional regression using data for October 1984:

$$s = 1.766 + .1024\sigma - .3328P - .1990V - .5675MM$$
$$\quad (25.86) \quad (18.15) \quad (-24.23) \quad (-25.73) \quad (-26.43)$$

$$\text{observations} = 2326$$
$$\text{r-square} = .8401$$

where :

$s \quad = \ln \left[\text{average} \dfrac{(P_a - P_b)}{P} \right]$, where the average is taken over all trading days in October 1984.

$P_a \quad$ = lowest closing ask price of any dealer.

$P_b \quad$ = highest closing bid price of any dealer.

$P \quad = (P_a + P_b)/2$

$\sigma \quad$ = ln[standard deviation of return in October 1984]. Return is defined as $(P_t - P_{t-1})/P_{t-1}$ and is adjusted for dividends and splits.

$V \quad$ = ln[average daily dollar volume of trading in October 1984].

MM = ln[average number of market makers in October 1984].

The above regression result is consistent with the results of previous investigators: A positive sign on the risk variable and negative signs on volume, price and the number of market makers. The coefficients in the regression are interpreted as elasticities since the variables are expressed in logarithms. For example, the coefficient on the variability measure means that a 1 percent increase in the variability of the stock causes the spread to go up by .1024 percent. The variables in the regression explain 84 percent of the cross-sectional variation of spreads. This substantial explanatory power indicates that underlying economic factors determine observed differences in spreads.

Dealer Structure

Other than the requirement for at least two market makers in each NASDAQ security, entry and exit from dealing in a particular stock are relatively free. Therefore, it is instructive to observe how the dealers align themselves, for it tells us how dealers, left to themselves, would choose the securities in which to make a market.

It could be possible, for example, that each security would have only the minimum number of dealers—two. Such a result would suggest the existence of substantial economies of scale from concentrating all trading activity in a stock in a particular dealer. Table 1 shows that this is not the case, however. Most securities have more than two dealers, and many have in excess of 20 dealers. This implies that market making is not a natural monopoly with unlimited economies of scale.

Ho[15] examines the factors that determine the number of dealers in a particular stock. The basic argument is as follows: A dealer makes a market in a stock if he believes he has sufficient opportunity to price above his reservation price so he can cover the fixed costs of entering that market. The opportunity to earn more than his reservation spread depends on the volume of trading in the stock and the number of other dealers in the stock. If volume is high, he has correspondingly more opportunities to earn above the reservation fee. If the number of dealers is high, it limits a dealer's opportunity to quote above his reservation spread. These two factors balance each other in such a way that the number of dealers increases with the volume of trading in the stock, but it increases at a decreasing rate.

Another factor influencing the distribution of dealers among stocks is the number of stocks in which a dealer decides to make a market. A dealer who concentrates on one or relatively few stocks may acquire a larger market share of those stocks, but he is subject to unexpected imbalances in relatively few stocks and is dependent on activity in those few stocks. On the other hand, the dealer who makes a market in a large number of stocks has greater flexibility to move resources from stocks that are currently inactive to stocks that are currently more active.

Dealers may view these tradeoffs in different ways. As a result, one sees not only differences across stocks in a number of dealers; one observes, as well, differences across dealers in the number of stocks. Table 3 illustrates that some dealers make markets in relatively few stocks while other dealers make markets in a large number of stocks. In

---

[15] Thomas Ho, *Market Making and the Changing Structure of the Securities Industry*, "Dealer Market Structure and Performance," In Amihud, Ho and Schwartz (eds.), Lexington Books, 1985.

Table 3

DISTRIBUTION OF THE NUMBER OF MARKETS MADE
IN NASDAQ COMMON AND PREFERRED STOCKS
BY NASDAQ MARKET MAKERS
(As of December 31, 1986)

Number of Markets Made	Number of Market Makers
1 to 5	131
6 to 10	60
11 to 20	80
21 to 30	51
31 to 40	32
41 to 50	27
51 to 100	59
101 to 200	40
201 to 300	20
301 to 400	6
401 to 500	6
501 to 1,000	6
More than 1,000	8
Total	**526**

December 1986, of the 526 NASDAQ market makers, 131 made markets in one to five common or preferred stocks; eight dealers made markets in more than 1,000 common and preferred stocks.

Dynamics of the Dealer and the Realized Bid/Ask Spread

The profits earned by a dealer depend on the dynamics of the price over time. A dealer who buys at the bid price hopes to sell later at an ask price that is above that bid price. If there is no systematic tendency for the ask price to fall after a dealer's purchase, the dealer will, on average, realize a spread that is equal to the spread he quotes. On the other hand, if there is a systematic tendency for the ask price to fall after a dealer's purchase and for the bid price to rise after a dealer's sale, the dealer's realized spread will be less than the quoted spread. If it is assumed that prices have a systematic tendency to move against the dealer and that transactions are reversed in one period, the relation between the dealer's realized spread and his quoted spread can be expressed as follows:

1. Dealer purchase followed by dealer sale:

$$P_{t+1}^a - P_t^b < P_t^a - P_t^b$$

2. Dealer sale followed by dealer purchase:

$$P_t^a - P_{t+1}^b < P_t^a - P_t^b$$

where, $P_t^a - P_t^b$ is the quoted spread at time t, and the left side of the inequality spread realized between t and t+1.

Two factors lead one to believe that realized spreads will tend to be less than quoted spreads, as indicated in the above inequalities. First, in managing his inventory, the dealer will tend to lower both the bid and ask prices after a dealer purchase because he is less anxious to buy additional shares and more anxious to sell the shares he has just acquired. Similarly, after a dealer sells, he will tend to raise both the bid and ask prices because he is more anxious to buy shares and less anxious to sell additional shares.

Second, the presence of adverse-information costs associated with the existence of public traders who may have superior information causes similar adjustments in prices. If someone sells stock to a dealer at the dealer's bid price, the dealer reasons that there is a greater probability of adverse information about the stock than positive information about the stock. Thus, he will tend to lower both his bid and ask prices to reflect the information conveyed by a public sale transaction.

Similarly, if an investor purchases stock from a dealer at the dealer's ask price, the dealer infers that there is a greater probability of good news than bad news about the stock; as a result, the dealer increases both his bid and ask prices. The dealer's attempts to limit his inventory exposure and to adjust for adverse information cause bid and ask prices to move systematically in a way that reduces the realized spread relative to the quoted spread.

Empirical evidence supports the view that the realized spread falls short of the quoted spread. Stoll[16] shows that there is a systematic tendency for prices to fall after a dealer purchase and to rise after a dealer sale. The data in Stoll[17] and Roll, in 1984,[18] suggest that the realized spread on the New York Stock Exchange is about one half the quoted spread on that exchange. Similar empirical work has not yet been carried out for the NASDAQ System.

The realized spread measures the amount the market maker earns. The difference between the quoted spread and realized spread measures the amount he loses to informed traders and the price concession he makes to induce the public to take unwanted inventory off his hands. Traders who possess superior information can, in effect, cut the

---

[16] Hans R. Stoll, *Journal of Financial and Quantitative Analysis,* "Dealer Inventory Behavior: An Empirical Investigation of NASDAQ Stocks," September 1976, pp. 359-380.

[17] Hans R. Stoll, *Market Making and the Changing Structure of the Securities Industry,* "Alternative Views of Market Making," In Amihud, Ho, and Schwartz (eds.), Lexington Book, 1985a.

[18] Richard Roll, *The Journal of Finance,* "A Simple Implicit Measure of the Effective Bid/Ask Spread in an Efficient Market," September 1984, Vol. 39, No. 4, pp. 1127-1139.

quoted spread by making trading gains from their knowledge. Traders who do not possess superior information pay the full, quoted spread. On average, the dealer's losses to information traders are offset by his earnings on the full, quoted spread from traders who do not possess superior information. This point was first made by Bagehot.[19]

The Future of Dealer Markets

Two forces have been instrumental in the past growth of dealer markets and are likely to be important in the future growth of such markets. The first of these forces is the institutionalization of savings in the hands of pension funds, mutual funds and similar institutions.

Institutional investors have, for a long time, dominated the debt markets, and with the development of the telephone, most trading in debt instruments moved off exchange floors to the OTC competing-dealer market. In the 1960s and 1970s, as the role of institutions in equity markets increased dramatically, the locus of institutional trading in equity instruments also moved off-floor to the dispersed trading desks of major dealers—although much of this trading continues to be brought to or reported to the floor of stock exchanges when executed.

The second of these forces is the technological change in communication and order execution. Technological developments have also made possible dispersed dealer markets in non-institutional-sized orders. Automation has extended the range of transaction sizes for which such markets are feasible. A major characteristic of the NASDAQ System is its ability to accommodate inactively traded securities as well as actively traded securities.

---

[19] Walter Bagehot (pseud.), *Financial Analysts Journal*, "The Only Game in Town," March-April 1971, Vol. 27.

Modern communications technologies make face-to-face trading on the floor of a stock exchange increasingly obsolete, and these technologies have resulted in the transfer of trading activity to systems connecting dispersed trading rooms.[20] Even in floor-type exchange markets, many transactions are executed more or less automatically. The improvements in technology and the enhancement of existing execution systems—to accommodate automatic execution and to incorporate a consolidated limit-order book, for example—hold the prospect of even further growth in off-floor dealer markets.

The future of dealer markets in general and the NASDAQ System in particular is much rosier today than in the 1960s when the over-the-counter market relied on the pink sheets to provide price quotations. The NASDAQ System provides a flexible framework in which the demand for and supply of market-making services can be equilibrated. Market makers are free to enter in response to a demand for additional market-making services, or they may exit if trading activity no longer warrants their participation. NASDAQ provides a communications network within which competition among market makers can take place, and that competition helps to assure that the bid/ask spread reflects the economic costs of providing market-making services in each security traded through NASDAQ.

---

[20] This process was dramatically illustrated by the shift of the bulk of trading in London from the floor to the NASDAQ-like Stock Exchange Automated Quotations (SEAQ) system over a period of weeks after the October 27, 1986, introduction of SEAQ, unfixing of commissions and removal of the trading rules. See " 'Big Bang' Killing a Tradition,'' *The New York Times*, November 28, 1986.

PART VI
The Financial Media Look at NASDAQ

Chapter
twenty-four

Jordan Goodman is a Senior Reporter who covers investing at Time Inc.'s *Money* magazine. He has also co-authored two books, published by Barron's Educational Series, *The Dictionary of Finance and Investment Terms* and the *Barron's Finance and Investment Handbook.*

Making the Most of Your Investment Opportunities in NASDAQ

by Jordan Elliot Goodman

If you're an investor who is looking to profit by trading shares of NASDAQ companies, you first have to learn how to make the system work for you. This chapter explains how to get the information you need for picking and following their securities.

Buying OTC stocks used to be a daunting experience, but things have changed greatly since the advent of NASDAQ, which has brought information flow, liquidity and ease of access to the OTC market. Today 1,800 of its stocks could just as easily trade on the New York or American stock exchanges. Many of its stocks, particularly those in the NASDAQ National Market System, are issued by well-known, established companies that are widely followed by securities analysts. In particular, hundreds of banks, savings and loans and insurance companies fit such a description. Now that NASDAQ is well established, trading is much faster, easier and fairer.

Let's say you're convinced that you should put at least some of your assets into NASDAQ stocks, either directly or through a mutual fund. Where do you go to find out more? The three best places to get information about over-

429

the-counter stocks are (1) the companies themselves; (2) securities analysts and brokers who follow the companies; and (3) the press: magazines, newspapers, investment newsletters and the broadcast media.

Let's take a look at what you can expect to learn from each of these sources.

The Company and Its Annual Report

Say you just heard a hot tip at a cocktail party that Unlimited Future Inc. is a sure-fire investment no one knows about and that you can get in on the ground floor if you buy shares now. Are you going to call up your broker and buy 10,000 shares on blind faith? Let's hope not. If the company is a good long-term investment, it'll still be a good investment in a few weeks, *after* you've analyzed its prospects for yourself.

The first step in that analysis is to obtain more information about the company. You can get a quick overview of Unlimited's numbers by looking in Standard & Poor's Stock Guide or possibly the Value Line OTC Special Situations Service. For more detail, ask your "hot tipper" where the firm is located. Then call or write its investor relations department to get an annual report and the latest two or three quarterly reports. These reports might seem a bit overwhelming at first, but hidden amidst all of those numbers is the answer to your question: Is this company's stock a good long-term investment?

Most annual reports contain these basic elements: highlights, a letter to shareholders, a review of operations, financial statements, investor's information, and a list of Directors and Officers. Here's a look at what you might watch in each of those sections.

- **Highlights.** This gives you a brief overview of the company's sales and earnings over the last two years, expressed both in total dollars and on a per-share basis. To make its results look better to shareholders, the company often uses fancy graphics to augment the numbers.
- **Letter to Shareholders.** Here the company's president and chief executive officer tell you what happened to the company over the last year and what can be expected in the coming year. It is usually written in the most upbeat manner possible, within the bounds of reason. If the letter says the year was "challenging," the company probably had a pretty rough time. If the tone is very optimistic, look at last year's annual report to see if top management's predictions from last year were actually fulfilled. In any case, the letter is a good place to get an overview of the company and its future direction.
- **Review of Operations.** Here's where you get all the pretty pictures of happy employees working, new products being launched or new factories being opened. While all this can seem impressive, don't get distracted. See if any important parts of the company's operations aren't pictured—those areas that might not be doing too well. Companies with diversified operations are required to provide financial information about important business segments, so you should be able to quickly identify all the firm's areas of operations.
- **Financial Statements.** This is the heart of the annual report. The Securities and Exchange Commission regulates what companies must report to their shareholders, and this is where all the facts are laid out. First a brief letter from the firm's independent accountants says whether they give an unqualified opinion of the firm's finances. An unqualified opinion means the accountants

have confidence in the numbers and that the numbers were compiled in conformity with generally accepted accounting principles. If the accountant qualifies his opinion, that means he has doubts about the viability of the company's business, and serious trouble may be about to affect the firm.

The remaining financial statements are broken into two main areas: the balance sheet and the income statement.

1. **The Balance Sheet.** This section of the annual report describes the financial condition of the company. On the balance sheet, items such as cash and short-term securities, accounts receivable, inventories, prepaid expenses, property, plant and equipment, and other assets such as goodwill or copyrights are totaled and compared to the figures from a year earlier. The same is done for the company's liabilities, such as accounts payable, taxes due, long- and short-term debt and dividends payable. The balance sheet also includes a listing of shareholders' equity—what the value of the company would be after creditors' claims were satisfied. This section lists common and preferred stock outstanding, any capital and surplus and retained earnings.

2. **The Income Statement.** Instead of comparing assets and liabilities like the balance sheet, this section details sales, costs of doing business and profits. The income statement compares this year's sales, cost of goods sold, depreciation, selling and administrative expenses, and profits with last year's figures. The statement also shows such items as depreciation and the provision for income taxes. Your eye might be attracted to the line that says "Net Income"—that's the bottom line that everyone speaks about so much.

The rest of the financial report is made up of a statement of changes in the company's financial condition, footnotes to the financial statements and supplementary tables that include a five-year summary and two years of quarterly data. Don't neglect this part of the report because a company often places important facts here that could affect the firm's prospects in the coming year.

- **Investors' Information.** Here you find what you need to know about trading in the company's stock—who the transfer agent is, what the stock symbol is, when and where the annual meeting will take place, if a dividend reinvestment plan is available and other such matters. This section also invites you to request a 10-K form, which is an even longer and more detailed version of the annual report.
- **Directors and Officers.** The people to whom you are entrusting your money are all listed here—both the inside management of the company and members of the board of directors who work outside the company. If the company has very few outside board members, you can tell it is dominated by the top executives. It is usually healthier to have several outside people on the board: They lend a fresh view to management's decisions.

To make sure you don't overlook another NASDAQ company in the same business that might make a better investment than Unlimited Future Inc., you might extract numbers from the annual report in order to calculate a few ratios which will allow you to compare companies. One important area of comparison is profitability. Here you can calculate the net profit margin by dividing net income by net sales; you can also look at return on equity by dividing net income by total stockholders' equity. You'll be able to tell quite quickly if Unlimited Future's profit margins are equal to, better than or worse than its competitors.

To see if Unlimited Future has taken on too much debt compared to its competitors, you can figure out the debt-to-equity ratio by dividing total liabilities by total stockholders' equity. In general, the lower the debt/equity ratio, the better.

Finally, you should take a look at how Unlimited Future's stock is priced in relation to others in its industry. Look first at the price-to-earnings (P/E) ratio, which is calculated by dividing the current stock price by the latest reported earnings per share. The higher the P/E ratio, the higher the expectation by investors that Unlimited Future will live up to its name. If the P/E ratio is significantly above the P/E ratios of others in the same industry, it can be a sign of over-enthusiasm, which could endanger the stock price if enthusiasm wanes.

The other ratio to look for is the price-to-book-value ratio, which is obtained by dividing the stock's market price by its book value. This shows you if the stock is selling above or below the value of the company's assets as stated on its books. But often book value is understated, since assets such as real estate may have appreciated sharply from the time they were put on the books.

After you've looked through all these sections of the annual report and compared the company to its competitors, you should have a much better sense of whether Unlimited Future Inc. can live up to its lofty name.

Securities Analysts and Brokers

You don't have to rely solely on a company's literature to decide whether or not it's a good buy. Securities analysts on Wall Street closely follow hundreds of NASDAQ companies and constantly express their opinions on which stocks are good buys. Although their opinions can be helpful, you must still use your own judgment in deciding what makes sense for you and your investment goals.

Securities analysts' reports contain most of the same information found in annual reports, but analysts' reports are much more timely. Annual reports can take months to grind out of the corporate bureaucracy, while analysts react to events constantly, either upgrading or downgrading their opinions of the company. Soon after a company reports its quarterly earnings, analysts write their reports. As an investor in the company, this timely information gives you an advantage over someone who is relying solely on the annual report, which summarizes last year's news.

Most analysts' reports provide a small summary of the key features of the stock under discussion: this year's and next year's earnings projections, the price/earnings ratio, dividends, and the analyst's buy or sell recommendation. While most analysts get the majority of these facts from the companies themselves, their opinions are also shaped by discussions with competitors, suppliers and customers. This can be key input for a small NASDAQ company, which may have a pioneering product or service. By talking to competitors, an analyst can ascertain if the company has a niche it can sustain or if competition is about to overwhelm it.

Analysts speak a vague language that you should learn if you want to know when to bail out of a stock. They might cut their rating from a "buy" to a "hold." Or they might say, "This stock could be a source of cash." Or they might announce that the stock is "fully valued." In all these cases, the analyst is really saying, "Don't buy more. In fact, you should be thinking of selling."

If possible, look at the research reports of analysts from a few different brokerage firms. If analysts generally agree about the quality of the company, you're better off than if they disagree sharply.

The Press

The fastest way to get news or investment ideas about NASDAQ companies is by reading some of the voluminous material being published on investments today. Newspapers such as *The Wall Street Journal* and *Investor's Daily* are filled with the latest events affecting companies, as well as news of earnings and top management changes. Magazines such as *Money, Fortune, Business Week, Venture* and *OTC Review* provide constant coverage of NASDAQ stocks. A bevy of investment newsletters with names like *Growth Stock Outlook, America's Fastest Growing Companies,* and *Smart Money* write up emerging over-the-counter companies.

Even the electronic media is now in on the action. Company news is reported on *Financial News Network, Cable News Network, The Nightly Business Report* and a growing array of syndicated business and investment TV shows. Many more radio shows, often featuring a call-in format, also devote time to investment topics.

If you want up-to-the-second information on NASDAQ companies, you can subscribe to one of the many computer data bases that spew out massive amounts of data on an ongoing basis. You can hook into Dow Jones News Retrieval, Quotron Systems, CompuServe or Source to get news, earnings announcements and price quotes on every company in the NASDAQ System. You can also get monthly balance sheet and income statement data on a computer diskette by subscribing to services such as Standard & Poor's Stockpak 11 or Value Line's Value Screen Plus packages. These and other competing services allow you to screen data on OTC companies so you can identify good investment opportunities. For example, you might narrow the kinds of companies you look at by asking for companies with earnings growth of 10 percent a year and price/earnings ratios of 15 or less.

For most people, the pages of a local newspaper or *The Wall Street Journal* provide the handiest and most timely method of finding and following over-the-counter companies. Pay particular attention to sections on key market indexes, market statistics, stock tables and earnings and dividend reports. Here's a rundown of these four sections and an explanation of each.

Key Market Indexes

Most papers give you the daily price changes of the major NASDAQ indexes. By taking a quick glance at these tables, you'll be able to see how the various components that make up NASDAQ have performed recently. Here's what the box in *The Wall Street Journal* looks like:

NASDAQ

411.16	326.69	OTC Composite	389.95	+	3.55	+	0.92	+	61.76	+	18.82	+	41.12	+	11.79
414.15	329.43	Industrials	396.80	+	5.76	+	1.47	+	64.87	+	19.54	+	47.47	+	13.59
467.05	382.76	Insurance	446.08	+	3.05	+	0.68	+	60.67	+	15.74	+	41.94	+	10.38
457.59	349.08	Banks	454.48	+	3.53	+	0.78	+	103.38	+	29.44	+	41.95	+	10.17
174.84	138.59	Nat. Mkt. Comp.	167.02	+	1.57	+	0.95	+	27.62	+	19.81	+	17.98	+	12.06
155.55	123.28	Nat. Mkt. Indus.	151.14	+	2.34	+	1.57	+	26.63	+	21.39	+	18.57	+	14.01

The columns on the far left show the highest and lowest levels at which the OTC Composite Index has traded over the last 12 months. The three numbers immediately to the right of the index name show the latest closing value for the index, the amount it changed from the close of the last trading session, and the percentage change, up or down, that this move represents. The middle two numbers show the amount the index has moved up or down over the last 12 months and the percentage change that the move represents. The final two numbers on the right show the amount and percentage change of the index since the beginning of the year.

Here is a brief rundown on each index:

NASDAQ OTC Composite: This index is a measure of NASDAQ/NMS stocks (except warrants) and domestic common stocks traded in the NASDAQ market. It is a market-value-weighted index, meaning that the representation of each security in the index is proportional to the last-sale (for NASDAQ National Market System issues) or bid (for regular NASDAQ issues) price times the total number of shares outstanding, relative to the total market value of the index. The index is constantly adjusted for additions and deletions to the NASDAQ list, changes in market capitalization, splits and stock dividends. Cash dividends are not figured into the index. The index and all sub-indexes to follow were based at 100 on February 5, 1971.

Industrial: This is the broadest of the sub-indexes and is filled with a wide range of manufacturing and service companies.

Insurance: This index represents all types of insurance companies, insurance brokers and agents, and insurance-related services.

Banks: This index contains all types of banks, including trust companies not engaged in deposit banking and establishments performing functions closely related to banking—such as check-cashing agencies, currency exchanges, safe deposit companies and corporations engaged in banking abroad.

NASDAQ/NMS Composite: This index includes all the stocks except warrants in the NASDAQ National Market System—almost 2,700 stocks.

NASDAQ/NMS Industrial: The final index listed by *The Wall Street Journal* incorporates the manufacturing and service company stocks in the NASDAQ National Market System.

NASDAQ also keeps track of three other sub-indexes: transportation companies, utilities, and other financial companies such as savings and loans and securities brokers.

Market Statistics

In addition to watching the ups and downs of NASDAQ market indexes, you should watch what is happening to the internal dynamics of the marketplace. The listing of the "Diaries" section of *The Wall Street Journal* can tell you at a glance. It looks like this:

NASDAQ	TUE	MON	WK AGO
Issues traded	4,488	4,485	4,480
Advances	1,452	1,307	1,691
Declines	930	1,053	650
Unchanged	2,106	2,125	2,149
New highs	233	186	144
New lows	27	19	22
Adv Vol (000)	99,694	66,449	104,229
Decl Vol (000)	30,120	43,384	17,210
Total Vol (000)	172,351	143,385	154,452
Block trades	3,079	2,523	2,596

Issues traded: This shows the total number of NASDAQ stocks that were traded in the latest session, the day before and a week earlier.

Advances: This is the total number of stocks that went up in price over the previous day's price.

Declines: This is the total number of stocks that fell in price compared to the previous day's price.

Unchanged: This is the number of stocks that ended the day at the same price at which they started. This does not mean that these stocks did not change prices at all during the trading day, however.

New Highs: This is the number of NASDAQ stocks that, on this trading day, reached their highest price in the last 52 weeks.

New Lows: This is the number of stocks that hit their lowest price in the last 52 weeks.

Advancing Volume: This is the number of traded shares, in millions, that went up during the day.

Declining Volume: This is the number of traded shares, in millions, that went down in price during the day.

Total Volume: This is the total amount of shares, in millions, traded in the NASDAQ market on that day.

Block Trades: This is the total number of trades of 10,000 or more shares that were executed on NASDAQ on that day. A large amount of block trades indicates heavy institutional activity, since most individual investors do not trade in lots of 10,000 or more.

Each of the numbers in these market diaries compares the latest figures with the number from the previous day and the number from the week earlier. Technical analysts frequently use all of these indicators to look at the condition of the market. Such analysts find it much more significant if the market is rising on heavy volume, with far more advances than declines, than if the market rises on low volume and an even advance/decline ratio. Other technical analysts chart the number of new highs versus new lows to see if the market is strengthening or weakening. You can learn to interpret these numbers, too, with a little practice.

Most newspapers also highlight the NASDAQ stocks that were most actively traded on the last trading day. The listing shows the name of the stock, the volume of shares traded, in millions, the closing price of the shares, and the dollar change for the day. Large volume can either be a sign of the importance of the company—MCI, for example, is often near the top of the list because it is among the largest of NASDAQ stocks—or it can be an indication that a major event, such as a takeover announcement or an earning's release, raised investor interest in the stock. A typical "Most Active Issues" table looks like this:

NASDAQ				
Intel Cp	3,652,900	27⅞	+	2⅛
US Hlthcr	2,861,600	11¼	+	¾
Seagate Tch	2,426,500	26⅛	+	1⅛
Apple Cptr	2,252,600	48⅛	+	3½
MCI Comm	2,004,700	6¾	...	
LSI Logic	1,800,100	14⅛	+	1¼
Miniscrb	1,603,600	12¼	+	¾

Finally, *The Wall Street Journal* and many other newspapers include a box listing the biggest percentage gainers and losers on NASDAQ on the previous trading day. The first column shows the stock's closing price, the second column shows the dollar amount the stock rose or fell, and the third column shows percentage change in price from the previous day. The stocks are ranked by the greatest percent gain or loss. By scanning this list, you can often spot stocks that have had some kind of important corporate development or that have rumors about takeover activity.

OTC											
Frankln Cmptr	3⅜	+	⅞	+	35.0	Satl Auct wt	3⅞	–	1¼	–	24.4
Chapmn En pf	2⅛	+	½	+	30.8	Sweet Victry	3¾	–	1⅛	–	23.1
Ctl Fd SL	9	+	2	+	28.6	NCA Corp	4⅝	–	1⅜	–	22.9
Stud Aide	4½	+	1	+	28.6	Diag Medic	3¾	–	1	–	21.1
J Hansn Sv	8	+	1⅝	+	25.5	Utilitech	3¼	–	¾	–	18.8
Cardplm TC	2½	+	½	+	25.0	VR Bus B	2¾	–	½	–	15.4
Image Mgt	3¾	+	¾	+	25.0	AC Teleconnec	3¾	–	⅝	–	14.3
Tylan Cp	3¼	+	⅝	+	23.8	ECI Telecom	2¼	–	⅜	–	14.3
East Weym	13¼	+	2½	+	23.3	CMS wt	5	–	¾	–	13.0
Elec Missl	2	+	⅜	+	23.1	Comptr Med	3½	–	½	–	12.5
Pinch Pd	4	+	¾	+	23.1	CMS Advertis	7¼	–	1	–	12.1
Cosmo Com	5⅝	+	1	+	21.6	Presid Aril	2⅞	–	⅝	–	17.9

Stock Tables

Once you've observed how the NASDAQ market in general is doing, you will probably want to look up individual stocks. NASDAQ stocks have much more information available today than in the past, in part because of the advent of the NASDAQ National Market System.

Here is a typical table that you'll find in *The Wall Street Journal* or your local newspaper and an explanation of the various columns, which are numbered for your convenience.

NASDAQ NATIONAL MARKET

7		1	2	3	4		5	6
52-week				Sales				Net
High	Low	Stock	Div	100s	High	Low	Last	Change
32	17	ABC	1.00	467	30 1/4	29 3/4	30	+1/2

1. This is the name of the stock, as abbreviated by the Associated Press or United Press International.
2. The dividend that the company is paying on an annual basis, if any. This number is stated in dollars and cents.
3. The volume of shares, in hundreds, that were traded in the last session. Many of these trades were made between dealers, as well as between investors.
4. The highest and lowest prices at which the stock traded during the latest session.
5. The closing price at which the stock finished that day.
6. The net-change column shows how much the stock went up or down compared to the closing price of a day earlier.
7. The highest and lowest prices at which the stock has traded over the last 52 weeks.

For the stocks on NASDAQ that are not traded on the National Market System, you will find less information in newspapers. These companies, whose securities are usually listed in columns titled "OTC" or "Additional OTC," should not be shunned just because they are small. Indeed, the additional NASDAQ listings are the most fertile field for finding big winners. Certainly not every company will live up to its promise, and some will sink into oblivion. But to enjoy the substantial capital appreciation these securities offer, you have to take above-average risks.

Here is the information these listings offer:

1 Stock & Dividend	2 Sales 100s	3 Bid	4 Asked	5 Net Change
XYZ Corp. 1.00	230	25	25 3/4	+ 1/2

1. The name of the stock and the annual dividend it pays, if any.
2. The volume of sales in hundreds of shares in the latest trading day.
3. The price a dealer is willing to pay you if you want to sell your shares.
4. The price you have to pay a dealer if you want to buy shares. The difference between the bid and asked price is the dealer's spread for risking his capital in making a market in the stock.
5. The net change in the bid price from the closing price of the previous day.

Earnings and Dividend Reports

Once you've bought shares in a company, you'll want to follow its quarterly earnings and dividend reports, which are both reported in the newspapers.

The earnings reports detail the latest quarterly results from the company's operations and compare them to results for the same quarter last year. A typical earnings release looks like this:

ABC Co. (ABC)

Qtr to June	1987	1986
Revenue	$10,456,000	$9,365,000
Net Income	1,000,000	900,000
Share earns	.32	.31
Shares outstanding	3,100,000	2,900,000

Most of these reports are released during the trading day, so investors have already reacted to the news by buying or selling the stock. If you read these reports in the next day's newspaper, it's still not too late for you to decide whether to sell your shares or buy more because most investors take their time evaluating the report. The key number that most investors remember and act on is the per-share earnings. This number takes into account any increase or decrease in the number of shares outstanding in the last year.

If your company pays a dividend, you'll want to watch for the announcement of that payout in the "Dividend Reports" section of *The Wall Street Journal* and other newspapers. A typical report looks like this:

		Regular	Stock of	
	Period	Rate	Record	Payable
ABC Corp.	Q	$1	7-15	7-30

This table tells you that the regular dividend for ABC Corp. is paid quarterly at $1 per quarter, that the dividend will be paid to those who own the stock at the end of trading on July 15, and that the actual dividend payment will be paid on July 30th. Therefore, if you bought ABC shares on July 16th, you wouldn't be entitled to the dividend. The dividend reports also list other special dividends under the columns for Irregular, Increased, Reduced, and Stock Dividends.

Now You're Ready to Buy

Armed with an ability to find, analyze and follow NASDAQ stocks, you can now go about selecting the mix of securities that best meets your investing needs. As with any investment, you should first analyze your investment goals, the amount of risk you're willing to take and the amount of money you're willing to put into each stock. You also should set a target-price objective for every NASDAQ stock you buy, as well as a downside percentage of loss you're willing to tolerate before you bail out.

With the rapid development of the NASDAQ market in recent years, investors with small and large portfolios are finding that it is foolish to ignore it. If you're properly informed about the risks and rewards of over-the-counter investing, you too can take advantage of the tremendous growth opportunities that continue to be available from NASDAQ stocks.

Chapter
twenty-five

Monica Roman is a New York financial writer who specializes in the structure and operations of the equity, options and futures markets. She has been on the staff of *Investor's Daily* since the paper's inception in 1984.

NASDAQ—A Market on the Move

by Monica Roman

Today, the markets for U.S. government securities, Eurobonds and oil are under pressure to distribute price and volume information more widely. Dealers in these markets consider this data proprietary and are willing to share it only with those with whom they do business. These dealers are concerned that if prices for their transactions become public knowledge, their profits, per transaction, would be reduced—and they are right.

The creation of the National Association of Securities Dealers Automated Quotations (NASDAQ) System for trading over-the-counter stocks has proven, without a doubt, that greater exposure of price information will narrow the spread between the bid and ask quotes for a security. But any resulting decline in a dealer's profit per transaction has been more than offset by the stunning volume growth NASDAQ has experienced since it began electronically displaying firm quotations on computer screens in brokers' offices across the nation.

449

NASDAQ Brings a Market Into the 20th Century

The National Association of Securities Dealers, Inc. (NASD), was founded in 1939, and its primary responsibility is self-regulation of the OTC securities market. In the Maloney Act amendment to the Securities Exchange Act of 1934, Congress authorized the creation of an organization to function ''as a mechanism of regulation among over-the-counter brokers and dealers operating in interstate and foreign commerce or through the mails.'' The NASD was established pursuant to the legislation and operates under Securities and Exchange Commission (SEC) oversight.

Although the NASD's charter permits it to standardize the principles and practices of the investment banking and securities business, the Association's leaders were not sure in the early 1960s that this mandate would allow them to create a central marketplace.[1] The SEC's Special Study of Securities Markets, presented to the 88th Congress in July 1963, sowed the seeds for the development of the NASDAQ System.

The SEC study noted that, at the time, three vendors were offering quotations for both listed and OTC stocks. ''There is strong reason to believe that expanded electronic systems, similar in principle to those used by the quotation companies, would be technically capable of processing information on every stock traded over the counter,'' the report stated.

''These devices could receive and store, among other things, all bids and offers in each stock and reports of all consummated transactions. The information could be made

---

[1] Robert Sobel, *Inside Wall Street*, W. W. Norton and Company, New York, 1977, p. 76.

instantly available for professional and public dissemination and compilation relating to price and volume could be prepared in permanent form," the study added.[2]

While securities industry leaders like NASD President Gordon S. Macklin, who assumed his post in 1970, believed that wider distribution of OTC stock prices would ultimately increase volume, the NASDAQ concept was opposed by many broker-dealers who were concerned with the potential impact on transaction profits. Nevertheless, the SEC pressed the electronic trading network on the market makers after the bull market of 1968 left Wall Street's back offices buried in paper. While the SEC received 3,991 complaints about broker-dealer inefficiency in 1968, the following year it was swamped by 12,494, almost 50 a day.[3]

The NASD was also motivated to computerize the bid and ask prices for over-the-counter stocks by the development in the late 1960s of competing electronic trading systems, such as Autex and Institutional Networks Corporation, which are still operating today. The computer terminals supplied by Autex allow subscribers to broadcast certain quantities of stock. If a dealer is interested, he contacts the firm advertising the block of securities and completes the transaction over the telephone. Instinet's system keeps the names of its subscribers confidential and permits automatic execution via a computer terminal.

Before the NASD advanced into the computer era, broker-dealers in the OTC market relied on "pink sheets" listing each market maker's bids and offers near the close of the previous day's trading. When an investor wanted to buy

---

[2] *Special Study of Securities Markets,* Securities and Exchange Commission, Washington D.C., 1963, p. 657.

[3] "From Over-the-Counter to Over-the-Computer," *Euromoney* supplement, March 1985, p. 4.

or sell a security, his broker was required to telephone three market makers, but there was no firm guarantee he would receive the best price.

That changed in 1971 with the introduction of the NASDAQ System, which was built and operated by Bunker Ramo Corporation under a 1968 agreement with the NASD. The agreement also included an option to purchase the electronic trading network, which was exercised by the NASD in 1976, when its subsidiary NASDAQ, Inc., took over ownership of the System.

The heart of the NASDAQ System is its main computer center in Trumbull, Connecticut, which boasts an uptime rate of more than 99 percent. When it opened in 1971, the NASDAQ System was powered by two Sperry UNIVAC computers; now Trumbull's data processing plant includes a warehouse full of mainframes. In September 1986, the NASD opened a $17.3 million operations center in Rockville, Maryland, to help support a daily volume capacity of 200 million shares. The facility will house the first complete back-up system for any securities market in the world, allowing NASDAQ to continue operating if the Trumbull plant becomes temporarily disabled.

The NASDAQ National Market System Debuts

While dissemination of current quotations and daily volume reporting dramatically changed the OTC market, many believe it was the creation of the NASDAQ National Market System slightly more than a decade later—and the SEC requirement that its stocks be subject to continuous last-sale price and volume reporting—that put NASDAQ on an equal footing with the exchanges. Like the introduction of NASDAQ itself, transaction reporting was resisted by some broker-dealers, who threatened to stop making markets in NASDAQ/NMS securities.

The NASDAQ National Market System began modestly in April 1982 with 40 of the most active OTC issues. All had a minimum average monthly volume of 600,000 shares and a bid of $10 a share or more. In February 1983, the first 100 securities entered the NASDAQ National Market System on a voluntary basis. The criteria for these stocks were a minimum volume of 100,000 shares a month and a minimum bid of $5.

After a three-month study concluded that last-sale price reporting did not have a negative impact on the securities involved, the NASD recommended that eligible issues continue to be added to the NASDAQ/NMS list on a voluntary basis. While market makers were certain that transaction reporting reduced the difference between the bid and offer prices for NASDAQ/NMS stocks, the NASD's study found that the effect of last-sale reporting on spreads was not statistically significant.

Although it is not yet known by how much spreads have been reduced since NASDAQ's introduction in 1971, everyone agrees they have continued to tighten as more information about transactions has been disseminated. For instance, until July 1980, NASDAQ displayed the "representative" prices, or median bid and ask prices, for each stock. But after NASDAQ began publicizing "inside quotations"— the highest bid and lowest offer for each security—spreads narrowed for 86.5 percent of NASDAQ stocks. For 10.8 percent of NASDAQ securities, the difference between the price at which dealers were willing to buy and sell remained unchanged, while spreads widened for only 2.7 percent.

A controversial decision by the SEC in December 1984 paved the way for expanding the number of NASDAQ National Market System issues from 1,100 to the 1986 level of almost 2,700. Despite objections from the exchanges, the

SEC approved the NASD's request to use financial criteria, rather than volume criteria, to determine the standards for NASDAQ National Market System inclusion.

The SEC approved two different sets of qualifications—one for operating companies and one for development companies. Under the rules, operating companies must have net income of at least $300,000 in the last fiscal year or two of the last three fiscal years and a minimum bid of $3 a share, while development companies must have a four-year operating history, $8 million in capital and surplus and a market capitalization of at least $8 million.

Another major breakthrough for the NASDAQ National Market System came in September 1984, when the Federal Reserve Board ruled that NASDAQ/NMS securities automatically qualified for purchase in margin accounts, like issues listed on the New York and American stock exchanges. While the battle for parity with listed securities has been won on the federal level, it is still being waged on the state level. In December 1984, Georgia became the first state to exempt companies in the NASDAQ National Market System from the requirements to register their securities under its "blue sky" statutes. Since then, many other states have followed Georgia's lead.

The NASD will have greater authority to decide which NASDAQ issues can be called NMS securities under a recent SEC proposal. In December 1986, the SEC proposed that the NASD be permitted to set standards for National Market System stocks, subject to SEC approval, similar to the way exchanges determine their listing requirements. Currently, criteria for NMS issues are determined solely by the SEC.

The SEC's proposal sets the stage for the NASD to impose corporate governance standards—such as having at least two outside directors—on companies whose securities are traded in the NASDAQ National Market System. These issuers will be asked to sign listing agreements with the NASD for the first time.

NASDAQ Success Inspires Others

Although the purpose of NASDAQ was to provide a central marketplace that would reflect all price information on OTC stocks, the System has evolved into an automated trading mechanism. In December 1984, the NASD began operating its Small Order Execution System (SOES), allowing orders of 500 shares or less in NASDAQ/ NMS stocks to be filled electronically. SOES was extended to all NASDAQ stocks by September 1985, and the maximum order size for NASDAQ/NMS issues was raised to 1,000 shares.

The success of the NASDAQ System recently inspired the London Stock Exchange to follow in NASDAQ's footsteps. As part of the revolution that took place on October 27, 1986, dubbed "Big Bang Day," the venerable British market installed the Stock Exchange Automated Quotations (SEAQ) system. "London is reinventing the stock exchange," said NASD President Macklin. "They are moving from a marble hall to a global system that meets the needs of international traders and customers."[4]

The compatibility of the SEAQ network with the NASDAQ System was demonstrated in April 1986 when the NASD and the London Stock Exchange began swapping price quotations in 580 securities. Like the NASDAQ System, SEAQ allows dealers to display the prices at which they are willing to buy and sell on computer screens in brokers' offices.

---

[4] Monica Roman, "London Exchange Follows NASD's Lead In Preparing For Electronic Trading Era," *Investor's Daily*, July 25, 1985, p. 1, col. 4.

London Stock Exchange members are no longer required to come down to the floor to trade stocks and bonds, and the exchange has predicted that the floor will not be necessary within three years. For now, members strike deals over the telephone, but the London Stock Exchange is working on automatic execution facilities for small orders and block trades.

The London Stock Exchange decided to transform itself into NASDAQ's British cousin because "the exchange of the future is invisible," said George Hayter, its Director of Information Services. "Anyone looking down from heaven at an exchange in the year 1800 would have seen coffee-houses. By the beginning of this century, a trading floor could be seen. In the year 2000, the exchange will be an electronic network connecting terminals all over the globe."[5]

The internationalization of NASDAQ seems destined to continue. The NASD has been talking with Reuters Holdings PLC, the London-based news and financial information company, about distributing prices for NASDAQ stocks over Reuters' worldwide network of more than 70,000 terminals. In addition, a proposal by the Association of International Bond Dealers (AIBD) to build an electronic trading system similar to NASDAQ could lead to a link with the AIBD, the Zurich-based organization which operates the Eurobond market.

At its annual meeting in May 1986, the AIBD membership approved hiring the NASD to study whether an automated quotations system could be built for the Eurobond market—a market in which borrowers issue debt outside their home countries. Whether the network will be installed

---

[5] Monica Roman, "Around-the-Clock Trading Moves Closer," *Investor's Daily*, September 17, 1986, p. 1, col. 4.

remains uncertain because of opposition by dealers, who are afraid their profit margins will be reduced if price quotations are electronically disseminated.

Perhaps Eurobond traders find it difficult to believe that a NASDAQ-like system could increase their volume, which totaled some $3.57 trillion in 1986 and was second only to the turnover in U.S. government securities. But if the NASD's experience is any indication, the development of an electronic marketplace could lead to further growth in the already booming Eurobond market.

Chapter
twenty-six

Paul Kangas is the Financial Commentator of *The Nightly Business Report*. A former stockbroker, he has been doing national television broadcasts about the stock markets since 1981 and radio broadcasts since 1965.

NASDAQ on TV

by Paul H. Kangas

The Nightly Business Report is broadcast on 240 public television stations across America and each of its nightly programs includes the following NASDAQ information:

- The NASDAQ Composite Index close and change.
- NASDAQ issues that advanced and declined.
- NASDAQ volume for the day.
- The top 10 NASDAQ stocks by dollar volume, with their symbols, closing prices and changes.
- *Stocks in the Spotlight*, which offers significant news about NASDAQ stocks that are not in the top 10 by volume.
- NASDAQ market performance news, such as the 21 times in 1986 that NASDAQ daily share volume exceeded NYSE volume.

Growing With NASDAQ

The Nightly Business Report devotes eight of its 30 minutes to the stock market. Why do we carry such extensive NASDAQ information?

461

We realized early on that NASDAQ was growing at a geometric pace, much faster than the stock exchanges, and rapidly gaining market share. That made it headline news. Investors flocked to it, providing a steadily increasing, nationwide audience for our NASDAQ coverage.

Viewer inquiries from all across the country have confirmed our judgment. When our guest analysts talk about NASDAQ stocks, phone calls and mail increase. Viewers ask for follow-up information on the issues we discussed. Analysts covering exchange-listed stocks do not generate that kind of feedback.

In recent years, the individual investors we hear from have grown more sophisticated. They realize they are much more likely to make gains in NASDAQ growth stocks than they are in NYSE blue chips such as General Motors or IBM. The risk factor may be greater with growth companies, but so is the reward factor, especially if investors closely watch market developments. Our show helps them do that.

This is one of the reasons why our show has grown in scope and popularity much as the NASDAQ market has grown. We started in 1979 as a 15-minute program aired solely on WPBT, Channel 2 in Miami. In mid-1981, we premiered a half-hour pilot program for the public television affiliates of the Interregional Program Service network, and that fall, 126 public television stations began to carry our show. When we celebrated the fifth anniversary of our half-hour syndicated program in October 1986, 240 public stations were carrying *The Nightly Business Report*, a significant growth. Our weekly audience is approximately 5 million viewers. (A.C. Nielsen, February 1985.)

Servicing NASDAQ Investors

We closely attune our program to the investing public's changing interests in the categories of NASDAQ stocks. When interest peaked in Silicon Valley high-tech stocks, which are concentrated in the NASDAQ market, we covered them copiously. In late 1986, we devoted a lot of time to home TV shopping stocks, then the rage. The same was true of savings and loan stocks, as interest rates dived. The genetic engineering stocks on NASDAQ—Genentech, Cetus, and others—have also captured viewer interest and our coverage.

We service many, many viewer inquiries about NASDAQ issues, providing price histories and basic background on them. I like to think our show is an information booth that directs people to specific NASDAQ companies and issues about which they want to know more. The *NASDAQ Company Directory* helps us do that. This directory is updated twice a year and provides the industry classification of each NASDAQ company, its stock symbol, its address and the name and telephone number of the company officer who is in charge of investor relations. It is an invaluable resource for our service to viewer investors.

The *NASDAQ Company Directory* also demonstrates the NASD's responsiveness, its aim to please. When I addressed the October 1983 conference of NASDAQ company CEOs, I suggested that the NASD publish such a directory. Lo and behold, the NASD put out the first issue of the NASDAQ Company Directory in 1984. By now, it is a regular publication with some 160 information-packed pages. That's responsiveness.

NASDAQ Responsiveness on Short Selling . . .

From my experience as a stockbroker, I have been concerned about the damage that "bear raiders" can do with abusive short-selling tactics and about NASDAQ's lack of short-selling rules, and I spoke to the NASD about it. In 1986, the NASD Board of Governors required the marking of order tickets long or short and tightened the prompt receipt and delivery requirements for trades initiated by public customers.

Then the NASD Board retained Irving M. Pollack, a former SEC Commissioner and a recognized expert in the field of securities regulation and surveillance, to make a comprehensive study of short-selling practices in the NASDAQ market. Mr. Pollack's principal recommendation, released by the NASD in July 1986, was to report and publicly disseminate short interest in NASDAQ securities. The NASD began to publicly disseminate this information through the financial media in November 1986 and is now doing it on a monthly basis. The NASD's alacrity in studying and acting upon alleged OTC short-selling practices demonstrates the organization's eagerness to solve problems and improve service.

One additional step might further pre-empt excessive short sales. For some time now, the Securities and Exchange Commission has required any individual investor or corporation who buys 5 percent or more of a public company's common stock to disclose that information by filing Form 13-D in timely fashion so it will become known to the investing public. This regulation, a good one, would be complemented by requiring any investor or corporation who sells short 5 percent or more of a public company's stock to disclose this information to the SEC. Furthermore, just as those 5 percent or more buyers of a firm's stock must, by law, state their reasons for such action, so too should heavy short sellers be required to announce their reasons.

In the days ahead, I see many opportunities for the NASD to take the leadership role in tailoring stock market rules so they will measure up to the expanding needs of the investing public.

...And on Investor Relations

In the area of investor relations, I suggested some time ago that NASD member firms could be more active in informing the public about interesting and promising public companies in their home areas. Broker-dealers might encourage these companies to sponsor open houses once or twice a year to give informative tours of a company's facilities and distribute the latest sales and earnings statistics to stockholders and potential stockholders.

I am delighted to see that the NASD itself has jumped into this area. NASDAQ Company Services now employs seven corporate consultants, who are former senior executives in the financial services field. These consultants advise some 1,600 NASDAQ companies a year on how to improve their investor relations programs. In addition, NASDAQ Company Services publishes a practical guidebook on this subject and conducts several conferences a year for NASDAQ company executives concerned with investor relations.

Once again, that's responsiveness.

Moving Into the Global Market

NASDAQ is becoming a major force in building the global securities market. In April 1986, NASDAQ initiated its "London Bridge," an intercontinental exchange of quotations with the London Stock Exchange. We covered the story extensively through our London Bureau. *The Nightly Business Report* has news bureaus located in the major financial centers of the United States and abroad.

NASDAQ and the London Stock Exchange are now planning to link their communications with the Tokyo Stock Exchange and other Pacific Basin markets. When they do, they will find *The Nightly Business Report* waiting for them. We have already established a Tokyo Bureau to permit our coverage of the entire global market.

...Which leads me to another suggestion: The NASD, because of its long record of successes, growing influence and, most importantly, innovation on an international scale, is well positioned to lead the way toward an IASD... *INTERNATIONAL* Association of Securities Dealers.

I'll drink to that with my favorite cocktail...the *"NASDAQUIRI,"* of course.

Chapter
twenty-seven

*P*adraic M. Fallon is the Managing Director of Euromoney Publications PLC, publisher of *Euromoney*, the monthly publication covering the world's capital and money markets. A financial journalist for nearly 20 years, Mr. Fallon is the recipient of the Wincott Foundation Trustees Special Award for Outstanding Journalism.

The View
From Overseas

by Padraic M. Fallon

In October 1984, we published an article in *Euromoney* entitled "The Final Days of the Trading Floor." With it we ran a mock plaque, similar to those at historic sites in the City of London, which read: "On this site stood the trading floor. It was demolished in 1988 when floor trading became obsolete."

We were attacked for doing so. The traditional London stockbroker, regarded as the backbone of the City, complained loudly: How could we be so irresponsible? Did we not accept that the floor of the London Stock Exchange was the center of gravity of the City? How could we possibly maintain that it would become a museum piece?

We were wrong, of course. I now concede that. But our mistake was to believe the process would take four years. It took two. Today, the trading floor of The Stock Exchange in Throgmorton Street is a deserted, echoing chamber, a monument to yesterday. The traders have moved upstairs.

Before we're very much older, the world's securities markets will have merged into a single, global exchange. Investors will be free to buy promising securities wherever they are listed. Dealers in one location will be able to build local liquidity in foreign stocks by trading, in their own markets, securities issued by corporations based not just in their own countries but on the other side of the planet too.

Corporations seeking to raise capital will look to investors the world over, not just to those in their own capital cities. The trading day that starts in Tokyo will roll westward through Asia, recharge itself in Europe and America and slide seamlessly into the following day by the time it reaches into Japan again. Securities houses will chase the liquid trading hours around the clock, passing their assets and liabilities from city to city in a ceaseless dealing network.

Of course, it's been known for many years that the notion of a single, expensively vaulted forum for traders would eventually be rendered obsolete by the new technology. But it has taken the emergence of the NASDAQ System to demonstrate how efficient and how liquid a computerized, over-the-counter stock exchange can be.

NASDAQ Becomes a Model

NASDAQ was slow to enter the consciousness of capital markets outside America. By 1980, Europe had more than 5,000 NASDAQ terminals, but they rated little more than a passing interest because they were low-level, passive lists of prices on stocks that few investors in Europe wanted to buy. All that changed when the great boom in sovereign lending, which fueled the growth of the Euromarkets through the 1970s, stalled in 1982. Suddenly, investors who had been happy to pack portfolios with government-guaranteed debt began to look harder at direct investment in foreign securities. They could not have done this, of course, had technology not been able to deliver— almost instantaneously—meaningful prices on these securities. And so the recent surge in international equities was born.

There were other factors. It wasn't until some of America's most fashionable stocks—like Apple, Intel and MCI—remained in the NASDAQ System long after they had become eligible for listing in New York, that Europe's traders and investors started to take the U.S. over-the-counter market more seriously. This was partly because they equated it with their own OTC markets, which were small, illiquid and third rate, as indeed they had been in America until 1970. NASDAQ changed that too. Unlisted markets in Europe have grown geometrically since 1983, especially in London, Paris and Holland.

The result of this coincidence of pressures was that NASDAQ quickly became the model for most European efforts to reorganize and automate securities trading. Traders and brokers began to understand that a stock exchange is no more than an old-fashioned switch in an inefficient communications system; and from then on it was only a matter of time before they adopted new habits.

NASDAQ proved not only that it was technologically feasible to lift trading away from the exchange floors; it demonstrated that competing market makers, properly policed, were a bold and efficient alternative to dealing through exchange-sponsored specialists. This system, which NASDAQ has proved is as logical for trading securities as it is for trading currencies, caught the imagination of traders overseas.

Thus, the London Stock Exchange—pushed toward negotiable commissions by Margaret Thatcher's deregulating government—has adopted the competing market-maker system and has built its own version of the NASDAQ System. London's Stock Exchange Automated Quotations (SEAQ) system lets broker-dealers post bid and offer prices on stocks that used to be visible only on the stumps inside The Stock Exchange.

SEAQ Links NASDAQ

Perhaps the most significant innovation of all is the international equity trading link. SEAQ is now directly linked to NASDAQ. Dealers in London can see moving two-way prices on selected NASDAQ stocks on their TOPIC screens, and NASD broker-dealers can see an equivalent number of London-listed stocks on their NASDAQ terminals.

The link was forged with a pragmatic lack of fuss, and quotes on 558 securities are being swapped. One day, the markets will merge, probably in a fiber-optic cable somewhere beneath the Atlantic or in a collision of satellite signals in space.

Of the European stock exchanges, London is both the biggest and the most advanced in terms of automation. The early days, immediately following October's Big Bang, were a horrid embarrassment—enthusiastic dealers overloaded the system on the first morning. But the concept is unshakable. Securities markets—which means borrowers, traders and investors—now require high-speed electronic delivery of price information on the full range of financial instruments offered in the international market.

It is especially important to European corporations that their securities can flourish in a large, liquid, international market because their domestic markets are no longer powerful enough to maintain enterprises with global ambitions. That is why Ericsson, Philips, Nestle and ICI have permitted large numbers of their shares to be traded in America and Japan; only by exposing them to the full array of potential investors can they retain a capital base strong enough to carry their business plans.

Big Corporations Look at Foreign Listings

It has long been a complaint in Europe that the biggest corporations do not enjoy the benefits of a large domestic market for either goods or capital. So finance directors are eager to obtain foreign listings and to launch new issues into the most competitive market available at the time.

That is no more than common sense: Capital markets exist to bring borrowers together with investors. So corporate finance departments will begin to look beyond their own local, competing market makers to something that, in practice, is nothing less than a worldwide system of competing stock exchanges.

It is as if the world were a single room full of brokerage pits, with one difference: Dealers won't have to turn up in person; they will simply peer at the world through remote electronic windows. This will significantly alter the culture of international finance. To be a trader, it's no longer necessary to be a stentorian bruiser; tomorrow's dealer will be more likely to hold an M.B.A. or a Ph.D. than a rugby blue.

NASDAQ was the first electronic stock exchange. But it will not be the last one. And it will not be the only one. Because technology is not only eroding the obstacles that used to limit trading patterns, it is generating in its wake a shift in the very nature of the instruments that are being traded. "Securitization," the buzz word of the early 1980s, began with the decline of the sovereign state as a credible borrower, but it rapidly became much more than a passing trend. Today, the bulk of the transactions in the international capital market is in the form of tradable paper.

The Eurobond market, which is also developing NASDAQ-compatible technology, has already given to the international equity market the innovative over-the-counter techniques that drove it from peak to peak through the 1970s and early 1980s. International equities may not be Euro-equities in the sense that they are neither bearer certificates nor unregulated; but they are underwritten, sometimes by syndicates, priced and placed in classical Eurobond style.

Changes Take Place Too Quickly

In some ways, the changes have taken place too quickly. The phenomenon known as flowback—when securities placed overseas are sucked back into the domestic market, thwarting the ambitions of finance directors—happens because investors in one country are still attracted to their own domestic stocks, even if they have to buy them from a dealer 7,000 miles away. Large slices of Reuters and British Telecom distributed initially in the U.S. flowed back to Britain within months of the issue.

Sometimes, too, chief financial officers have been forced to look on helplessly as their stocks take a beating in a foreign market because of a sudden local hiatus. This is what happened to Ericsson, which saw the value of its shares fall from over 300 to almost 200 Swedish kroner in 1985 because of heavy selling in New York. It is at times like this, when no friendly local banks help maintain steady trading in a stock, that CFOs wonder whether the much-vaunted internationalization of their capital base is such a wonderful idea after all.

Not that they have a choice. In 1984, *Euromoney* predicted: "The threat is simply part of a global phenomenon, a phenomenon that may spell the beginning of the end for the very symbol of trading everywhere: the market floor. In fact, there are some who contend that the development of the market floor is at the same stage now that the battleship was in 1939, or the traditional Swiss watch in 1970: that is, on the brink of obsolescence. NASDAQ...is probably the prototype for all attempts to establish an off-floor securities market."

In 1984, that was a speculative remark. Now, it's common knowledge. No one argues that hectic, computerized, round-the-clock trading comes free of risks; but pricing risk has become the everyday business of investment banks and brokers, and the rewards are great for those who seize the day.

These rewards, however, will come in unusual packages. Even when the securities industry appears to investors, borrowers and traders to be a single global market, there will be rival stock exchanges. New technology will allow them to swap price information, and, hopefully, to share a streamlined clearing and settlement system. An elaborate fee structure will be attached to this arrangement. The New York Stock Exchange will not expect to swap data on its listed stocks with The Stock Exchange in London without some sort of premium to compensate for the fact that it is giving away much more than it receives.

Old Distinctions Must Disappear

Before anything like this happens, the old distinctions between listed and unlisted stocks need to disappear. The most important step taken in this direction was the connection established between The Stock Exchange in London and NASDAQ in 1986. London's listed stocks became accessible, through NASDAQ's screens, to players in America's unlisted securities market, an implicit if untrumpeted obliteration of the distinction. One of NASDAQ's achievements has been that by keeping major corporations happy with the way their shares are being traded, it has made the notion of an unlisted stock purely theoretical. Naturally, the market will always have securities of corporations that are either very young or very risky; but in the future, this may be simply something to be pointed out by brokers' research reports, rather than by any heavy-handed drawing of the line between first-class and second-class paper. These days, even the biggest companies can issue junk bonds.

Much has not yet been built. The lack of an effective global clearing system for securities still bedevils most attempts to build truly international liquidity in any one stock. Those who were able to benefit from the enormous gains in the Italian stock markets in 1985 and 1986, for example, found it far from easy to liquidate their assets, purely because of the obstructive inefficiency of the settlement process at the local stock exchanges. But this is not a technical problem, and change will be forced, willy-nilly, on the oligarchies that persist in maintaining barriers to the smooth trading of securities in any one market. Just as the most powerful NASDAQ stocks have withheld their liquidity from the established American stock exchanges, so, elsewhere, growing companies will decide for themselves where their shares are to be traded.

Problems Will Arise

Of course, there will be problems. Revolutions overthrow regimes. In London, at least, the old guard has been handsomely paid to make way for the new generation of investment houses; but some of the ruptures won't be healed so easily. Of these, the most significant is the open question: Who will regulate the global securities exchange? Technically, there is no problem. The electronic surveillance technology at NASDAQ, and the obligation on traders to display, transaction by transaction, the prices at which they are dealing, makes policing the market a straightforward enough business for sharp-eyed administrators.

But the political difficulties will be considerable. Domestic electronic networks, be they national telecommunication agencies or dealing systems, can interlock as cleanly as the hexagons on a soccer ball; governments find it harder to do so. Yet a supra-national agency of some sort—whether it be a self-regulating body along the lines of an NASD, an Association of International Bond Dealers or a politically sponsored secretariat—will be essential. Scandals, like those surrounding Dennis Levine and Ivan Boesky, ricochet nastily through markets; if capital is to flow efficiently, according to the logic of the marketplace, from investors to borrowers, there must be no interference on the line.

PART VII
NASDAQ Systems, Services and Regulations

Chapter
twenty-eight

C. Richard Justice is Executive Vice President, Automation Division, of the National Association of Securities Dealers, Inc. Mr. Justice serves on the Boards of Directors of the Depository Trust Company, the National Securities Clearing Corporation and the International Securities Clearing Corporation. Before joining the NASD in 1968, he was with the Mitre Corporation.

The NASDAQ System: State of the Art, Growing and Global

by C. Richard Justice

The NASDAQ System is the computer and communications facility for the NASDAQ market. A state-of-the-art system that is growing very rapidly, the NASDAQ System is pioneering communications for the forthcoming 24-hour global market.

The central computer complex for the NASDAQ System utilizes a Sperry 1100/84 system and 16 Tandem TXP processors. Four additional Tandem VLX processors with over 15 gigabytes of on-line storage support the NASD's Central Registration Depository, a related system with a data base of every individual registered to deal in a public securities business in the U.S. Three regional concentrators connect 3,000 terminals, leased to securities firms and financial institutions, to the central processors over approximately 80,000 miles of leased telephone lines. Through this network and computer complex, NASDAQ processes 1.7 million transactions (queries, updates, trade and volume reports, and supervisory activities) each day, with an average response time of two seconds.

The System delivers high reliability, with total downtime experienced at the average terminal of only .8 percent, almost all of which is due to telephone line and terminal outages. Central processor availability has been a consistent 99.9 percent or higher. Automatic-recovery software limits most central processor outages to 40 seconds.

The basic architecture of the NASDAQ System and its associated support systems is complex.

The Services the System Provides

This architecture provides three basic services: the NASDAQ Quotation System, the Small Order Execution System and the Trade Acceptance and Reconciliation Service.

- **NASDAQ Quotation System.** One of the System's primary functions is to collect, validate and distribute quotation information to our subscribers. The System provides subscribers with quotation display through both its own terminals and the terminals of market data vendor organizations.

  Level 1 Service is distributed through more than 150,000 terminals leased by subscribers from market data vendors, such as Quotron, Reuters, Telekurs, ADP/Bunker Ramo and others. Of these terminals, 134,000 are located in the U.S., and 17,500 in 36 other countries. This service distributes the best bid and asked prices in all securities to salesmen and dealers, giving these securities broad visibility. To support the vendors, the System broadcasts the inside quotation and share volume on all NASDAQ securities over 78 lines leading out from it. In addition, this service broadcasts periodic information about several market indices.

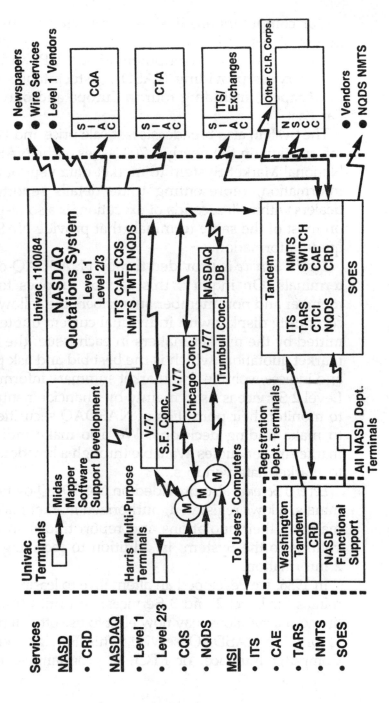

NASD – NASDAQ – MSI
BASIC SYSTEM ARCHITECTURE

Our computers are likewise connected to the computers of research bureaus, such as Datastream and Telerate, and to the computers of AP, UPI and other wire services providing NASDAQ stock tables to 165 newspapers, including four in Europe and one in the Far East.

The System also broadcasts last-sale price and volume information on the nearly 2,700 issues of the NASDAQ National Market System to market data vendors. This information, representing trade details reported by dealers within 90 seconds of execution, is also displayed on most of the same terminals that provide NASDAQ quote information.

Level 2 Service is provided through NASDAQ-owned terminals. On inquiry, this service supplies to both member and non-member subscribers the following: a composite display with individual current quotes submitted by the market makers in each issue; the inside market quotation, which is the best bid and ask prices; and indices, volume and market summary information. Level 2 Service is used mainly by financial institutions to monitor their portfolios of NASDAQ securities and to make trading decisions. We also make individual market-maker quotes available through a broadcast feed to market data vendors.

Level 3 Service, also provided on NASDAQ-owned terminals, allows registered, authorized market makers to maintain their quotations and report trades and daily volume to the System, in addition to receiving Level 2 information.

In 1986, we developed an alternative to leasing our terminals for Level 2 and 3 Services: securities firms and financial institutions may now elect to use other terminals to provide NASDAQ service. This Foreign Terminal Computer Interface, or FTCI, is programmed by the customer to emulate NASDAQ functions and may also be used for access to other trading-related data bases.

In early 1987, we also implemented plans to extend the reach of Level 2 and Level 3 Services to two countries outside the U.S. In response to numerous requests, NASDAQ made full interactive service available in the United Kingdom and Puerto Rico. This permits NASD member firms in those regions to monitor and maintain markets, as well as to enter orders through the NASD's Small Order Execution System (SOES).

- **The Small Order Execution System.** A Tandem-based system, SOES is one of NASDAQ's most successful enhancements. Through SOES, orders in all securities can be executed automatically by computer, without the customary telephone call from one trader to another. The size limit for a single trade is 1,000 shares for the nearly 2,700 NASDAQ National Market System issues and 500 shares for about 2,500 other NASDAQ issues. SOES executes all trades at the inside price being quoted on the NASDAQ System. In addition, SOES automatically reports all executions to the clearing system as compared, locked-in trades and automatically reports each trade to the trade information distribution system for public dissemination and surveillance purposes.

  NASD members participate in SOES through one of two means. First, a firm with sufficient automation capabilities can elect to have a Computer-to-Computer Interface, or CTCI, between its in-house system and SOES. We also make CTCI available to service bureaus, allowing multiple firms' orders to be routed to SOES on one line. Alternatively, firms may elect to use their standard NASDAQ terminals or PCs to enter orders into SOES, using a quick-entry mask displayed on the screen. Execution reports can be received by both the order-entry and market-making firms on their NASDAQ terminals or through CTCI via an in-house computer system. Printers are available if a hard copy of an execution report is required.

SOES is unique among automated trading systems because it offers automatic trade-detail reporting for clearing and compliance. Volume in SOES averages about 8,000 trades and 2 million shares per day. On heavy volume days, SOES volume increases far more rapidly than overall volume. SOES accepts any order size up to the 500- or 1,000-share limits—odd lots are no problem. By eliminating a great deal of telephoning and paperwork, SOES contributes significantly to high-volume processing.

We are studying new enhancements in the trading area, such as the Trade Confirmation Transaction and the Internalized Trade Transaction. The Trade Confirmation Transaction combines the dealer market's traditional telephone negotiation with the automatic trade-detail reporting feature of SOES to permit semi-automatic dealing in any block size. Upon completion of the telephone negotiation, the market maker involved in the transaction enters the trade through his terminal, and the computer displays it to the contra-party and reports it to the last-sale information system. If the contra-party confirms the transaction within an allowable time period, submission to clearing is automatic. Without ceding total control to the computer, brokers and dealers can use the Trade Confirmation Transaction to process increased order flow without increasing trade comparison problems.

The ITT, or Internalized Trade Transaction, will allow integrated firms with retail orders internalized and executed by their trading departments against their own principal positions to use the trading facilities of NASDAQ—CTCI and SOES—to route their orders and gain the advantages of automatic transmission to clearing and trade reporting.

- **Trade Acceptance and Reconciliation Service (TARS).** Another Tandem-based system, TARS helps the back offices of member firms in resolving their uncompared and advisory OTC trades processed through participating clearing organizations. TARS permits subscribers to view on their terminals all information contained on daily OTC contract sheets received from the clearing corporation and to take actions to resolve problems. TARS users can display all of their trades—compared, uncompared and advisory—prior to settlement date and reconcile and correct problem trades on-line. Corrections entered by one side are immediately displayed to the other side. Recently, we added trades in U.S. municipal bonds to this data base.

  TARS also can handle the original entry of trading information for transmission to clearing houses. As linkages with clearing organizations worldwide are developed, this feature will greatly enhance the processing of international trades.

The Next Steps: Rockville, Satellites, PC Data Bases

To support and accelerate the growth of the NASDAQ market, we are continuing to develop the System for even greater reliability, transaction volume and technological sophistication.

In September 1986, we began to phase in the new NASD Operations Center in Rockville, Maryland, 20 miles away from the NASD headquarters in downtown Washington. This second central computer complex, separated by 200 miles from the main computer complex in Trumbull, Connecticut, will serve several key purposes.

First, it will provide back-up computer systems and telecommunications circuits to help assure uninterrupted NASDAQ service in the event of a major physical disaster at the Trumbull location. Our target is to restore service in one to two hours if a major problem occurs, such as fire or other catastrophic damage to the main computers. NASDAQ is the world's first equity market to establish such a safety resource.

Second, the duplicate Rockville facility is part of a restructuring of our telecommunications network, which adds four network nodes and rebalances the terminal load so that no concentrator site handles more than 500 terminals. This will ultimately contain or reduce the costs of local lines and long-distance trunks. When combined with a streamlined dial back-up capability, it also will minimize the impact of the loss of a single node on the general subscriber population. At the same time, the new network architecture and its control software will help rationalize the maze of inter-computer links at the heart of the System.

Third, the Rockville facility serves as the new primary site for the NASD's computerized registration system and other systems established to support regulatory and administrative functions. The site provides full state-of-the-art security and power back-up to insure continuity of operations.

Further, to contain communications costs, we are exploring several satellite-based alternatives to the use of private terrestrial circuits. SCPC links—a single-channel-per-carrier, satellite-transmission method—can provide highly reliable, high-capacity backbone trunks, while a point-to-multipoint VSAT (very small aperture terminal) network can move large volumes of market data at a very low cost. We are also working with satellite service providers to help specify and develop a hybrid broadcast and interactive service that can be delivered through a single rooftop dish measuring less than 7 feet across. This architecture would permit huge volumes of data to be broadcast to intelligent workstations, with little or no contention with interactive transactions, thus making optimum use of channel capacity.

Another current project is aimed at developing personal computers (PCs) into high-powered trading workstations for delivering NASDAQ information. We are now able to deliver Level 2 and Level 3 Services over standard, IBM-compatible PCs. In 1987, our PCs will be able to maintain a full data base of securities locally, with a wide array of value-added functions. These functions will allow subscribers to customize the display of the information to their individual needs. Quotation and trade information will be broadcast from the central computers and stored in the PC's memory. Simple instructions will allow a trader to update his or her markets and to display quotations in many formats, including market minding and ticker-like displays. Dynamic screen updating and eventual access to other information systems are other important features of this service.

Also, as part of our general system and network upgrade, we are pioneering the use of local area networks to provide gateways between our host processors and terminal network. Our newly installed HYPERchannel™ will permit the network processors and the Sperry and Tandem host processors to communicate among themselves at the rate of 50 million bits per second. The new DCP-based network, which combines local area networking with wide area networking, promises greatly enhanced System capability in the future. With the ability to offer internationally standard communications gateways, NASDAQ will be guaranteed a pivotal role in the automated, global marketplace.

Systems for the Global Marketplace

Just as modern technology enables high-volume markets to operate in their own national environments, it also opens up the prospect of internationally linked markets. International standardization of communications interfaces and protocols, the extremely low error rates of satellite links, and the processing capacity of even the smallest computers will permit practically any market, regardless of its size or location, to link with practically any other.

This technology is also very low cost. It has been estimated that if jet aviation technology had progressed from the introduction of the Boeing 707 to the present as quickly as computer technology has progressed, a commercial transatlantic flight would take 10 minutes and cost $2. The low cost of computer and communications technology enables markets of all types and sizes to automate, brokerage houses of all sizes to automate, and markets all over the world to link together.

The NASDAQ/London Link

The link between NASDAQ and London's International Stock Exchange (ISE), the first intercontinental market-to-market linkage, provides a good example. At 4 a.m. in Trumbull, Connecticut, our computers begin to receive live price information on some 300 ISE-listed issues from London, where it is 9 a.m. American traders, arriving at their desks at 8 a.m. New York time, can look at their terminals for continuously updated, actual prices from London's competing dealers. Similarly, prices being quoted by U.S. dealers in 300 of the largest NASDAQ issues are received by the London exchange's computers. Five-thousand London traders, also starting work at 8 a.m., can look at their TOPIC screens to find NASDAQ's closing prices for the previous day. Starting at 12:30 p.m. and lasting until London's market closes, TOPIC screens also have live NASDAQ prices.

During the hours of overlap, when markets are open and traders are active in both time zones, the automated systems and the information they exchange permit investors to choose the most advantageous market for their deals. Through nearly 18 continuous hours, these two automated systems have bridged the gap between time zones and the gap between traders. The forthcoming continuous international marketplace will not mean that traders have to be at their desks 24 hours a day—it means that when traders are at their desks, they can make informed decisions based on accurate and timely information.

The NASDAQ/London quotation exchange is the first stage of a more comprehensive, automated market linkage. It will soon include transaction information, automatic execution of small orders, and facilities for collecting U.S. market-maker quotes on London stocks and London dealer quotes on NASDAQ stocks.

A parallel development of vital importance in the evolution of international trading markets is the new link between the International Securities Clearing Corporation in the U.S. and the London Stock Exchange's Talisman settlement system. In the U.S. securities industry, the cornerstones of the high-volume marketplaces are continuous net settlement of trades and the option to take book-entry delivery of shares; the NASD played a pioneering role in both developments. Rationalizing the international clearance and settlement process is not nearly as glamorous and exciting as building international trading links, but marketplace development will be slow without it.

The Shape of the International Marketplace

A variety of linkages and relationships will shape the international marketplace.

OVERVIEW OF INTERNATIONAL TRADING

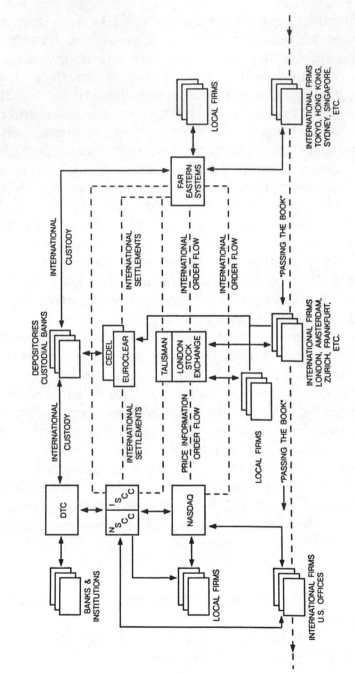

In the accompanying diagram, NASDAQ, the London Stock Exchange, and Far Eastern systems are representative of the electronic marketplaces in the world's three major trading zones. It is just a matter of time before a compatible, dealer market in the Pacific Basin links with western systems.

In each trading zone, local firms are shown. These are firms whose business will remain local to their primary marketplace and whose access to the international marketplace will be through market center linkages.

At the bottom of the diagram are the international firms. Examples of these are Merrill Lynch, Morgan Stanley, Nomura and Salomon Brothers. These firms are linked to a market in each zone and linked internally so as to "pass the book" among their various offices. Firms in each zone are also linked to their local clearing and settlement systems, for example NSCC and Talisman. Shown also are U.S. banks' and institutions' links to the U.S. depository, the Depository Trust Company, and the links among the Depository Trust Company and the clearing organizations with banks around the world providing global custody services, thereby reducing or eliminating the physical delivery of certificates.

The 25,000-Mile-Long Trading Floor

The NASDAQ System's technology has turned the U.S. into a 3,000-mile-long trading floor and enabled the NASDAQ market to become the third-largest market in the world.

Tomorrow, the technology that NASDAQ has pioneered will turn the world into a 25,000-mile-long trading floor— and into one vast, international confederation of automated dealer markets.

Chapter
twenty-nine

John T. Wall is Executive Vice President, Member and Market Services, of the NASD. He is responsible for the overall development of the market for NASDAQ securities, through NASD services to NASDAQ issuers, NASD members and public investors. Mr. Wall has been with the NASD for 20 years, and he currently serves as a director of the Options Clearing Corporation.

NASDAQ
Market Services
by John T. Wall

The administration of the NASDAQ market is handled by 11 departments in the Member and Market Services Division:

- *NASDAQ Company Operations* processes the inclusion and the maintenance of NASDAQ companies' securities in the market and provides the companies with essential information services.
- *NASDAQ Member Operations* enters securities information into the NASDAQ System and administers the Small Order Execution System (SOES).
- *TARS/Uniform Practice Department* simplifies the processing of member businesses by administering various transaction-related, computerized services and a code of procedure for facilitating the clearance and settlement of securities transactions.
- *NASDAQ Company Services* assists companies in their investor relations programs through individual consultations and group conferences.
- *NASD Membership* supplies administrative services to 6,700 NASD member firms and their 18,000 branch offices.

- *Central Registration Depository* maintains the professional records of some 400,000 registered principals and registered representatives who sell securities.
- *Qualifications Department* develops and administers examinations for these professionals.
- *Communications Group* conducts economic research and informs the investing public, NASDAQ companies and NASD members about NASD and NASDAQ developments.
- *The Treasurer's Office, Human Resources Department* and *Administrative Services* are also key operating units of the Member and Market Services Division and are responsible for the day-to-day administration of the NASD's finances, staffing needs and general operating requirements.

NASDAQ companies and NASD members participate extensively in the direction and oversight of these departments. For example, the NASD's Trading Committee guides NASDAQ Company Operations and NASDAQ Member Operations; the Corporate Advisory Board develops policy for NASDAQ Company Services; the Registration Committee guides the Membership Department and the Central Registration Depository; and the Qualifications Committee supervises the Qualifications Department.

NASDAQ Company Operations

When a public company wants to apply for a listing, it works with the NASDAQ Company Operations Department at NASD headquarters in Washington, D.C. If the security is already registered with the SEC, the company submits all Forms 10-Q and 10-K and proxy statements filed with the SEC during the past year. It also files a proposed four-letter trading symbol and the names and titles of its designated corporate contacts.

If the security is a new issue, the company must state whether the security will be offered on the basis of firm commitment (the underwriters commit to purchase a stated amount of shares) or best efforts (the underwriters agree to use their best efforts to sell the shares). A best-efforts offering is included in NASDAQ only upon written confirmation that the offering has closed and that the company has received the net proceeds. The confirmation must also include the number of shares that have been sold.

A qualifications analyst verifies that basic requirements are met. For a domestic common stock, these include: SEC registration; total assets of at least $2 million; capital and surplus of at least $1 million; public float of 100,000 shares; and 300 shareholders of record. Securities meeting these qualifications are displayed on NASDAQ terminals so dealers can register to make markets in them. Each company must secure at least two market makers before its stock can be traded.

The qualifications analyst assigned to the security reviews the company's quarterly financial reports (10-Qs), annual financial reports (10-Ks) and other SEC-required filings to determine its continued eligibility for trading.

Companies that no longer meet minimum maintenance requirements for inclusion and are slated for deletion from the System may appeal this action at hearings. If a company demonstrates that it can shortly return to compliance by meeting the minimum qualifications, an exception may be granted, permitting the company to remain on the System. The letter "C," signifying the exception, is appended to the company's stock symbol.

NASDAQ Company Operations also designates NASDAQ National Market System (NASDAQ/NMS) securities. In addition to the basic qualifications, NASDAQ/NMS inclusion requires net income of $300,000 in the latest fiscal year or two of the last three years; a float of 350,000 shares, with a minimum market value of float of $2 million; and a minimum bid of $3. Development-stage companies must additionally have a four-year operating history, capital and surplus of $8 million, a float of 800,000 shares, and a market value of float of $8 million. All company and security information that is pertinent to initial and continuing qualification is stored in a computerized data base and in document files.

NASDAQ Company Operations also provides issuers with these information services:

- **Monthly Statistical Report (MSR).** The MSR is a report on the performance of a company's security or securities in the preceding month. It contains daily price and volume information, index data and the market makers in the security. The MSR Section responds to questions about the reports, fills orders for back copies and accepts subscription requests for MSRs on hard copy or microfiche.
- **Historical Research.** The MSR Section receives hundreds of requests for historical data each week from issuers, NASD member firms, lawyers and researchers. Issuers and member firms receive most information at no charge; if their requests are extensive, they are billed on a reimbursement-of-cost basis. Others are charged a base fee of $25 for written confirmation of trading data and additional fees as appropriate.
- **Newspaper Visibility.** NASDAQ Company Operations provides up-to-date trading information on NASDAQ securities to the newswire services, adding securities as they qualify for the NASDAQ/NMS List, the National (bid/ask) List and the Additional List, and deleting securities as appropriate. The department also assists a nationwide network of 150 Local Quotations Committees, which select securities not included in the major NASDAQ stock tables for publication of local lists in newspapers.

- *NASDAQ/CQS Symbol Directory.* NASDAQ Company Operations issues the *NASDAQ/CQS Symbol Directory*, which is distributed to subscribers to NASDAQ data and sold to others at $3.50 per copy. The directory lists NASDAQ securities by company name and by symbol. In the Consolidated Quotations Service (CQS) section, the directory lists all stocks, rights and warrants multiply traded in the over-the-counter market and exchange markets. It also lists NASDAQ market makers, their symbols, addresses and telephone numbers, and the rules and procedures for market makers. In 1987, the information in the directory was made available on-line on NASDAQ terminals.

NASDAQ Member Operations

Market makers, registered representatives and investors are informed of securities newly quoted on NASDAQ or NASDAQ/NMS by the Member Operations Department located in New York City. A principal function of NASDAQ Member Operations is to enter new securities information into the NASDAQ computers. The department also advises the newswire services of additions and deletions of securities.

The NASDAQ daily list, distributed by the department to market data vendors and wire services, includes:
- Security additions effective that day.
- Anticipated additions.
- Security deletions.
- Security name and/or symbol changes.
- Newspaper list changes.
- Mutual fund and money market fund additions, deletions and changes.

NASDAQ Member Operations collects daily mutual fund and money market fund prices and enters the data into the computer for delivery through the wire services to newspapers. The department collects stock exchange and third market-maker quotations on listed securities and enters them into the Consolidated Quotations Service. NASDAQ terminal subscribers may subscribe to CQS and thus retrieve quotations on listed issues as well as on NASDAQ securities.

Member Operations also administers the NASD Small Order Execution System (SOES). The department clears NASD member firms for participation in SOES and enters authorized securities for trading in the system.

TARS/Uniform Practice Department

Also located in New York City is the Uniform Practice Department, which administers NASD rules for the clearance and settlement of securities transactions between member firms. These rules govern the delivery of securities, entitlements to dividends, rights and warrants, and reconciliation of uncompared trades. The Uniform Practice Department is responsible for the administration of the Trade Acceptance and Reconciliation Service (TARS), which permits NASD members to see their trades on-line and to adjust problems through their terminals.

NASDAQ Company Services

Once their securities are quoted on the System, companies receive continuing assistance from the NASDAQ Company Services Department, particularly on how to increase the visibility of their securities and to work effectively with the securities industry.

The Company Services Department consists of a staff at the NASD's Washington office and a team of corporate consultants and regional managers. The corporate consultants, who are based across the U.S. and meet with some 1,500 companies annually, include former executives of NASDAQ companies and NASD members. They provide free advice to companies on matters such as:

- Attracting more market makers and maintaining productive relationships with market makers.
- Working with securities analysts.
- Working with financial media.
- Planning and managing investor relations programs.
- Gaining access to problem solvers in the securities industry and in governmental regulatory agencies.
- Interpreting and responding to regulatory changes.
- Evaluating and selecting investment bankers for additional offerings of securities.

Company Services also conducts investor relations seminars for company executives. The sessions, which include presentations and small discussion groups led by experts, are held in or near major cities that are easily accessible by air.

NASDAQ chief executive officer conferences are held each fall in eight to 10 cities. Discussions center on the market and its facilities, regulatory developments, capital formation and internationalization of the markets.

Companies contribute advice and initiate changes in the market. The Corporate Advisory Board, a national standing committee of the NASD Board of Governors, reviews all aspects of NASD and NASDAQ policy and operations from an issuer's perspective. The Corporate Advisory Board is made up of company chief executive officers who meet several times annually. The Board has made recommendations on such matters as qualifications standards for NASDAQ/NMS securities, corporate governance standards, the shareholder voting-rights issue and short-sale regulation.

The Financial Communications and Investor Relations Committee focuses on financial and investor relations. Made up of executives of companies and investor relations firms, the subcommittee recommends to the Corporate Advisory Board additional services that the NASD might provide to companies. It also proposes to the Board changes in rules and, on behalf of the Board, drafts comments on proposals advanced by other organizations and the SEC.

As a member of the NASD Board of Governors, the Chairman of the Corporate Advisory Board brings the views of a NASDAQ company chief executive officer directly to the NASD's primary policy-making body. Several other Governors-at-Large represent NASDAQ companies and serve three-year terms on the Board.

NASD Membership Department

The Membership Department in Washington, D.C., reviews NASD membership applications by securities firms. If an initial application appears to meet all requirements, including qualification of officers and net capital, the Membership Department assigns the application to an examiner in one of the NASD's 14 district offices. The examiner verifies the data and conducts a pre-membership interview. The Membership Department authorizes final approval.

The department also provides continuing administrative services to the 6,700 NASD member firms and their 18,000 branch offices.

Central Registration Depository

As of year-end 1986, the NASD's member firms had over 400,000 professional employees selling securities. Some 260,000 of these employees had passed the General Securities Registered Representative examination (known as Series 7) and were qualified to sell nearly all financial products. The remaining salesmen had passed limited qualification examinations and were authorized to sell investment company products (mutual and money market funds), variable contracts, direct participation programs (tax shelters)—but not stocks and bonds.

The NASD maintains, through the automated Central Registration Depository (CRD), the qualification, employment and disciplinary histories of these professionals. Before CRD began in 1981, securities firms registering their professionals to deal with customers in several states had to file separate state registration forms and pay separate state fees. With the cooperation of the North American Securities Administrators Association (NASAA), the NASD streamlined this cumbersome and costly registration procedure. The NASD and NASAA developed standardized terminology and forms for broker-dealer licensing and registration of principals and representatives. In addition, the states adopted the Uniform Securities Agent State Law Examination.

Today, securities firms need to file only one document with the NASD and send one check to register new representatives, to transfer them, to renew their annual state registrations or to terminate their employment. The NASD verifies that the filing is complete, routes it to the appropriate states and disburses the checks for the required fees.

The NASD processes CRD documents for registrations in the District of Columbia, Puerto Rico and all states but Hawaii. It also processes registrations for the Boston, Midwest, New York, Pacific and Philadelphia stock exchanges and the Chicago Board Options Exchange. All participants in CRD are linked to the central facility through a nationwide network of CRT on-line terminals.

Securities firms may utilize the automated Firm Access Query System (FAQS) for a broad range of functions concerning their own employees' registrations: checking the status of effective and pending registrations; assessing qualification status examinations; reviewing disciplinary, employment and educational histories; transferring employee registrations to and from other firms; and scheduling qualification examinations for employees. Since the introduction of FAQS in 1983, the service has attracted more than 200 subscribers, ranging from smaller firms to national firms with 20,000 or more registered representatives.

Qualifications Department

The Qualifications Department of the Member and Market Services Division administers more than 200,000 examinations a year for the NASD, other self-regulatory organizations, the states, the SEC, the commodity exchanges and other certifying organizations.

NASD registered representatives may take the General Securities Registered Representative Examination and two limited representative examinations (Investment Company Products/Variable Contracts and Direct Participation Programs). Individuals may also take the Non-Member General Securities Agent State Law Examination and the Uniform Real Estate Securities Examination.

Principals of NASD member firms may take the following examinations:

- General Securities Principal.
- General Securities Sales Supervisor.
- Financial and Operations Principal.
- Investment Company Products/Variable Contracts Limited Principal.
- Direct Participation Programs Limited Principal.

• Registered Options Principal.

Almost 70 percent of these examinations are administered on the automated testing system of the NASD through its nationwide network of testing centers. Administered individually, candidates are able to take tests when they are ready, rather than having to wait until a group of candidates is assembled. The computer instantly scores the tests and informs candidates of results.

Communications Group

The Communications Group is the general research, news dissemination and publications arm of the NASD. It includes:

• **The Office of the Chief Economist,** which conducts studies of the NASDAQ market and assists with studies performed by outside consultants. This office recently established a data base of historical prices for all NASDAQ securities at the University of Chicago's Center for Research in Security Prices (CRSP). The NASD co-funded this project, and CRSP will make the data available to 150 colleges and other subscribers. This section also assists with economic research, performing statistical research and data analyses of NASDAQ securities and the NASDAQ market.

• **The News Bureau,** which disseminates NASD and NASDAQ information to the print and electronic media. This unit operates a computer-to-computer interface with financial wire services and makes daily transmissions to television and radio stations and networks. It also issues NASD and NASDAQ news releases, as well as monthly disciplinary press releases announcing NASD penalties for firms and individuals.

- **Communication Services,** the principal publishing operation of the NASD and NASDAQ. Among other items, it produces:
  1. The *NASD Annual Report,* the *NASDAQ Fact Book,* the bi-annual *NASDAQ Company Directory* and *Introduction to the NASD.*
  2. *Investor Relations: A Practical Guide For NASDAQ companies.*
  3. Monthly *NASDAQ Notes* for issuers and *NASDAQ Subscriber Bulletins* for terminal users.
  4. A monthly *Q&R* (Qualifications and Registration) *Report,* which documents CRD and Qualifications Department requirements and procedures.
  5. *Executive Digest,* which summarizes actions taken by the NASD Board of Governors at its six meetings each year.
  6. *Committee & Staff Report,* a quarterly review of major regulatory and market developments.

The Overall Function

The overall function of the Member and Market Services Division is to provide an orderly, progressive and responsive environment for investors, companies and NASD members in the NASDAQ market and to keep them all informed of market developments.

Chapter
thirty

*F*rank J. Wilson is Executive Vice President and General Counsel of the National Association of Securities Dealers, Inc. He heads the Legal & Compliance Division of the NASD, whose primary responsibility is implementation of the NASD's regulatory programs. A former Assistant United States Attorney, he has served in various other senior officer and attorney positions since joining the NASD in 1963. Mr. Wilson has taught law and participated in many industry seminars as well as served on a variety of industry and governmental study groups and task forces. He is a member of the American Bar Association, Federal Bar Association and the District of Columbia Bar and has been active in various committees and organizations of the securities industry and the American Bar Association.

How NASDAQ Trading Is Regulated

by Frank J. Wilson

The NASD has regulated the over-the-counter market for nearly 50 years and the NASDAQ market for 16 years.

Regulatory personnel, which represent more than half of the NASD's full-time professional staff of 1,500 people, have significantly increased in both numbers and expertise in recent years. Most of our regulatory employees are stationed in 14 district offices across the United States. District office professionals conduct the on-site examinations of members, which include detailed inspections of the financial and operational condition of the firms, reviews for sales practices, checks to determine the adequacy of books and records and reviews of supervisory procedures.

Other regulatory personnel are primarily concentrated in the Market Surveillance Section, the Corporate Financing and Advertising Departments and the General Counsel's Office, among other departments at the Executive Office in Washington, D.C.

INCREASES IN REGULATION DIVISION STAFF

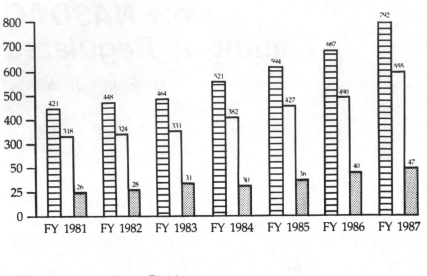

☰ Legal & Compliance Division
☐ District Staff
▨ Market Surveillance Section Personnel

Market Surveillance

The Market Surveillance Section is the front line of the regulation of trading in NASDAQ securities. This department helps maintain fair and orderly markets for these securities, deters manipulative practices and insider trading and investigates such practices when they appear to have occurred.

The department works with a great deal of computer power. As soon as a security is entered into the NASDAQ System, it is programmed with price and volume parameters reflecting historical patterns in comparable stocks. As market makers key their quotations into the System during the day and as trading volume is recorded, the computer compares the entries with the parameters. Whenever parameters are broken, the computer alerts the Market Surveillance Section in Washington, D.C., with a printout of the exact nature of the parameter break.

A professional analyst responds to the alert and examines the nature of the break. The analyst reviews the newswire tickers to determine whether material corporate, industry or market news may have prompted unusual activity. In the absence of news, the analyst contacts the company or its market makers for explanations; the analyst may interrogate a NASDAQ terminal for up-to-date quotations and historical data on the stock and study corporate records for perspective; and the analyst may program a terminal to flag all significant further news and market developments in the stock.

Various information resources help track market activity, including:

- NASDAQ terminals, which can access not only market-maker quotations and general market data but also the historical price and volume profiles of securities.
- Vendor terminals, which can retrieve news articles about securities published in *Barron's* and *The Wall Street Journal* during the preceding 90 days.
- Dow Jones, Reuters, Business Wire and PR Newswire tickers.
- Corporate records and news from issuers, including annual reports, 10-Q and 10-K filings and newspaper articles.
- Over 40 regulatory reports generated by the NASDAQ computers. Among these are:
  1. *Market Maker Price Movement Report*, informally known as NASDAQ's "instant replay," records each change in a market maker's bid or asked quotation and produces a record of each market maker's

activity in an issue at each moment throughout the day.

2. *Pricewatch* monitors intra-day fluctuations in each NASDAQ security and provides automated alerts to significant movements.

3. *Volumewatch* follows real-time, intra-day volume fluctuations in NASDAQ/NMS issues and flags those with substantial increases as they occur.

4. *Blockwatch* provides real-time notification of block-sized trades in NASDAQ/NMS securities, with the identity of the reporting firm and the price, size and time of the trade.

5. *Quote/Trade Comparison System* monitors compliance with NASDAQ/NMS trade-reporting rules. For the nearly 11.5 million trades in NASDAQ/NMS issues in 1986, 99.4 percent were reported at prices equal to or better than the prevailing market.

6. *Insider Exception System* identifies price and volume movements before and after news releases by NASDAQ companies to determine the potential for insider trading.

7. *All-Securities Report* identifies the market makers, their reported volumes and the high and low bid and asked quotes in each issue during the day. This report makes it easy to determine where the concentration of activity occurred.

8. *NASDAQ Stockwatch Report* signals unusual price and volume fluctuations over weekly periods for each NASDAQ issue and shows which firms were responsible for the largest percentages of total volume. The on-line Stockwatch Report signaled a parameter break over 16,500 times in 1986.

9. *NASDAQ Equity Audit Trail* provides a fully integrated data base of second-by-second quotation, transaction and clearing information for all

NASDAQ securities on a firm-by-firm basis.

10. *Retail Account Name Search* provides a cross-reference capability to allow analysts to identify firms and individuals who have been cited in previous investigations as engaged in questionable trading activity.

When all these sources fail to explain unusual activity in a NASDAQ security, the Market Surveillance Section initiates an investigation. The section may request trading data from NASD member firms active in the issue and statements from individuals at the firms to obtain pertinent data that could have affected the stock. The section may also ask how news was released to the newswire services in order to verify the timing coordination with certain corporate activities.

The Market Surveillance Section conducts thousands of routine reviews each year; 250 resulted in formal actions in 1986. The Market Surveillance Committee, a national standing committee of the NASD, supervises the work of the section and reviews every case the department develops. In 1986, the NASD Board of Governors, as a result of Market Surveillance investigations, collected more than $723,000 in fines and suspended three member firms from making markets in NASDAQ stocks and four of their personnel for malpractice in the market. In 1986, Market Surveillance referred 115 cases to the SEC, and NASD referrals have silently figured in some of the highly publicized actions the SEC has successfully brought.

Besides conducting inquiries and investigations, the Market Surveillance Section implements over 1,000 quotation halts a year. The purpose of a quotation halt is to alert the marketplace that important corporate news which could affect the value of a security is about to be released or has just been released. This provides an opportunity for investors and potential investors to evaluate the news and subsequently make an informed investment judgment before entering into a transaction.

Most quotation halts occur when NASDAQ companies are releasing corporate news. The NASD strongly recommends that companies notify Market Surveillance of impending news. The major newswire services are notified when quotations are halted and reinstated.

Broker-Dealer Surveillance

The financial and operational condition and the selling practices of broker-dealers are closely monitored by the 14 NASD district offices located in Seattle, San Francisco, Los Angeles, Denver, Kansas City, New Orleans, Dallas, Atlanta, Chicago, Cleveland, Washington, D.C., Philadelphia, New York and Boston. The district offices are supervised and supported by Surveillance Department staff at the NASD's Washington, D.C., headquarters.

The NASD requires that each firm trading NASDAQ securities have a qualified general securities principal and a financial and operations principal. These principals must pass the appropriate examinations administered by the Qualifications Department. Sales personnel must pass the General Securities Registered Representative examination, or the Investment Company Products/Variable Contracts Limited Representative examination and/or the Direct Participation Programs Limited Representative examination. Examinations are also required of persons engaged in municipal securities activities.

The SEC has designated the NASD as the examining authority for most NASD member firms. Approximately 180 NASD members are also members of the various regional exchanges including the Boston, Cincinnati, Midwest, Pacific and Philadelphia stock exchanges. The NASD has responsibility for examining these firms and shares the examination findings with the exchanges. Another 437 NASD members that are also members of other exchanges, such as the New York Stock Exchange and the Chicago Board Options Exchange, are designated to the appropriate exchange. Notwithstanding this designation, the NASD examines their over-the-counter and municipal securities activities.

Firms for which the NASD is the designated examining authority must file every month Part I of the SEC's FOCUS (Financial and Operational Combined Uniform Single) Report. This report identifies selected financial and operational items, including a firm's volume, cash position, customer exposure, inventory, monies and securities due to or from other broker-dealers, profits and losses, and net capital position. The report is reviewed at the NASD district offices and is key to the NASD's early-warning system for financial and operational monitoring.

Member firms complete Part II of the FOCUS Report quarterly. It is a more comprehensive financial statement than Part I. Members also submit annual financial reports that have been certified by independent auditors. These reports are required by the SEC and reviewed by the NASD.

In examining its broker-dealer members, the NASD checks for and enforces compliance with the NASD By-Laws and Rules of Fair Practice and with federal laws and regulations. These standards govern the qualifications of broker-dealer personnel and the firms' financial responsibility, financial reporting, management and dealings with customers.

On-Site Examinations

Broker-dealers designated to the NASD and engaged in a general securities, municipal securities or options business are subject to at least one extensive, on-site examination a year by NASD staff. The firm's books and records are examined for accuracy and currency. Sales practices are reviewed for compliance with suitability, best-execution and mark-up requirements and standards. Market-making and underwriting activities are examined, as are activities in a wide range of products, including corporate bonds, municipal securities, mutual fund shares, options, tax shelters and variable contracts. Examiners review for compliance with the anti-fraud provisions of the Securities Exchange Act of 1934, including market manipulation and insider trading, as well as the registration requirements of the Securities Act of 1933, disclosure-of-capacity require-ments, advertising rules and other matters. The routine examination also includes a check for compliance with the Federal Reserve System's Regulation T, which governs the extension of credit by broker-dealers.

A financial and operational examination is part of the routine examination, providing information on the sound-ness of a member firm's financial and operational condition. It includes a review of all financial-responsibility rule require-ments, a verification of the FOCUS Report, Parts I and II, and a net capital computation prepared in accordance with the SEC net capital rule. A reserve requirement computa-tion is made pursuant to the SEC's customer-protection rule. The examination also covers bank and omnibus account reconciliations and a cash-flow analysis.

Every NASD district office has professional staff on duty to receive customer complaints against member firms. Most complaints involve matters such as slow delivery of securi-ties certificates or delayed transfer of customer accounts and are readily resolved. More serious customer complaints may result in special examinations of firms.

Special NASD Responsibilities

The NASD also has authority for many areas of member activity that are beyond the purview of any other self-regulatory organization. For example, the NASD is responsible for regulating members' over-the-counter market-making activities (wholesaling) and trading practices; their underwriting arrangements in connection with public distributions of securities; their new-issue distribution practices; their advertising practices; their activities in a wide range of products, such as NASDAQ issues and other over-the-counter securities, exchange-listed securities traded over the counter, debt securities and options; their sales of direct participation programs; their mutual fund and variable contract business, including mutual fund and variable annuity sales charges; and their municipal securities business.

Determining member compliance with the rules of the Municipal Securities Rulemaking Board is an important part of the NASD's examination program. Because of this statutory responsibility, the NASD conducts annual examinations of all municipal securities firms, as well as the municipal securities departments of large firms, even if these large firms are designated to another self-regulatory organization for financial-responsibility reviews. Late in 1986, the NASD was also given the responsibility for examining the government securities activities of its members.

Action on Examination Reports

Each of the NASD's districts has a District Business Conduct Committee (DBCC) consisting of securities industry professionals elected by their peers for three-year terms. DBCC members are volunteers and serve without pay. The DBCCs review all examination reports prepared by the staff. When a report indicates a firm's conformity with applicable rules and regulations, the committee orders the report filed without action.

When an examination report indicates apparent violations and the DBCC orders formal disciplinary action, the firm and individuals involved are entitled to a hearing. If a DBCC finds violations, it may impose penalties ranging from censure to the expulsion of the firm from NASD membership and the barring of individuals from association with any NASD member firm. Fines may also be imposed. In addition, the Association has the authority to impose "any other fitting sanction." In discharging this authority, it has ordered disgorgement of illicit profits; prevented individuals from continuing to participate in given aspects of a firm's business; required retesting of individuals; and imposed a variety of other unique sanctions designed to fit the improper activity found. All actions by the DBCCs are reviewed by the NASD Board of Governors, which may modify or affirm them. NASD penalties may be appealed to the SEC and, ultimately, to a United States Court of Appeals.

1986 NASD Investor Protection Highlights

4,479	On-site broker-dealer examinations conducted
4,252	Customer complainte received
1,357	Special sales-practice reviews made
668	Formal disciplinary actions ordered
504	Disciplinary decisions rendered/letters of Acceptance, Waiver and Consent accepted
10	Firms self-liquidated under NASD supervision
$67.9	Million distributed to customers and broker-dealers
16,556	Parameter breaks triggered by NASDAQ automated surveillance systems
260	Formal investigations launched
1,065	Quotation halts instituted
3,694	Corporate equity and debt, real estate investment trust and direct participation program filings by members for review
20,951	Pieces of advertising and sales literature filed by members for review

In 1986, the NASDS's district offices conducted 4,479 regular and special examinations. They also reviewed 4,252 customer complaints and 1,357 other special sales-practice-related situations. On the basis of their reviews, DBCCs ordered 668 formal disciplinary actions. These led to 322 disciplinary decisions; the acceptance of 182 letters of acceptance, waiver and consent; and the acceptance of 16 summary complaints.

Arbitration Service Resolves Disputes

The NASD can discipline member firms and their employees but cannot recover monies for customers who make claims against firms as a result of disputes. For such customers, the NASD operates an arbitration service. To utilize the arbitration service, individuals or organizations file claim letters and submission agreements—by which they agree to be bound by the decision of the arbitrators—and deposit the appropriate fees.

In 1986, the NASD Arbitration Department received over 1,500 claims. The Arbitration Department's workload has increased nearly five times since 1980.

Rulemaking for the NASDAQ Market

The NASD develops rules for the improvement and expansion of the NASDAQ and the OTC markets. The rulemaking process generally involves:
- Determination by the NASD Board of Governors that new procedures and practices are necessary or that existing rules need to be modified.
- Referral of the matter to the appropriate national standing committee.

- Provisional Board approval of a proposed rule.
- Solicitation of NASD membership comment on the proposal, and committee review of the comments received.
- Board approval of the proposed rule.
- Membership vote on the rule.
- If the membership vote is favorable, submission of the proposed rule to the SEC for its approval.

In recent years, the NASD developed and adopted, with SEC concurrence, five major new rules. These include:

1. Procedures for the NASD's Small Order Execution System, which began operation in late 1984.
2. Qualifications criteria for the NASDAQ National Market System (NASDAQ/NMS).
3. Rules for the NASDAQ/London Stock Exchange link, which began in April 1986.
4. Regulation and reporting of short sales in the NASDAQ market, accomplished in stages during 1986.
5. Authority for the NASD to impose trading halts in NASDAQ securities (currently awaiting final SEC action).

A proposed NASD rule, approved by the Board and awaiting approval by the SEC, will require NASDAQ National Market System companies to meet a series of corporate governance requirements, as a condition for remaining in NASDAQ/NMS or being admitted to it.

These requirements, among others, are:

- Each NASDAQ/NMS issuer shall maintain a minimum of two independent directors on its board of directors.
- Each such issuer shall establish and maintain an audit committee, a majority of the members of which shall be independent directors.
- Each issuer shall hold an annual meeting of shareholders, solicit proxies and provide for a quorum of no less than 33⅓ percent of the outstanding shares of common stock.

- Each issuer shall utilize the audit committee for the review of potential conflicts of interest.

These forthcoming NASDAQ/NMS corporate governance requirements were developed by the NASD's 17-member Corporate Advisory Board. They essentially codify the existing practices of the great majority of NASDAQ/NMS companies. They have also been strongly endorsed by U.S. and overseas institutional investors in the companies' securities.

The Purposes of the NASD

The NASD's regulatory programs are crucial to achieving its stated purposes, which are:

- To promote the investment banking and securities businesses.
- To standardize its principles and practices.
- To promote high standards of commercial honor and to promote among members observance of federal securities laws.
- To provide a medium through which the membership may consult with governmental and other agencies.
- To cooperate with governmental and other agencies in the solution of problems affecting the securities business and investors.
- To adopt and enforce rules of fair practice in the securities business.
- To encourage self-discipline among members.
- To promote just and equitable principles of trade for the protection of investors.
- To investigate and adjust grievances between the public and NASD members.

Glossary

GLOSSARY

American Depositary Receipt (ADR)—A receipt or certificate issued by a U.S. bank, representing title to a specified number of shares of a foreign security. The actual foreign shares are held in a depository in the issuing company's country of domicile.

Association of International Bond Dealers (AIBD)—The association of 800 dealers from 39 countries, including major European banks and financial institutions, for the trading of Eurobonds. Eurobonds are debt obligations issued by borrowers outside their home countries in any one of several currencies. The AIBD has its headquarters in Zurich, but most Eurobond trading takes place in London.

bid/ask spread—The difference between the highest price which any buyer is willing to pay for a security and the lowest price at which any seller is willing to sell the security.

best efforts—An agreement whereby a securities firm promises an issuer that it will do its best to sell an issue, but does not guarantee the sale by purchasing the entire issue for its own account.

block trade—The purchase or sale of stock in a large quantity, generally 10,000 shares or more.

block volume—The aggregate volume of trades of 10,000 shares or more.

blue-sky laws—State laws that require issuers of securities to register their offerings with the states before they can be sold there.

broker-dealer—A firm that both buys and sells securities as an agent for public customers (broker) and also buys and sells securities for its own account and risk (dealer).

Central Registration Depository (CRD)—A computerized system in which the NASD maintains the employment, qualification and disciplinary histories of more than 400,000 securities industry professionals who deal with the public.

Computer-to-Computer Interface (CTCI)—A link between a securities firm's in-house computer and the NASDAQ System. It permits a firm to report its trades simultaneously to its internal computer for recordkeeping purposes and to NASDAQ for trade-reporting purposes by a single set of entries to a single terminal.

Consolidated Quotations Service (CQS)—A service available on NASDAQ Level 2 and 3 terminals, providing quotations of all participating exchange specialists and market makers on all stocks, rights and warrants listed on the New York Stock Exchange and the American Stock Exchange, and in selected securities listed on regional stock exchanges.

continuous net settlement—An on-going accounting system used by a clearing corporation which settles transactions between securities firms. The system generates net tallies of firms' accounts with the clearing corporation on a daily basis, and substantially reduces the need for certificate deliveries and cash payments for the settlement of individual transactions.

Direct Participation Program (DPP)—An investment program that provides flow-through tax consequences to investors. Such programs include real estate, oil and gas and agricultural ones; they do not include real estate investment trusts.

Financial and Operational Combined Uniform Single (FOCUS) Reports—Financial reports filed by broker-dealers with their self-regulatory organization on a monthly (Part I) and quarterly (Part II) basis.

Firm Access Query System (FAQS)—A service that provides NASD member firms with computerized access to their employees' records in the Central Registration Depository.

firm commitment—An agreement by which an underwriter buys an issue of a company's securities for its own account, and then assumes the risk of being able to resell them.

firm quotation—A bid or offer quotation on a security which is good for at least 100 shares or for a specified larger amount.

float—The portion of a company's outstanding shares which is held by the investing public, not by management.

flotation costs—The expenses that a company incurs in connection with offering securities to the public, including underwriter's compensation, legal and accounting fees, printing costs and others.

Foreign Terminal Computer Interface (FTCI)—A link that permits a securities firm to connect a non-NASDAQ terminal, which is linked to various data bases, to the NASDAQ regional network. It permits a firm to consolidate streams of data from various sources into a single terminal.

Initial Public Offering (IPO)—The first offering of a company's equity securities to the public.

inside quotation, or inside quote—The highest bid and the lowest offer in a security from any market maker.

International Securities Clearing Corporation (ISCC)—An organization formed to facilitate the clearance and settlement of international securities transactions between U.S. broker-dealers and others. ISCC is a subsidiary of the New York-based National Securities Clearing Corporation, which is jointly owned by the NASD and the New York and American stock exchanges.

last-sale reporting—Notification to the NASDAQ System, by a securities firm, of the price and number of shares involved in a transaction in a NASDAQ/NMS security, within 90 seconds of the execution of the transaction. Transactions in listed securities are similarly reported to the exchanges.

Level 1—A NASDAQ information service provided through market data vendor organizations to more than 150,000 terminals around the world, mostly used by brokers and other professionals. The service includes the inside quotations on all NASDAQ securities, last-sale information on NASDAQ/NMS securities and market summary data.

Level 2—A NASDAQ service provided through NASDAQ-owned terminals to the trading rooms of broker-dealers and financial institutions. In addition to Level 1 information, Level 2 service provides all the quotations of all the market makers in all NASDAQ securities.

Level 3—A NASDAQ service provided through NASDAQ-owned terminals and authorized foreign terminals used by market makers. In addition to providing Level 2 information, it enables market makers to enter quotations and last-sale information into the NASDAQ System.

limit order—An order to buy or sell a stated amount of a security at a specified price or better.

liquidity—The resilience of the price of a security to buying and selling pressures.

locked-in trade—A transaction as to which all of the terms and conditions are agreed upon or accepted by the parties in advance of its being reported to an information dissemination system (e.g., NASDAQ) and a clearing corporation.

making a market—Standing ready to buy and sell a security at specified prices.

managing underwriter—In a public offering of securities, the firm which manages the offering and the syndicate involved in its distribution.

margin—The amount of money deposited by a buyer in connection with the purchase of securities on credit.

mark-down—The difference between the current wholesale bid and the price a retail customer receives when selling a security to a firm acting as a dealer, i.e., as principal, for its own account and risk.

mark-up—The difference between the current wholesale offer and the price a retail customer pays when purchasing a security from a firm acting as a dealer, i.e., as principal, for its own account and risk.

market maker—A securities firm that buys and sells securities for its own account and risk, at stated bid and offer prices.

market order—An order to buy or sell a stated amount of a security at the best price available at the time the order is executed.

Monthly Statistical Report (MSR)—A report, which the NASD provides to each NASDAQ company, containing daily price and volume information and the names of the market makers in the company's security during the prior month.

Municipal Securities Rulemaking Board (MSRB)—An independent, self-regulatory board established by the Securities Acts Amendments of 1975 and charged with primary rulemaking authority for the municipal securities industry.

NASDAQ Composite Index—A measure of the aggregate performance of all NASDAQ National Market System stocks except warrants, and all other NASDAQ domestic common stocks. It is a market-value-weighted index: the influence of each stock on the index is proportionate to its price times the number of shares outstanding.

NASDAQ National Market System (NASDAQ/NMS)— That segment of the NASDAQ market in which securities are subject to real-time trade reporting. It encompasses approximately half of all NASDAQ securities, accounts for more than two thirds of NASDAQ share volume and over 90 percent of aggregate NASDAQ market value.

NASDAQ System—National Association of Securities Dealers Automated Quotations System, the computerized communications facility for more than 5,200 securities of more than 4,400 companies.

National Association of Securities Dealers, Inc. (NASD)— The self-regulatory organization for the over-the-counter securities market, and the owner and operator of the NASDAQ System.

National Securities Clearing Corporation (NSCC)—A securities clearing corporation formed in 1977 by the merger of the National Clearing Corporation, owned by the NASD, and the clearing facilities of the NYSE and the Amex. It is a medium through which trades in the respective participants' markets are cleared and settled.

North American Securities Administrators Association (NASAA)—An association of securities administrators from each of the 50 states, the District of Columbia, Puerto Rico and several Canadian provinces.

open order—An order to buy or sell a security which remains in effect until it is either executed or canceled.

position—The number of shares of a security held by an investor or a broker-dealer.

quotation halt—A suspension of price quotations on a NASDAQ security to allow its issuer sufficient time to disseminate material news which may affect the price of the stock.

right—A privilege granted to shareholders in a company to buy shares of a new issue of common stock before it is offered to the public.

secondary market—Trading in a security after the initial distribution of an offering by the underwriter.

shares of beneficial interest—A security that represents an interest in a group of assets in a non-corporate entity, e.g., a partnership or trust.

short interest—The total number of shares of a security sold short by securities firms and their customers.

short sale—The sale of a security that the seller does not own or that he owns but does not intend to deliver. The seller expects to be able to later buy the shares at a lower price, and thus make a profit on the transaction.

Small Order Execution System (SOES)—The NASD's automatic trade execution system for customer agency orders of 1,000 shares or less in NASDAQ/NMS securities and 500 shares or less in regular NASDAQ securities.

Standard Industrial Classification (SIC)—A code developed and maintained by the U.S. Office of Management and Budget and predecessor agencies, which assigns identification numbers to industry groups and to companies falling into the groups.

Stock Exchange Automated Quotations (SEAQ) System—The electronic communications facility of the London Stock Exchange, which is modeled on NASDAQ. It collects the quotes of competing U.K. market makers and disseminates them over the Exchange's TOPIC System.

stock symbol—An identifier for a security, consisting of one or more letters, and used in stock market communications systems. NASDAQ symbols consist of at least four letters; additional letters are used to designate special securities or special circumstances affecting securities.

TOPIC System—The London Stock Exchange's computer terminal network that provides on-line information services to users in the U.K.

TALISMAN—The London Stock Exchange's facility for the clearance and settlement of securities trades.

Trade Acceptance and Reconciliation Service (TARS)—An on-line service on NASDAQ terminals that permits subscribers to review transaction details and to correct problem trades.

trading unit—Normally, 100 shares of a stock. Anything less is known as an "odd lot."

two-sided market—A market made by a dealer who stands ready both to buy and sell at his quoted prices.

Uniform Securities Agent State Law Examination (USASLE)—A uniform qualification examination, administered by the NASD, that is required by most states.

unit—More than one class of securities, such as a stock and warrant, trading together as one.

warrant—A certificate issued by a company giving the holder the right to purchase its securities at a stipulated price, usually within specific time limits.

Index

INDEX

NASD LIST OF PUBLICATIONS

The NASD publishes a variety of educational materials for its members, NASDAQ issuers and the public to describe its work, the rules and regulations governing the securities industry and the NASDAQ market.

Requests for single copies may be directed to:

NASD Communications Group
1735 K Street, N.W.
8th Floor
Washington, D.C. 20006-1506
(202) 728-6900

Publications are free unless otherwise indicated.

General:

NASD Annual Report. Highlights regulatory, automation and market-development activities in the U.S. and overseas. Contains lists of Board of Governors, national and regional officials and financial statements. (40 pages)

Guide to Information and Services. Names and telephone numbers of NASD staff members to contact on various subjects. (25 pages)

An Introduction to the NASD. An overview of the NASD's purposes, structure, regulatory programs and services. (16 pages)

NASD Manual (reprint). The NASD's By-Laws, Rules of Fair Practice, Code of Procedure, Uniform Practice Code and pertinent SEC and Federal Reserve Board rules. (Approximately 500 pages) $3.50

How to Become a Member of the NASD. Explains the process in step-by-step fashion, with a checklist and sample forms. (48 pages)

Compliance Checklist. Guidelines for securities firms to follow in establishing internal procedures for compliance with NASD and federal rules and regulations. (20 pages)

Disciplinary Procedures. The NASD's regulatory process, including informal and formal actions, hearing procedures, penalties, appeal machinery and publicity for actions. (28 pages)

Code of Arbitration Procedure. The NASD's Code, which incorporates the Uniform Code of Arbitration developed by the Securities Industry Conference on Arbitration. (16 pages)

Arbitration Procedures. Answers the most commonly asked questions by the parties to an arbitration. (12 pages)

How to Proceed With the Arbitration of a Small Claim. Explains procedures followed in disputes of less than $5,000 between a customer and his broker. Includes small-claims rules and the Uniform Submission Agreement form. (12 pages)

Recordkeeping, Net Capital and Related Requirements for Firms Specializing in Direct Participation Programs. Also of interest to investors in such programs. (44 pages)

NASDAQ Market:

NASDAQ Fact Book. Extensive data on the performance of NASDAQ securities and the NASDAQ market in the preceding year. (Available each year in April; approximately 125 pages)

NASDAQ Company Directory. NASDAQ companies, their securities' symbols, industry codes, addresses, media and investor-relations contacts and their telephone numbers. (Updated twice a year, on January 1 and July 1; 170 pages) $5.00

574

NASDAQ/CQS Symbol Directory. A listing of NASDAQ issues and market makers and their symbols; the names and symbols of exchange-listed securities included in the Consolidated Quotations System and available on NASDAQ Level 2/3 terminals; and the rules and procedures governing NASDAQ market makers. (Updated three times a year; 135 pages) $3.50

Reference Guide for NASDAQ Companies. How-to information for companies on the NASDAQ System or companies considering NASDAQ: qualification requirements, application procedures, initial and annual fees, financial reporting requirements, market-maker rules, news dissemination guidelines, etc. (Approximately 100 pages) $5.00

Investor Relations: A Practical Guide for NASDAQ Companies. Tested programs to improve company communications with shareholders, securities professionals and the media. (60 pages) $5.00

Reporting Requirements for NASDAQ Companies. (12 pages)

NASDAQ ADRs, The Preferred Way to Trade. Explains the use of American Depositary Receipts by foreign companies to gain access to U.S. investors and the selection of NASDAQ as their preferred trading market. (13 pages)

Trading in the NASDAQ National Market: A Question-and-Answer Guide for Investors and Registered Representatives. (pamphlet)

Trade Reporting in the NASDAQ National Market: A Question-and-Answer Guide for Market Maker Firms and Traders. (pamphlet)

Why NASDAQ? Why U.S. and overseas companies make NASDAQ their market of choice. (10 pages)

Have You Heard About the New London Bridge? and **NASDAQ/London Link Subscriber Guide.** These companion pieces describe the mechanics of the NASDAQ/London Stock Exchange electronic link through which quotation information is exchanged for hundreds of world-class stocks. (pamphlets)

Academic/Research Studies Currently Available:

NASDAQ/NMS Qualification Standards, Ohio Registration Experience and the Price Performance of Initial Public Offerings. Written by Ohio State University's Professor of Finance Stephen A. Buser and Assistant Professor K. C. Chan, this 1987 study analyzes the relationship between the price performance of NASDAQ/NMS-eligible IPOs and their Ohio registration experience and supports a blue-sky exemption for NASDAQ/NMS companies (48 pages)

Short-Sale Regulation of NASDAQ Securities. This comprehensive 1986 study of short-sale regulation for the NASD by Irving M. Pollack, a former SEC Commissioner, produced recommendations calling for added regulation of short selling in the over-the-counter market. (88 pages)

Organized Exchanges and the Regulation of Dual Class Common Stock. This 1986 study of shareholder voting rights by Daniel R. Fischel, Professor of Law and Director of the Law and Economics Program, University of Chicago, finds that while one-share, one-vote appears to be the preferred standard for the vast majority of companies, there is no pattern of abuse to warrant a legally mandated standard of one-share, one-vote for all companies. (36 pages)

Exchange Listing and Stock Liquidity. Published in the Winter 1984 edition of *The Journal of Financial Research*, School of Business Administration, Georgetown University, this study by Texas A&M University Professors David A.

Dubofsky and John C. Groth finds a decline in liquidity for stocks leaving the OTC market. (12 pages)

Exchange Listing and the Cost of Equity Capital. Pubished as Part 8 of the Securities and Exchange Commission's Capital Market Working Papers, dated March 1982, authors Susan M. Phillips and J. Richard Zecher find that listing status does not affect risk or the cost of capital for companies of similar asset size, industry group and trading volume. (32 pages)

The Impact of Exchange Listing on the Cost of Equity Capital. This 1982 study by H. Kent Baker, Professor of Finance, Kogod College of Business Administration, The American University, and James Spitzfaden, Internal Auditor, Textron, finds that issuers in the NASDAQ market have no higher cost of capital than issuers of comparable listed securities. (22 pages)

Liquidity, Exchange Listing and Common Stock Performance. A 1983 study by Kerry Cooper, Professor of Finance, and John C. Groth, Associate Professor of Finance, Texas A&M University, and William E. Avera, Principal of FINCAP Inc., finds that exchange listing does not provide greater stock liquidity than the NASDAQ market. (22 pages)

Listing and the Liquidity of Bank Stocks. In this study of banks listing over a four-year period, researchers Donald R. Fraser, Professor of Finance, and John C. Groth, Associate Professor of Finance, Texas A&M University, conclude that there is no evidence that listing contributes to greater liquidity: Their regression results suggest that listing reduces liquidity and to a substantial degree. (14 pages)